Down A Bumpy Road

But Not Alone

Joe Neill

Down A Bumpy Road

But Not Alone

Brighter Outlook Publishing

Published in the United States of America
by Brighter Outlook Publishing

International Standard Publishing Number (ISBN): 0-9763028-0-2

Table
of
Contents

Introduction and Acknowledgment

Down A Bumpy Road
But Not Alone

Many of us have read books on famous, very successful businessmen such as Lee Iococca and Sam Walton. These people usually started very modestly and either worked their way up the corporate ladder or built a ground up business that grew and grew. Stories like this always intrigued me and I admired how the folks accomplished what they did.

This book, however, is very different. This is my story of thirty-five years in small business. A family business in the third generation in one sense, but also very unique in how the third generation has had to deal with a very changing world and the industry it revolves in. As with a lot of small businesss there are side investments into other business ventures with other partners. Failures and successes are both looked at in depth. A successful partnership goes bad when two of the partners betray their trust. There are countless hours of work in the business; meeting payroll; paying bills; managing employees' quirks; blending their style with yours; dealing with customers and their wants, needs, and desires (reasonable or not); and finally, looking down the road of planning for the future and its changes for both the business and the family. Then, there are the government regulations to contend with in regard to employees, tax matters, and the ever-threatening EPA environmental regulations.

The manner in which a small businessman handles all the above challenges affects him or her, but also his family, employees and their families, customers, and other small business suppliers to the business. Also, in many cases of rural small business, the business may be one of the largest employers in town, bringing a lot of related traffic of vendors, suppliers, and delivery truck drivers to the area. This all impacts the rural economy very much.

We will look at my four pillars of life to serve. They are very important for a rounded, fulfilled life. In order, the four pillars are Service to God, Service to Our Family, Service to Our Community, and Service to Our Industry or Vocation. We will look at my concept for the small business owner's own board of directors. This board can help guide you through all the perils looming in the business world. The business world can seem so lonely if you forget to utilize your board and forget to ask your Maker for His guidance.

We will take a look at how we should all cherish our friends and nourish them. We will look at the customers and employees. A changing industry and how to deal with the change is examined. My theory of plan, research, and execution are laid out.

We will also look at my struggle with chronic fatigue syndrome since 1988. If you have or know someone with a chronic ailment I hope my own dealing with chronic fatigue syndrome will add hope and confidence that you too can carry on a normal business life in many cases such as I have. If you cannot, maybe, you will have a better perception of how an illness can change and impact your life.

After winding thru the all the pitfalls, please remember that the rewards of seeing your own business work and the thrill of making it happen justify all it takes to get there.

The fourth generation in business is looked at, and some important thoughts in helping ensure the next generation's success are laid out. Laying out the options and how to analyze each in my big decision are looked at in depth.

I will try to show at each point of adversity how trusting in God and treating people how you would like to be treated will make the path of life so much easier. We all have times of trial in our life. These times are made so much easier with God's help. He will be there for you, if you only ask for His help. A good point to remember.

Two people have provided the inspiration for this book. One, my mother, Kathryn Neill wrote her book "God's Hand In Mine" just two years before she passed away in 1993. Her last days were spent writing about dealing with family and raising four boys, three of which had Cystic Fibrosis. Mom was a vibrant lady who dealt with all the hard days of caring for my three brothers. She spent countless hours working for the Lord in our local church. Hundreds of funerals and weddings as well as all church services were played by Mom on the organ or piano. She started a weekly after-school Bible school and taught a Sunday school class for most of her life. She also was the secretary/treasurer of the church. In the family business she handled all the accounts payable, receivables, and banking. She always had a smile on her face, no matter what was happening. The other inspiration comes from my good family friend, C.L. "Stu" Parker. After my father died in 1986 and I was dealing with a changing cattle industry and a troubled bank at the same time, Stu would come by to visit and just listen to my troubles. I would call Stu my "shrink." He would listen to all going on in my life and just shake his head. Many a time Stu would tell me I should be taking notes for a book on my adventures. I didn't take the notes, but I haven't forgotten the memories of a wild, but great, ride in business. Well, here it is, Stu. I wish you were here to read it.

Let's get into it. Hope you enjoy my thoughts very much.

Stu Parker – friend – customer – cattleman
"my shrink"

Kathryn Neill, author's mother

C.E. Neill, Jr., author's father

Dee Ann Neill, author's wife

Joe Neill, author

1

Making My Own Mark

Everyone has a point of time in their life that they remember as being a defining point. I am no exception. Fresh out of high school and newly married, I considered where to start my working life. I grew up in the cattle business. My father, and to an extent my grandfather, had started a custom cattle feeding business when I was four-years old. I grew up around the feedlot and worked after school and summers most of my life. It was a fun business that involved a lot of hands-on cowboy work, riding horses and looking after cattle. There also was the downside of scooping feed bunks when it snowed and painting fences in the summer.

While I liked this business very much, enjoyed working with Dad, and already had a nice start of some cattle of my own, I longed to go out on my own and prove myself. This was not out of rebellion, as my folks and I always got along very well. I just knew that I needed to make my own mark, make my own mistakes, and learn to do something entirely on my own. However, I do not have a mechanical mind and fixing broken feed mills or welding gates was something I just could not ever be very good at.

I always have liked nice cars, new or old and enjoyed working with them. Here, also, I was at a disadvantage as to the mechanical side. However I could get the help I needed in this area and not have to learn to do the actual work. In high school I owned two Model A Fords. The first one was a 1929 model I bought in the mid

'60s. I was its third owner. The man I bought it from had bought it in 1930 and was the only car he ever owned. I saw it through a complete restoration. The other was a 1931 Model A with a rumble seat. I had a blast with both and drove them all week on an eight-gallon tank of gasoline.

In looking at career paths I decided I would like to be in the automobile sales business. I wanted to go to the Northwood Institute in Dallas, Texas where a compressive program geared for running the automobile dealership was offered. Dad really did not want me to move to Dallas so I did not pursue this avenue. Our family was always very close. I grew up across the street from my mother's folks and as I said Dad was in the cattle business with my grandfather. I had three brothers, all with cystic fibrosis, a very bad inherited disease of the pancreas and lungs. One died at six months before I was born, one passed on at two years of age when I was four. My other brother was four-and-one-half years older than I and lived to be twenty-three before the disease took him. I was the only one not affected. I guess that this made our family much closer because we all knew how precious life is and how short of time we can have here on earth. I started looking for ways to go to a regular college and work my way thru selling cars. I went to Tulsa, the closest larger city, about seventy-five miles from our home. I went to all the dealerships and of course all looked at me kind of funny when they saw a seventeen-year old wanting to be in charge of selling a piece of their inventory. The Milner Pontiac folks did talk positive to me and I thought I might land a job there, but nothing ever came of it. I came back home and made a visit to the local Ford, Lincoln, Mercury Dealership, Kissee Motor Co. Darrell Kissee, the owner, had sold my folks several automobiles over the years. When they wanted a Buick he had even made a deal for one for them with a Buick dealer. I guess that since he knew our family and had seen me off and on as a kid growing up he thought he would take a chance on me.

I had my start. I started the second week of August 1967 at the car lot. I will never forget, one of the salesmen a few years older, Jerry Garroutte, took me home for lunch that first day. I thought that was so nice. Sometimes something small we do for someone else will have a long-lasting effect on another as this act by my new friend did. The only problem with starting a new car job in Miami, Oklahoma when I did was that the local B.F. Goodrich Tire Co. plant, the biggest employer in town, had been on strike all summer. No one at the plant could buy anything after the long strike, and local business had been slow for other businessmen so they also were holding back. The strike got settled by the end of August and things started looking up until Ford Motor Co. went on strike. The Ford strike caught us without any inventory after going thru the long Goodrich strike. Now people were ready to buy and Ford was out. Mr. Kissee did find seventeen cars in Pampa, Texas that a dealer would transfer to us. All the personal were loaded up and hauled to Pampa and each assigned a car to drive home. In those days, I am sorry to say, most dealers would unhook or roll back speedometers to suit. For this four-hundred mile trip, the speedometers were unhooked and we were all told to follow our lead car that had taken several of us to Pampa. He would be our speed gauge. Of course the younger guys and myself had to make a party out of this. We would lag back a long way on the four-lane roads and then race up to our lead car. I watched several of these cars for several years and all ran forever with little mechanical problems. Our fun had broken them in right with lots of slowing down and running fast. The varying speeds were really good for the cars. I am sure some of the sedans that were purchased by older couples got a real tame ride after our wild first four-hundred miles that they knew nothing of.

College started after Labor Day and Dee Ann, my wife, and I enrolled in the same classes. We would go eight to one straight through three days a week and for an hour on Tuesday. That left me a lot of time to work at the car dealership. We took business classes and the basics such as English. Dee Ann would read the chapters assigned and tell me about what was in each. I did my written homework while working at the car lot. The head bookkeeper, Ms. Pat Ruth, helped me learn accounting and was always helpful in the other subjects too. We worked four hours on the "floor" at the dealership and had the rest of the day to go out and beat the bushes selling cars. I knew a lot of the farmers, and with homework finished on floor time if not with a customer, I would go to the country. Many a night I would work the country till ten o'clock. Soon I was the number two salesmen at the lot out of six to eight total salesmen. Number one salesman was a Gob Taylor, who knew everyone and had been in the business a long time. He was kind of gruff but really a good salesmen and took a liking to me and often gave me pointers that helped. Car selling was paid on straight commission. We received four percent of the gross for a used car and twenty-five percent of the profit with a twenty-five dollar draw on a new car with the balance after all trades had been sold. If we sold nothing, we got minimum wage for our "floor" time only, nothing for the hours worked away from the lot. With a two-week pay cycle, I had one pay period that I got the minimum in two years I was at the dealership.

One of my first cars sold was to a strange guy from Pitcher, Oklahoma. who came in driving an old wore out Oldsmobile convertible. He had taken a liking to a sixty-six yellow Thunderbird convertible that had been a demo and never got sold. Since it was at the end of the sixty-seven model year we had all been told it would be paid as a used car for commission purposes. I let the man test drive the Tbird and I, as required, went along. He gave me the wildest ride I ever took and remember I was just a kid myself and knew a lot about wild rides. We made it back safe and sound and we arranged financing for the man and traded for his piece of junk. The trade price was $4,000 and I got $160. This car selling was going to be all right. I promptly bought my friend Gob a present for helping me with the close and finance on this deal. It was money well spent, because Gob and I always got along and never had any of the customer fights so many of the salesmen got into when someone came in and did not ask for the first salesman if this was their second visit to the lot. To this day, I always try to treat people I think work on commission with a greater respect and ask for them if I return to their place of business.

The "dogs" of the lot were taken to the car auction in Joplin or Springfield, Missouri, usually on Friday night dealer-only auctions. The salesmen had to drive a car without pay, but we did get a great free supper at a local eating favorite. Sometimes we would push these clunkers up the freeway all the way for the twenty-mile trip to

Joplin. We had fun on these trips and just figured it was a part of the job that we really did not get paid on, but at least it would wash out the final trade and we would get our final new car pay check.

I often had to go pick up a dealer transfer car I had sold at another town. These trips always came unexpected and usually caught me without any money. I needed a credit card. In 1967 getting a credit card for a seventeen year old was unheard of. I would not have either, if not for the local bank president, Charles Stoner, going to bat for me and seeing that I got one. I really appreciated this. Watch the Stoner name as we go on, as he will be both a friend and a turncoat through the years. We never know what life holds for us and who will present the opportunities and challenges. Keep this in mind as you read this book and go through life.

My biggest thrill in selling was to a father/son duo at Afton. I had heard that they were looking for a new pickup, so I went to their farm for a visit. I knocked on the door and Delmar, the son, answered. I told him I was from Kissee Ford and was there to talk new pickups. He said they only bought Chevys. Howard, the father was in the other room where they had just finished lunch together. Hearing us, he told Delmar to let me in and hear what I had to say. I went thru my sales and product speech. I must have done all right because they got interested enough to come in to our dealership and look. On the second visit to our lot, I sold them two new Ford pickups and two new Ford two-ton grain-hauling trucks. Was I ever on cloud nine? Four units sold to one family and a family that wouldn't have anything but a Chevy before I met them. I always credited part of this success to the Ford training classes I had taken. Ford taught us well and their lessons would serve me even later in my cattle business career. When I purchase a new car today, I am sometimes bewildered by the lack of product knowledge and people skills that some of the younger sales reps exhibit. Automobile selling has always had a bad reputation, but I found it to be a very rewarding and satisfying business. I don't know if I have not met some of the right salesmen today or if today's crowd is different. One exception to this was the Ford salesmen that recently sold me a new Ford pickup from the same location I sold at so many years ago although now under different ownership. Tim Jones really treated me right and did the right things to make the sale. He is a rarity at the city dealers I have visited.

Salesmen would come and go during the two years that I sold Fords. I always was amazed that some salesmen would look like they had everything it took to be a success in sales. They would look successful, talk a good talk, and knew the product. However many could not close the sale, spent too much time with dead beats instead of qualifying the customer before spending all day with them, and some just could not manage their time wisely. They would sell three or four cars a month and soon be gone. I averaged about eight cars per month and sometimes would sell as many as twelve. That kept me a steady number two behind Gob, who sold three or four a month more than I. Of course, he worked full time and I went to college. I carried fifteen hours at school and made only two B's in my two years of classes. The rest were A's. Dee Ann did as well; she did the reading and we studied for tests together. I worked at selling cars about fifty hours per week. This is the kind of hours I have been used to putting in for the past thirty-five years. Dee Ann and I made Who's Who In American Junior Colleges, made the grades, enjoyed college, and worked a lot. We had a routine that included lunch at the local Kuku Drive Inn for two fifteen-cent hamburgers (ketchup only). I got to drive a new demo car and received a twenty-gallon of gasoline allowance per week for it. If I ran short of gas (we still lived in Welch about fifteen miles away) I would simply find someone to show a used car to that had been traded in with a tank full of gas. I might not get the car sold, but it was a free ride home. This helped keep our college expenses down. I was on a full tuition scholarship that also paid for our books. I averaged about five hundred dollars per month working at the car agency, which was not bad for a working family in 1967-69 years.

In January of my second year my older brother Steve passed away. While we knew his life would probably be short, he had completed four years of college and was married. His last bout with the disease had taken its toll and he had a heart attack and died. The funeral registration of guests included my boss, Darrell Kissee, and the Ford area dealer rep, Cy Barnes. I never knew Mr. Barnes real well and he probably only went because of Darrell, but I have remembered to this day how much I thought of him for coming by the funeral home. We never know when we will have a lasting impact on someone else's life. I never really told Mr. Barnes how much this had meant to me, but all these years later it still stands out in my memory. In March of the same year my grandmother that had always lived across the street passed away from a stroke. This was a tough time for my family. Dad was having some back and other health problems and could not get anyone to help manage the feedlot. He needed help and I decided it was best for all the family and me if I went back to the cattle business. Darrell Kissee, my car lot boss, offered to teach me the whole business and eventually partner on a dealership for me to run. He had taught me well and I really wanted to stay, but knew I shouldn't. Watch for Darrell Kissee's name many years later that would show in a much different light in the chapter dealing with the troubled bank. Yes, Darrell, would be one of the partners and problems at the troubled bank. While the last experience made me very angry with Darrell for what he did, I never showed it and always respected him for the start in business life I got from him. It was a good thing I did not stay and partner with him as he went broke from other sour investments and would have surely taken me along. The training at the dealership taught me people and negotiating skills that would help me so much in the cattle business. You see most of my cattle business revolved around obtaining customers, haggling over a penny a bushel of corn, a quarter per hundred on the price of finished cattle, or a dime a bottle on the vaccine we bought for the cattle. Same skills, just different products.

I gained the confidence I had been lacking to work with Dad. I miss not having gone on for my four-year college degree, but Dad was a good teacher on the cattle business side. Had I not gone back to his business when I did, the opportunity might have never happened again.? I think he would have sold out before I finished two more years of college. We became friends as well as being father/son and enjoyed seventeen years of work together. I will tell you more about it as we go along.

The main point of this chapter is to relate that you can gain valuable experience for one vocation in a completely different one. The next chapter will move from cars to cattle.

2

Cars to Cattle

This was to be quite a change from two years in the automobile business. Coming home to the family cattle business would prove to be challenging, rewarding, fun. and a lot of work. I started out with the cowboy crew, doing what any new hire would do, such as cleaning feed bunks, checking cattle, processing new cattle, and even a little painting of the pipe fences in the summer. I did not mind and enjoyed everything as long as I did not have to do the same thing every hour of the day. This was never the case at the feedlot as we had so many varied tasks to be done during the day. I think it is very important for a next generation starting new in the business to start at the bottom and work up. Too many times the owner's son or daughter wants to start with an upper-rung position in the company. This sends the wrong message to the employees and does not properly prepare the next generation to know just how the business works. Conversely we will look later at how many parents never let siblings assume leadership or responsibility roles in the company. The sons or daughters are simply left as a grunt worker and never learn to manage and think of how to manage change that comes with time in any business.

The feedlot was a five-thousand-head capacity lot that fed about 15 percent company cattle and 85 percent custom ownership mostly local ranchers that did not have facilities, time, or expertise to feed their own. It had been located at this location three miles south of our town for nine years. The feed mill, however, was still located at the south edge of town where cattle had been fed from 1954-1960. The old location proved to be too close to town and would have soon caused problems. It also did not have as good of drainage and the pens could get very muddy in the winter. The new location had excellent drainage and was close enough to the highway for semi truck access without having too much gravel road to keep up and out of town enough to not bother the neighbors.

In looking back, the two mistakes my dad made early on were not planning ahead enough when building the first lots at the edge of town. A costly mistake, which all of us do at times. The second was deciding after only two years of having me on the job to invest in a new feed mill at the new location. The new mill was much higher tech and less labor intensive. It also saved hauling each load of feed from town, a six-mile round trip. Then what was the mistake? Remember Dad had health problems when I came back and I figured that he probably would have sold out had I not came to help. Now two years later, me the son, a ripe old age of twenty-one with two years of feedlot experience we start a mill that was to cost one hundred twenty thousand dollars. This was a huge sum of money for our family and for the time to be spent. If I had not stayed solid in the business, the folks would have been stuck with a large bank note and been forced to feed cattle whether health permitted or not. I guess the folks knew me better than I at the time because I stayed and ran the custom feedyard for thirty-two years. However, a lot of twenty-one-year olds are not settled down enough to make the kind of investment we did and certainly would have caused much heartache and financial burden on the senior generation.

Everything went smoothly and Dad and I got along great working in the business. I soon found out, and I am sure Dad did too, that we did not work together on the same project very well at all. I would always assume Dad could do a better job than I, which in most cases was true, and I would hang back and let Dad figure out and do whatever we were working on. However, if we took separate projects, I had to do my own thinking and doing and directing the help for results. This proved to work just wonderfully. Dad and I would eat lunch together and talk over what each was doing and make sure the other was comfortable with the plan. Then after lunch we did our separate projects.

Soon, with some of the pressure off, Dad's health seemed to be better. The ulcers and stomach problems in his forties did not bother him much and while the back surgery did not cure all back problems the rest of his life, he got along. I never knew if the stomach problems had to do with work or dealing with my older brother's illness. I am sure most was related to the illness of Steve and the financial burden that went along with it. Steve's daily medicine alone would cost around one hundred dollars per month back in the sixties when Cokes cost a dime and a new Ford pickup cost less than two thousand dollars. The cattle business has always been a very stressful business dealing with the ups and downs of the markets, the harshness of winter weather, the toll of hot, humid summers on cattle, and all else that goes with running a small business.

We thought markets were fickle back then but looking back the cattle market made a big move if it changed twenty-five to fifty cents per hundred pounds. Corn, our main feed item, went all winter at $1.27 per bushel the first year I bought the corn in 1971. Today, we often see weeks where cattle prices move three-five dollars per hundred and corn moves fifteen to twenty cents per bushel. When I started, the era of sending finished cattle to terminal markets and letting commission companies sell the cattle for us in Kansas City, St. Louis, St. Joseph, or Omaha were just about over. Cattle were starting to sell direct to packers at the feedlot. This was best for the industry, but also would prove to put more work and pressure on us to do not only a good job of feeding our customers' cattle, but now also a good job of selling them.

After the first couple of years working entirely outside, I was now spending about half my time in the office buying corn and learning the markets. You had to see and experience our office to get the full feel of what I will now try to describe. It was a 16'×20' tin building without air conditioning. In the summer we had all the windows open and the dust would fly everywhere inside. We had given up the old "yellow sheet" market letter that came in the mail and gave the markets two days late for a new modern mechanical tele-type that gave almost instant market news. The Teletype was great, but it was also very noisy. We also now had a constant stream of company coming by. Some were customers coming to see their cat-tle, some were local ranchers who would come by for a soda pop break and read the markets on the Teletype. We also had started having many neighbors wanting to buy cattle-working supplies from us since we had such a large selection of what they needed. This has become a business within the business over the years and we now cater to the local ranchers. In the seventies though can you think of going to a 16′×20′ tin building with dust flying everywhere and buy-ing your input needs for your business? We also had several men coming and spending the day watching the markets on the teletype. They had become addicted to the new trading of commodities on the Chicago Mercantile or the Chicago Board of Trade. This all made for a dusty, noisy, and (in those days most all the old cowboys smoked and thus) a very smoke filled office. I soon was doing most of my phone business on the outside step if the weather was warm at all, sitting on a concrete block. The block on the step was much quieter and more comfortable than inside.

Like the other traders watching the markets, I soon had the bug to trade and formed a partnership with Archie Neill, my older cousin who worked at the feedyard and Carl Mayfield, who worked for a local cattle order buyer. We called our venture the "JAC" Cattle Company after Joe, Arch, and Carl. We put up a total of a thousand dollars between us and were off and trading. Arch and I would work outside in the morning, but always had numerous stops by the office to see how the futures market was trading. Pork Bellies was our trade of choice and we soon had made close to two thousand dol-lars in a very few days. We thought, boy this is it and we soon will be rich! If you have ever met many future traders they are not rich, at least the ones I have met over the years. We were no exception; we soon expanded our trading into the live cattle futures pits. This proved to not be good as we got on the market train backwards and soon had lost our profit made in trading pork bellies. Before we could get turned around we lost all our profits, our initial investment money, and an additional one thousand dollars that we had to send for margin money calls from the Chicago Brokerage House we did business with. This broke me of speculative trading. I have done some bona fide hedge trading to cover actual cattle owned or grain to be bought to feed the cattle as an insurance against cattle prices going down or grain going up too much. I do not think I have ever done very well even at the hedge, though some people do all right this way. I have never speculated in the cattle or grain futures since. A lesson well learned.

One of the traders and cattle order buyers that fed cattle with us was Woody Wilkins, a tall, dark old Indian. Woody could tell stories that would make you laugh till you hurt. He really knew cattle, but sometimes had a hard time being completely honest. Dad partnered with him because he knew their cattle would make money and it filled pens at the lot. One of Woody's stories was on Carl of our "JAC" Cattle fame and who worked for Woody hauling cattle. Now Carl had been married three times and Woody always said that the devil owed Carl a debt and paid him off in women.

Another one of the "traders" was a Keith Kugler who got to coming and watching the markets and trading. Keith is a small gentleman who talks a little "duchy" and was soon nicknamed "Kudeybear" by Woody. "Kudeybear" had a nice family and had built a successful dairy operation. Like all of us he made some money at first in the futures markets and soon was investing very heavily in this newfound gold. At one point he had bought so many contracts of soybeans that the Chicago Board of Trade would not let him under their rules buy any more. He went to town one day and decided to spend some of his new fortune on a new suit and a new station wagon for his family. As soon as Woody found out he immediately told "Kudeybear" that he had better not put a scratch on the new car or "toot" in the new suit because what the markets giveith they can taketh away. You guessed it, the sad story is the soybean market went opposite of Kudey's position. Soon the new car had to go back; I guess they didn't come after the suit, but he also eventually lost his dairy farm and his wife and family left him. In a short time he had gone from the Soybean King with a nice family and a well off dairy operation to nothing. I lost track of "Kudeybear" for several years and ran in to him at a farm show I was working in Springfield, Mo. Twenty-five years later. "Kudey" has a small sheep operation and while happy had never regained what he once had.

Woody also got to playing pitch card games at our office in between watching the markets. These games were for money and got to going on quite a bit. It got to be a little much. The last straw seemed to be when Woody who liked to drink often and a lot decided to share some of his booze with Homer, our night watchman and my wife's uncle. Now, Homer had been quite a rounder himself in his day, but had pretty well reformed as he was up in his seventies by then. Well, Woody got Homer drunk and he fell and cut his head pretty bad. I got the call and had to take him to get sewed up and deal with his drunken state. This was it for Woody, Dad ran him off. He never fed with us again, but none of us held any ill feelings against each other. Woody knew he had gone too far and we knew how Woody was. Several years later after Dad was gone Woody would come by once in a while to visit. He always was on his best behavior on these visits. On one visit, he heard us talking about going to the ranch to burn off the excess left over grass in the spring so the new growth could come on strong. Woody ask if he could join us. I said yes and we had a great time. Woody told stories to all of us and made the late hours burning at night after working all day go by seemingly quick.

Roy Davis was another order buyer who fed and partnered with Dad. Roy was a little wild, but quite tame compared to Woody. I learned a lot about cattle from Roy. He once went with me to Springfield to call on a Mr. Larson, a new potential customer. He had an office in the tallest office building in Springfield on the top floor. I was quite impressed. His cattle operation was several miles away and he had a foreman taking care of it. Mr. Larson had his foreman send his cattle to us. However, the foreman had not done his job well and several of the cattle got sick and some died soon after arrival. I had done all I could to lessen the blow, but it was not enough for our customer. He got drunk one night and called me at two- thirty in the morning and let me have it. I had never experienced this side of business and thankfully never had a call like that in the middle of the night again. I enjoyed Roy's company and learned many things about cattle from him especially on buying at the sale barn, but I learned on my own how to handle a drunken customer in the middle of the night.

Another one of our customers and buyers was Lee Scott. Lee was a retired school superintendent that had gone into ranching. He soon was order buying feeder cattle and got Dad to partner with him and Rex Jeans on a feeding company called the Welch Cattle Co. Lee bought the feeder cattle for the new partnership, Rex would grow the cattle and straighten the health out at his ranch, and we would feed them out and sell to the packers. The three worked well together until tough markets came and Lee and Rex decided to retire. Lee sold his Vinita ranch and moved to Texas which has no state income tax as Oklahoma has. I could not understand why Lee and his wife would leave their home and move ten hours away over a small tax payment he would owe if they lived in Oklahoma. Looking back, I am sure that the tax was only part of the reason Lee moved. The real reason was to start the next chapter of his life fresh with other retired people in a retirement community. He would not have to see his friends still working or watch someone else run his ranch. I learned many years later that this is not all bad.

I had obtained a pretty good start feeding cattle in about three years. Watching Dad with his partnerships, I decided I was ready to try one also. There was a section of 640 acres of grass for sale about three miles east of our operation. My old friend Charles Stoner wanted to get in on the cattle feeding so I talked to him about the ranch. Another friend, Duane Carter, had previously worked at the lot and now sold Moormans feed and fed cattle with us. He wanted to expand. The three of us got together and had a plan to buy the ranch together, fertilize the poor pasture with manure from the feed lot and buy cattle. We would straighten up their health on the ranch and put pounds on them with cheap grass and then them feed in the lot. We thought we would make a lot of money. We got to within $5,000 on the 640 acres and the owner would not come down another penny. The five thousand we were apart amounts to only $7.81 per acre, not much. Somehow, we held our ground and did not give in, but neither did the owner. The best thing that could ever of happened was that we walked away. A sixth sense kept us from jumping off what would have been quite a cliff. Like so many times in my life, God was watching over me. With in twelve months the cattle markets had tanked. For two years, cattle lost money like we had never seen. Duane had to sell his ranch and move back to Texas where he went into farming with his father. The cattle he was already feeding had lost all his equity. The bank run by Stoner was after him to collect all they could before more was lost on his loans. Charles Stoner would not have been able to survive financially nor had the fortitude to stay hooked in cattle till the prices came back had our venture went through. I lost $50,000 on cattle I was already feeding during this time. More losses would have done me in as well. Our proposed ranching venture would have broken all three of us within a year. I learned a good lesson on walking away from the deal when it's called for. I also learned that sometimes what looks really bad such as the fifty thousand dollar loss I incurred during this cattle downturn is actually just the tip of the iceberg I could have hit if God had not looked over my shoulder and guided my business decisions. God will not spare us from all of life's failures, losses, poor health, or death. He will always guide us through troubled times and not give us more than we can bear. We must learn to trust and look to Him in all our choices and dealings.

In the next chapter we'll talk about running out of beef, or should I say beef running out our ears?

3

Running out of Beef or Beef Running Out of Our Ears?

By 1973 I was getting adjusted to my life at the feed yard. We expaned the capacity of the lot thru the '70s, adding a few pens each year till we got to an 8,000 head capacity. I usually would take our plans for the lots and take charge of forming up the concrete pad aprons for the feedbunks and water tanks. We hired a full time welder and he would take our layout and put in the pipe fences. I have always been as dumb as a fence post when doing anything that entailed mechanical or "fix it" jobs. I struggled at this but enjoyed learning how to do things and soon learned that I could lean on more skilled employees and outside contractors when dealing in areas I had trouble in. In later years I have gotten pretty good at scouting out the needed repair contractor or part, but this only because I know I have to have help in these areas and I have learned how to figure out who to call.

I started learning to sell finished cattle and this is the area along with customer relations, that I have always liked best in the business. These two areas are also where the bottom line at a custom yard is transformed. In the August 1973 President Nixon placed a price freeze on the price of beef. Old time cattlemen thought we were going to run out of beef. I will always remember my friend Morris Barnes who sold cattle at a competing feedlot thinking we would only have beef in the grocery stores on weekends. Remember this prediction because it will cause Morris much grief that we will talk about later in this chapter. Somehow Dad and I didn't buy into the theory of running out of beef. When most feeders quit selling and elected to wait for the sure-to-come higher prices after the freeze went off in September we forged ahead and sold every hoof we could. By September you could have shot a rifle down thru the pens without hitting a thing.

One dear father and son team of Morris and Waymon Montgomery had some really plain cattle on feed during this time. They had fed with us for several years, but upon placing this pen on feed they told us it was to be their last. Morris had back and other health problems and they had decided to cut back so that Morris could slow down. Waymon farmed and liked cows and did not have time to do their buying of feeder cattle nor straightening up the cattle to make sure all sickness was out of them before placing on feed. I had a small locker plant come by and wanted to purchase five head for his locker. I sold him five of the Montgomery plain steers for fifty five cents a pound, the highest we had ever seen at the time and would prove to be the highest market for years. A larger packer buyer, Hull & Dillon, came by and wanted a pen of steers. Hull & Dillon had never been a large player in fed beef; they elected to process mostly old cows and hogs. However during the thirty-day price freeze they did more business than I would have ever dreamed. After the freeze we never heard from them again and they closed for good a few years later. On this day however, I told the buyer I had been selling out of this pen at fifty-five cents and he could have the rest at the same money if he wished. Now you never want to story to anyone and for sure not to a buyer, but remember I had sold five out of the pen. He bit, he bought, and we all chuckled a little about how many dollars the cattle brought. Had we waited till post freeze (to the amazement of many including my friend, Morris Barnes) they would have brought only forty-four cents. Before the slide was over prices fell to the low thirties over a period of time. This was to be a period of about two years of probably the darkest days ever in the cattle industry. The Montgomerys missed all the bad markets and several years later Waymon changed his farming operation so that he would have time to deal with cattle again. He was the only feeder we had who missed the bad years of feeding to come back in better times.

Many customers were not so lucky and lost their shirts before it was over. We often heard stories of people in Texas feedlots literally feeding their cattle until the feed bill ate up more than their whole value. It was a bleak time. I got to where I hated to go to work because I would have to listen to our customers and cattlemen coming by talk of all the horror stories going on in the industry. I guess it was getting to Dad also, because during this time he turned most all of the finished cattle selling over to me. I would spend hours on the telephone trying to sell cattle. Of course with the glut in numbers everyone else was also doing the same thing. In those days we had a nice network of independent packing companies both local and east of us from Arkansas to Florida. The locals would come by and look and we would trade over ten cents or even a nickel per hundred for seemingly hours before one of us would give in and we would have a trade. The major packers at the time were John Morrel & Company, Wilson Foods, Swift, Missouri Beef, American Beef, and a relatively new player Iowa Beef Processors—today simply known as IBP. I would sell some to all of these companies except Swift; they mostly were located in Texas and had a closer source of cattle. John Morrell even had two buyers call on us from different plants plus one who telephoned once in a while from a third plant. Each buyer would bid against his own company. I never understood that and today John Morrell is out of business. The only surviving packing company of the ones I just mentioned is IBP, and Tyson Foods, the chicken people, bought them in 2001. American Beef went broke during these bad years in the '70s. I had been trying to get their buyer to come and look at cattle and he just wouldn't come. To this day I think he realized where his employer was headed and stayed away on purpose. The cattlemen that did get cattle sold to American during this time did not get paid and lost even more money to add to their woes. None of us had seen their demise coming.

I ended up selling most of the cattle over the telephone to buyers I had never met nor had they ever seen our operation. Trust among cattlemen even today is a completely different world than other industries. I would just describe the cattle to the buyer over the phone; tell him how big they were going on feed and how many days they had been on feed. I would also guess at the figures in regard to quality grades such as choice and dressing percentage would be once the cattle were harvested and on the packer's rail. They would bid accordingly. Sometimes I would miss how well the cattle should have done, but never would I intentionally mislead a buyer. Our reputation was worth too much to screw up on one bad deal. I would sell to plants in Montgomery, Alabama; Quincy, Florida; Shreveport, Louisiana; Fort Smith and Little Rock, Arkansas; and Memphis, Tennessee. Today, these plants are all gone, as the industry has settled closer to the cattle feedlots. It was a very tough time in our industry for many months, which would take its toll on many cattlemen.

One such cattleman was a Duane Barr. Duane is a big, jolly, single man. He liked to buy and feed cattle and had several hundred on feed when the collapse hit. He had just by luck of the draw bought a Brahma cross steer that was on feed by the office. The steer must have been someone's pet bucket calf because most Brahma steers are very wild. Not this steer, he would hear the door slam on the office and he would come up to the fence. Soon everyone would go by and stop and pet the steer. When it came time to sell the pen, the steer led all the others out to the shipping corral. Duane couldn't part with him and had us transfer the steer to his next pen. He did this through five pens and the steer just kept getting bigger. After five pens of losing, the bank had given up on the market and Duane, and it wouldn't let him buy any more cattle. Duane ate his now one-ton pet steer and said that that was all that was left of $100,000. The steer was the only hundred thousand dollar steer I had ever seen. Of course he was not worth that, only what Duane had left to show for his huge loss feeding of cattle. My friend and almost partner, Duane Carter had to sell his ranch during this time and moved back to Texas to farm with his family. Carl Mayfield of our "JAC" commodity trading also bellied up during this time. A solid banker is the key to a lot of success stories and here also.

Our long time family friend and customer, C.L. "Stu" Parker struggled like all did during this time. Stu, however, a few months before the price fall had studied his program and decided it was too risky. He had been feeding a pen of about three hundred head once every four months. If the market was good when his were ready he was happy, but he had realized if the market sunk, which it did and he had that many ready at once it could break him.

Stu went to his banker, the First National Bank in Miami and laid out his plan. He would borrow enough money to feed a pen of one hundred per month. His plan laid out to have two pens of one hundred each at home learning to eat, get over any shipping fever, and get some grass gain on them before sending one hundred each month to the feedlot. The cattle would need four months on feed, so Stu would always have two groups at home getting ready and four pens in the lot, each one month apart. His plan was that if one set sold bad, maybe the next month would be better. The other feature of his plan was that each time he sold finished cattle, he was back to the sale barn buying on generally the same market news he just sold his fats on. If the market was down he would buy back cheaper. Stu never dreamed that this plan would save his career. He went thru pen after pen losing money till he had lost one hundred thousand dollars just like Barr. This was a huge sum in the seventies for these men to swallow. The bank quit Barr and he would not regain his former status for decades. Stu, however, had presented his plan to his banker and they stayed hooked up with him. Each time he sold a pen at a loss he went right back and bought more at the sale barn. When the markets finally turned he had four pens of one hundred in the lot and two more pens at home, all costing seventeen cents per pound or so. He made a hundred dollars per head on each of these the next six months and bought more back on the improved conditions that would enable Stu to earn his losses back in months, not years. Stu and his wife Betty worked together on the ranch and grew their numbers and prospered for years after this. The other three gentlemen never regained their former place in the cattle business even years later. A solid plan and a solid banker are two very important elements in any small farm or business.

My friend, Morris Barnes that I mentioned earlier found out we actually had beef running out of our ears. He had 10,000 head on feed of his own at the Parsons, Kansas lot he partially owned and in which he sold the finished cattle. The losses on this many did not break Morris immediately, but he never recovered. Interest rates in the mid seventies to early eighties were high and at one time Morris was paying two percent over New York prime rate which made his interest rate payable to the bank 21 percent. This was just too much to overcome; with the huge cattle loss and these record high interest rates. Morris lost his farm, which was quite large. Worst of all, he soon was drinking too much and also lost his health. Morris died virtually broke. His widow Norma, the nicest, sweetest lady you would ever see, had to move from their farm home to some nice apartments that were mostly government subsidized rent. Now, I have never once had a bad thought about my friend Morris because I know it is so easy to think something is an cinch and bet the farm on it. He certainly was neither the first nor the last to make the same mistake. However, all these years later I think of Morris at least once a week. I don't want all he and his family went through to be completely in vain. I use his example, not in a looking down on him in a foolish way, but as it could very well have been or could be me next. I realized that if cattle prices are good it won't take ten thousand to make a good profit and if they are losing money I sure do not want that many. Morris has kept me from going off the deep end many a time. For this I thank him, now. Wish I had when he was alive.

One of the small packers was Bauer and Son in Sand Springs, Oklahoma. Bobby Bauer, the owner was a very tough trader. He never quite played by the same rules most everyone else in the business did. His plant would use three to four loads of cattle per week or 150 to 200 head. He sold mostly on government contracts to Army and Air Force Bases. Bobby bought a load of cattle over the phone from my Dad in the early seventies. Later in the day the price broke. As the cattle truck pulled in to the plant on delivery day Bobby came running out and hollering that these cattle weren't good enough before he had even seen them. He thought he could call up Dad and "bush" him on the price since the market had fallen after their trade. Dad could be pretty stubborn and he was sure in the right. He wouldn't "bush" the price and told the driver to load them up and then call. In the meanwhile, Dad called another packer buyer and friend, Art Chaney of Cushing Pack just down the road and told Art the trouble he was in at Bobby's. Art listened to the same cattle description and then said send them on over, we will take care of you. When the cattle were processed they did even better than Dad had thought or told Bobby. Bobby would call every little while after that for years, but not until at least ten years would we ever let him purchase cattle from us again. Finally, I worked out a deal and let Bobby buy from us again using another buyer, Danny O'Brien, as our go-between. This went on for several years till Danny seemed to be taking advantage of Bobby by giving him the worst end of his buy and keeping the better ones for himself. This may have been their arrangement, but I didn't want any one taken advantage of so I went to selling Bobby direct again. I continued to sell Danny until he retired from his small packing operation. Bobby also bought from me till he closed down. He never completely changed and once in awhile I would have to get real mean, chew up some nails, and call Bobby and line him out. He never cared though, and would be all right for a few weeks until I would eat those nails again and call and straighten him out. We actually got to enjoy each other and I worked with him just fine in our own funny way. Bobby's sons Tom and Mike would come some of the time and in later years Tommy did some of the buying. He was a chip off the old block. We enjoyed each other and did many a trade, but I always had to be on guard.

Those long months in 1973 and 1974 were certainly hard on everyone in cattle country. As the finished cattle got cheaper so did feeders and the calves. Feeders made their money back first if they could just stay in and buy back the cheap calves. Eventually, of course, everyone started to rebound in all segments. It is a time that will be remembered by all who experienced it through their lifetime. I lost about fifty thousand dollars in my own cattle operation. Since I had only been in the business four years I had not yet built up my numbers. However, this was a huge sum for us at this stage in our life. We managed to stay in and buy cheaper inventory that allowed us to recoup our losses in short order. We did postpone buying a piece of land nearby that I really would have liked to own. We also put off building a house for a couple more years. I will talk about that experience in the next chapter.

Dad never said how much he lost, but I know it had to be a considerable amount. His salvation was owning the "hotel" for cattle we called a feedlot. Our customer business always paid the bills in bad times and made a living. So many small businessmen and farmers or ranchers do not realize just how much the daily living expenses cost. If living cost, losses, and interest all have to be made up it makes for a tall mountain to climb. Much harder than just making back the initial loss.

Our cattle industry has changed so much since this period of time. Our small, independent packers are all gone. Consolidation in the industry because of cost of operation compared to the giants of the industry forced each out over time. Some stayed until broke, others were smarter, saw what was coming, and got out before they lost their nest egg. Even the giants were not efficient enough and as I said earlier only IBP remains today and chicken people own them. Cattle in every phase is a very unforgiving, cutthroat business. It is fun and can be rewarding. However, you have to plan, watch your cost, and be a very sharp businessman to succeed.

Most businesses can be very unforgiving just as the cattle business. You must study and plan your investment from every angle. No matter how good a deal looks, do not bet the entire farm, or in other words, more than if the venture goes bad you can afford to lose. Build your business up over time. Expansions are great and risk with borrowed capital is a part of business. Just do not grow so fast that if you are wrong a sudden downfall will result in total business failure.

The next chapter will talk of my early days in my side venture of real estate sales.

4

Real Estate

The rule of business I learned early on was "You cannot get ahead if you live too high on the hog or spend too much living and not enough investing." Dee Ann and I lived in a 52′ × 10′ mobile home for nine years. This was the cheapest living we have ever had. It was parked on an empty lot my grandmother owned and let us use rent-free. We paid $3200 and a 1931 Model A Ford worth about $800 for the mobile in 1967. This was probably the worst trading I have ever done in my life. The home was a fairly plain, inexpensive model built by Champion. We had no trouble with it the entire nine years. I just gave more money for it than it could have been bought for at the time. I have learned to be a much more astute trader since. The mobile home was pretty cramped on space especially after Jodee, our daughter, started to grow and acquire more toys and clothes.

The utility bills and upkeep were cheap though. With only about five hundred square feet to heat and cool our bills were cheap. The first summer we spent without air conditioning, which was a real scorcher, like a sardine in a tin can. The second year we bought an air conditioner and life was a real breeze. Our only time of concern was when the wind started blowing. In those days most mobile homes were not tied down and you read often of them blowing over in storms. I always watched for storms and got out if the wind got too high. I probably stand much more chance of blowing away today living in a highly insulated, well-built stone veneer home. I never hear the wind or pay much attention. The tornado will probably sneak in and get us some day when we least expect it.

The money saved by living in the small mobile those nine years was plowed into our expanding cattle business. We lived on a very modest salary from the Neill Cattle Co., the folks' cattle corporation that had been formed in 1960 with my dad and granddad as partners. Any money we made on our cattle was plowed right back into cattle. We borrowed large sums of money to finance our cattle business. However, our small home and our car were paid for when purchased out of savings. So many young people today want to start out with two new cars and a house nicer than Mom and Dad's. While this is great, it puts the young couples usually in debt for assets that do not make them money. Yes, a house can appreciate in value. However, the cost of living in the larger house usually eats up a lot of the gain. Cars never make money and depreciate rapidly.

I started trying to think of ways to swing a new house without dipping into our operating capital. The first twenty years or so of my career I had a very high energy level and was always doing something productive. Chronic illness robbed me of this energy over the past several years, and we will discuss that later. In our small community there was only one part-time real estate agent. This looked like an area where some extra money could be earned without too much cash invested and earned during off hours in the evenings and Saturday or Sunday afternoons. I enrolled in the evening class for real estate at my old junior college, Northeastern A & M College in Miami, Oklahoma, and began to study. To sit for the salesman's license required one semester of three hours credit. Upon completion of the course, the state test for the real estate sales license was taken in Oklahoma City. After the successful passing of the test, I had to work under a licensed real estate broker. I visited with old family friend, W. A. Maxson. W. A. "Wauyaugh" had started the local cattle auction business at his home about the time I was born. My father was a partner in the business the first couple of years. The business flourished and Dad and Wauyaugh got the sale rolling. Soon, however, some of Wauyaugh's brothers wanted in on the sale.

It looked like this would be the best route for all concerned so Dad sold his interest out. The Maxson Brothers would continue in the livestock sale business for years in our community. I worked this same sale for the Maxsons as an extra yard hand on sale days while in high school. Wauyaugh and his wife Ruth had a son Rocky, a year younger than I. Rocky and I studied the real estate course together and enjoyed each other a lot during our learning. We both placed our licenses under Wauyaugh and started our part time careers in real estate.

I enjoyed meeting people and working with them on land or house deals. I did not spend too much time since I worked a full schedule plus at the cattle feedlot. Rocky and I both went back for the second semester real estate broker course at the college. We both completed it and passed the broker exam as well. Now, we had to spend one year under the sponsorship of a licensed broker. I stayed with the Maxson Agency for over that year. I enjoyed it very much and Wauyaugh was very nice to me. He, however, was used to working by himself and it seemed I kind of got in way, so like Dad I decided to leave this arrangement and start my own real estate company. Joe Neill Real Estate was formed in 1976. Wauyaugh and Rocky continued to sell together until Wauyaugh passed away. The Maxson Sale Company was sold in the late seventies and Rocky started teaching vocational agriculture in the Miami High School were he still is today. In our own high school years, I always thought that Rocky would be a large rancher and sale operator. There is certainly nothing wrong with school teaching; it is a very rewarding profession. It was just a completely different path than I envisioned for my friend Rocky. We had been close friends during these early years but have since gone different ways and rarely see each other. I, however, continue to respect and thank the Maxson family for their friendship and opportunities I had with them.

A person's spouse can make a huge difference in how things go in the business world. I have always been thankful that Dee Ann liked our business and could go with the flow. I always figured that Rocky's first wife Judy played a big role in his school teaching decision, as she should have. While Rocky was in business with his father, they lived in a remodeled farmhouse in the country. Judy never seemed to like this arrangement. One story of this comes to mind with a strong point to remember. Rocky and I were active in the local Jaycees chapter and were working late one night on one of their projects. Just as I walker in the door, Dee Ann handed me the phone. Judy was on it wondering where Rocky was. Not realizing what was going on, I was my usual joking self. I joked, oh he left along time ago and probably stopped by the local El Toro Bar. Now, Rocky was not in the habit of stopping at the bar and I knew he had not that night either. No sooner than I joked with Judy about this I realized she was scared or upset and immediately told her that Rocky should be home any minute. About an hour later, Judy called me and said that Rocky had got home very soon after our conversation and then proceeded to chew me up one side and then the other. I took it in fashion and decided then and there that I should be more careful when joking. We never know when we will make a bad impression on someone without realizing what we are doing. A good reason to always be careful before the words come out of our mouth. I don't know what had happened but we were never close to Rocky and Judy after that. I always missed their friendship. I wish I had handled things differently. Soon they left the cattle sale business and moved to Miami where both got teaching jobs. Judy and Rocky had martial problems several years later and divorced. One's mate can sure make a difference in how life goes. I hope both my friends found true happiness.

Real estate sales commissions were my plan to pay for our long-planned house of dreams. I never set the world on fire but in the last half of the seventies and thru the eighties I usually sold eight to twelve different deals in a year and usually made an extra eight to twelve thousand dollars a year to go towards our home. In the seventies a small twelve to fourteen hundred square foot house could be built for twenty five to thirty thousand dollars. Now, this is not the size so many young folks want today, but we enjoyed ours very much. The insurance and utility cost were also held down on this size home. If not for dear old Uncle Sam and income tax, I would have the cost of a new home earned in about three years selling real estate on the side. We saved this money and planned all along the way for our new home. I spent many enjoyable hours studying house plans with Dee Ann. Part of the joy of obtaining something is the planning and then working toward the goal. The fulfillment does not last long, if we rush out and buy something without the dreaming and planning and we have to look at the mortgage cost of it every month thereafter.

Dad had a housing subdivision he had started on the former feedlot sight joining town. I helped sell the lots after starting my real estate business. I never charged him a commission though. One large lot joined the school bus barn and needed a lot of fill. No one wanted it, so we decided to use it for our house. We hauled load after load of rotted cattle manure from the feedlot to this lot. Soon we had it built up and started our house construction. I acted as my own general contractor. This not only saved several dollars but also gave me more business experience. I always thought everyone was honest and honorable as the people I dealt with in the cattle business. The cattle business has always had its share of wild players who lived and played hard and many went broke. However, you can usually depend on a cattleman's word. They are a dying breed, I am sorry to say, in this world. I had come to expect this honesty in all my dealings. I soon learned that many in the building and construction supply or sub contracting business would just as soon tell you one thing and do the opposite as not. It was hard to adjust to this way of doing business, but I did. I wish the world would go back to God's Golden Rule of "Do Unto Others As You Would Have Them Do Unto You." The world would certainly be a much better place to live. We hired an old friend, Charles Williamson, to be the carpenter on our house. Charles had started his career as a carpenter, but later went into the meat locker and butchering business. We sold him his beef for the locker and I knew he would do as he said he would. He got tired of the long hours involved with the locker and had sold it and went back to carpentering. Charles was a dream to work with. Of course, Murphy's Law says that nothing will go smoothly and the house did not either. It was to have a concrete slab floor. I had a block foundation laid and I hauled the fill rock to bring up the foundation to the four-inch concrete slab for the floor. The day of the concrete floor was planned and started off well. Then an uncalled for change in the weather came and it rained hard on our newly poured cement. Charles and his helpers did a good job getting finished but the floor turned out pitted and rough. We had planned on tile floors in the kitchen, dining, and foyer areas. With the floor pitted and rough, but thank goodness solid, we changed plans and used kitchen carpet for the kitchen and dining areas. The rest of the house went on plan and turned out very nice and pretty. Dee and I spent our off hours once again doing the odd jobs involved that did not require special skills we did not have. We hauled not only the foundation fill but also found some really nice used bricks in Parsons, Kansas and hauled them on our old feedlot dump truck. We insulated the walls, painted the walls and stained all the wood and door trim, and painted the outside. I also searched all the newspaper ads for the best buys on building materials and made many trips to Tulsa with the dump truck or a trailer to pick up materials. We enjoyed every minute of the process and put a lot of sweat equity in the house.

As the end was in sight for the construction of our home I turned my attention to selling the mobile home that had served us so well. I sold it to Alford Schumacher sight unseen. Al lived in New York and was preparing to move back a widower to his hometown of Welch and retire. There were many Schumachers in Welch and they looked the house over well for Al and we made a deal over the phone for two thousand four hundred dollars. Mobile homes are known to depreciate, but ours only cost us sixteen hundred dollars for those nine years. If I had been a better buyer on the start the loss would have been even less.

After five or six years of planning and saving and many hours of labor in the building process we finally had our dream home. We lived in it for all of nine months. A chance of a lifetime came along and the house went. Next chapter will deal with the house trade. I think you will get a kick out of "Did Dee Ann Kick Me Out For Selling Her New Home? Or The Best Trade Of Our Life?"

5

Best Trade Of Our Life

You might say it would take a lot of nerve to sell your wife's dream home after years of planning and dreaming about how it would be built and then selling it after only nine months. Well, I did sell our home after only nine months, but Dee Ann and I jointly decided to do such. We did not have a plan to sell the home, it just sort of happened. You never know how some things will play out.

A local widow lady, Mrs. Phillips, had sold her farm and moved to town. Mrs. Phillips rented a nice home from our former neighbors and life long friends, Jewelle and Arthur "Boone" McAffrey. The home rented by Mrs. Phillips was the McAffrey old home place. It was directly across the back alley from my folks home, where I grew up. Boone took me on one of my first fishing trips and showed me how to garden. He was the town master at both catching fish and producing the best garden. Jewelle was also always very kind to me. While in grade school, any time I got sick which was quite often (I missed thirty-one days of my first grade due to various illnesses) Jewelle would bake me my favorite apple pie. They were always just like family to me and I always went by their house on Christmas Eve until they died.

The McAffreys had purchased my Grandmother's large two story home across the street from where I grew up and next door to the lot we used to park our mobile home in 1968 from my

Grandmother's estate. They retained their old home as a rental. Both homes were old, but well kept with a stately look to them. I was glad that they had bought my grandmother's, whom we called "Yoo Hoo," home. I could still visit it and feel like it was in the family. Our daughter, Jodee spent many an hour with Boone in his garden next to us just like I had done as a child. I always got along with the McAffreys but not all people did. They could be pretty set in their own ways and very opinionated. We all have our quirks and I just looked over theirs.

For some reason, Mrs. Phillips made the McAffreys mad over their rent house. I never knew what happened. I do know that Mrs. Phillips was probably as good of renter that they would ever find. However Jewelle and Boone told her to move and gave her just thirty days to do so. Mrs. Phillips called me, knowing I was in the real estate business and ask what I had available for sale. She had decided that maybe renting was not for her and that she would buy herself a home. I showed Mrs. Phillips several homes I had listed in our small town. Nothing was really anywhere close to what she wanted. One evening Mrs. Phillips and a friend whose name I cannot remember came by our new house to visit about houses. Time was running and she had to decide soon where she was moving. We talked for quite some time and nothing was appealing to her. She turned to her friend and asked, "what would you do if you were me?" The friend immediately replied, "I would ask Joe and Dee Ann if they would sell this very home we are in." That sounded great to Mrs. Phillips and she asked if we would sell her our home. Shocked, I said I would need some time to think about it and time to talk to Dee Ann. I told her I would call her with an answer the next day.

I was a little afraid to even mention to Dee Ann the thought of selling her dream home, but did. Always supportive of my business deals, she said sure. It will be fun to build another home and we can put our profits into a slightly larger home without dipping into our cattle fund. The next morning I called Mrs. Phillips our answer and priced the home somewhere in the low thirty thousand dollar figure. Mrs. Phillips and the friend came back and looked again. She sure wanted our home, but only had about twenty-eight thousand dollars in readily available cash. I know she had more savings, but I guess she felt like she needed to save it for living expenses. We both tried to think of a way for her to swing a deal we both could live with. We had something over twenty-five thousand dollars in hard cash in the home plus the value of all our own work on the project. We thought and thought, but to no avail. The two women left with all of us seeking a solution.

It came to me shortly after they left. Mrs. Phillips' grandparents had at one time owned the bank in our little town and I knew she had inherited a few shares of its stock. I thought that this bank stock might turn out to be a good investment some day. My father sat on its Board and owned some shares my Mother had inherited from her family. My grandfather and mom's father also back in the years had been president of the Welch State Bank. The controlling interest in the bank had been sold long ago to three gentlemen John Buford, John Wallace, and Ben Owens of Miami who also owned the Security Bank in Miami. They were starting to get on in years and I knew that there had been talk of someday selling the bank back to local ownership. I thought this might be a good investment in the long run. I called Mrs. Phillips and told her I had an idea. We met and I presented my plan. I would take her twenty-eight thousand dollars cash she had and for the balance I would take her bank stock in trade. At the time, the stock was worth in the neighborhood of one hundred twenty-five dollars per share. It paid no dividends and had not changed much in value in years. I still thought it would someday have potential if local ownership ever came about. It would be a big chance, but the cash Mrs. Phillips had would clear our cost of the house and the stock would be our profit and our pay for our long hard hours.

Mrs. Phillips thought this sounded just great. At her age, she did not think the stock would do her much good and it certainly did not offer any income. We made a deal. Mrs. Phillips felt good, she would not be in the street. Now the panic was in our court, where do we go so fast?

We thought and looked to no avail. There has never been many rent houses in our little town. We were getting close to the deadline and nothing yet in sight. Out of the blue one of our feedlot employees came in and said that he was leaving us for another job. Terry also just happened to be living in a one of our feedlot houses. We have three homes on places bought around the feedlot and have used them for employees to live in rent free in exchange for their being part of the security team and for helping the night watchman if a emergency repair was needed after hours. I was not about to put one of the employees out on the street so that I would have a place to live. I never dreamed Terry was looking for a change, but when he turned in his notice he was set that he was leaving. Terry moved out the front door and we followed him in the back door of the house. Problem solved.

I will never forget moving day. My State Farm insurance agent Jerry Gullet was a friend getting his start in the insurance business. He was working hard to build his business and today twenty-nine years later, he is still with State Farm and a very good agent. I called Jerry and told him about our sale to Mrs. Phillips and arranged for him to meet her. He sold her on keeping her insurance on the new home with him. Jerry in turn offered to help us on moving day, which was very appreciated. He knew how to get ahead in business and I have had insurance of some kind with him ever since. Another old family friend, Stu Parker, the cattle feeder, also offered to help. We had a good time moving. I about got Stu hurt when the back steps of the old house gave way with him as we were going in with a heavy dresser. We had a good laugh and Stu helped us move a couple more times before saying enough was enough and that we were on our own. Even though Stu was my dad's friend, Stu also grew to be my good friend. After Dad died, Stu was always good to come around just to visit and listen. Friendships are two sided and have to be cultivated over years. A good friendship is a very valuable asset. All is not measured in worth by the amount of money you have.

We got through the move. However, I have not told you the rest of the story on our new home. You probably guessed when I mentioned the steps falling in with Stu that this home was lacking in a few areas. The old house was an original three-room house all in a row that had had a living room, with a bathroom added later in an "L" fashion. The only heat in the home was a wall heater pointed in the direction away from the kitchen, toward the bedroom wings. We had been used to central heat even in the trailer home. Now we would spend a winter with little heat in our bedrooms. It also did not come furnished with a cooking stove and, not planning to be there long, we did not buy one. We cooked on a hot plate; this was before the microwave oven days. The winter we lived in the house was very wet and cold. The last quarter mile of the gravel road to our home was not well maintained as we were at the end of a dead end road. It got so muddy that we could not get our car down the road, only our pickup. We left the car in town the whole winter.

We soon found another house plan we liked, but could not get our friend Charles Williamson to be our carpenter as he was booked several months in advance. We found another father and son team to work on this house. They would prove to not be near as good to work with as Charles. We started the work and as before we did several projects of the construction ourselves during the evenings and weekends. We were building another concrete slab floor construction and I once again hauled the foundation fill. This type of construction always applies a pre-treat application of a chemical for termites before pouring the concrete. We had a chemical sprayer used for cattle that could be washed out and used to apply "Chlordane" as the pre-treat. I was working on this alone at the site a few blocks from my folks' home where I would go if I needed a phone or snack. I started to unscrew the faucet on the spray hose, bent over looking down at it. Instead of the faucet handle having a stop on it when all the way open, the handle just came out of the pipe thread and the spray water shot with full force at me. It soaked my face and got in my eyes so bad I could not see. I knew this was powerful stuff and that I had better get it off fast. I felt my way down the street the two or three blocks to the folks' house and washed and washed my face and eyes. All was fine; I had quite a scare that could have been very bad. The Lord above was watching over me as usual and all was to be fine. To this day I have not had any termites in my wooden head.

We decided to build two houses simultaneously this time, thinking that we could shift the contractors between the houses and buy materials for both in the same time. It didn't quite work like I envisioned but turned out all right in the end. My first framing crew, the Crosbys would not show up and work as promised. I got through the framing process on the first house with them and with a stroke of luck my old friend Charles Williamson had a cancellation and moved to us to do the finish part of the house. The bank in town was building a new facility and had a framing crew from St. Louis, Missouri in town working. I soon became acquainted with them and struck a deal with them to frame the second house we were building on speculation. They framed it and later Charles finished it as well. I drew my own plans for this home and thought I had did quite well until we discovered we needed a six inch plumbing vent wall in the bathroom instead of the four inch wall I had planned. We had to cut the vanity in the bath at a curve two inches to have room for the entry door. It looked fine when finished, but made me wonder for a while. The coal business was booming in our little town, which we will talk about later. I was having good luck selling houses during this time. I soon had a down payment on the speculative house and let the prospective buyers pick out the carpet. Just as the house was being finished, the buyer's employer, Russell Creek Coal Co. announced they were shutting down. This came as quite a shock to the buyers as they had been assured before buying that the coal business was there for the long haul. I had to start all over on the marketing of the now finished home. Interest was clicking away on the borrowed money I had used to finance the construction. I told the first couple I would refund their non-refundable down payment if I could get the house sold at the same money. This did not happen; it took quite awhile to sell the second time around, as the town was also shaken with Russell Creek Coal pulling out. I got the home sold at a small profit, but not allowing anything much for my own labor. We kept as agreed the first down payment, which I hated to do, but Russell Creek Coal did finally reimburse this to their former employee. I didn't try any more "spec" houses after that.

We did however at just a little over a year into our own new house, enjoying it more than we ever thought we could after the stint in the cold house in the country, have an offer to purchase it from an retired couple wanting to move to Welch. Dee Ann and I thought and thought this time. We really liked our home and Jodee was growing up, about ten years old at this time, and we wanted her to have a home to remember growing up in. We did however decide to price the home to the Turners. This time, though, knowing they were in no deadline to move from their present home in Chetopa, Kansas we priced our home at a fair cash profit for our work and investment and told them we needed four months to give possession. This was fine with them and we had a deal.

This time around, I was not lucky enough to get my friend Charles to construct the new home. I checked around and found the Williams family, Red the father worked with his sons, Mike, Rick, and Tracy building homes. I soon had a deal with them to do both the framing and finishing work on the new home. This time we had enough profit to build a bigger home. Our first home had been about 1,200 square feet; the second home sold to the Turners was about 1,450 square feet. This next home was designed to be eighteen hundred ninety-two square feet. We were really proud of it. More so, we were proud to have a home paid for by my side career in real estate. We had not used our business capital for a home. This is how you can get ahead when starting out. We all worked hard. Even Jodee at nine had helped plant the grass in the Turner house yard and had to do it all over again in this new house. She did not mind though. We always made some kind of fun in our family work projects. As you have probably guessed by now, we did not have a lot of free time to do normal family activities. I worked five full days at the feedlot, went to a cattle auction sale on Saturday to purchase cattle inventory for our cattle business, did chores back at the feedlot on Sunday morning before church. Evenings and Sunday afternoon were spent with real estate and the house building. I was fortunate to have employment in the family business that allowed me to get away to show real estate or see to the house projects from time to time as needed. Jodee grew up going with me to the cattle sales and helping with the house projects where she could, such as sowing the grass. We made time and still took off to help sponsor youth group outings at the church. We never took long vacations, but would always get in three or four days of camping and canoeing in the summer, an activity we all enjoyed very much. It also was a relatively cheap form of vacation.

That first trade to Mrs. Phillips turned out to be the best trade of my life. I will later discuss the bank in great detail. However, the twenty-five shares valued at one hundred twenty-five dollars per share in 1975 would prove to be worth well over two thousand dollars per share in 1997. The shares had also split as we had bought out other shareholders and retired their stock thru later years. This was a deal of a lifetime for a then very young and very green businessman. I certainly was not out to cheat a widow lady and had no idea the trade would turn out to be as good as it did. I just thought getting the bank stock as profit on the house would be a good investment for our future.

Be alert and ready for action when a good deal presents itself. They happen few and far between.

Next chapter will deal with the city slicker real estate firm against the country kid. I think you will get a laugh out of how it turns out as well.

6

The City Slicker vs. The Country Kid

I have learned many lessons dealing with people over the years. I have always tried to bend over backwards to do the right thing in a deal or trying to collect a past due account. However, I can get pretty stubborn if someone tries to really stick it to me. This chapter will deal with friends and business. The important lesson here is to learn to forget past hard feelings and get on with life. Life is too short to harbor grudges.

I sold mostly houses and small tracts of land in my real estate business since it was only part time. I tried to have just a few listings and work them hard. I did not want to get more than I could give the time due to the seller nor did I want to neglect my cattle business. I also had to leave time for family, church, and civic duties. A later chapter will deal with how I feel we all should do our part for church, family, industry, and civic activities in the community. If I did not think I could sell a listing property because of what it was or how it was priced, I would either decline the listing or make sure I listed it only as an open listing leaving the seller with the right to list with other brokers or sell himself. Of course, like all real estate brokers, I tried to get exclusive listings on homes or land I thought I could do a good job of selling. Many of these listings involved absentee owners who lived away and had local property to sell.

In 1979, only a few years into my real estate sideline, I came on a listing with old friends who had 590 acres to sell. This listing was going to be difficult. The Ruark family owned the land. Mrs. Ella Ruark was a ninety-plus-year-old widow who had lived next door to my folks while I was growing up. Her granddaughter Cindy often stayed with Grandma and we often played together growing up. We have been life long friends.

Cindy's father, James "Buster" Ruark had title to the land with Mrs. Ella Ruark granted a life estate in the land. This meant the land went to Buster upon Mrs. Ruark's death, but that Mrs. Ruark while she could not sell the land got the income off it while alive. Buster, of course, was Mrs. Ruark's son. Buster's wife and Cindy's mother, Lee Ann had died very young (in her early thirties) and left Buster to raise Cindy and her two brothers, Randy and Kevin. Buster worked at the Goodrich tire plant, so he hired a nanny to stay with the kids. Della did a nice job, but of course eventually Buster found a new love and married Joann. Joann tried hard with the kids, but while she got along, her relationship with the new kids was not great. Joann did persuade Buster to go to school and get an easier job. He went into the funeral home business, as were many of Joann's relatives. They eventually moved to Bartlesville, where Buster worked in a funeral home. Mrs. Ruark getting on in years was persuaded by Buster to move to Bartlesville also into an assisted living type of apartment complex. Buster would be near by to look after her. As is often the case in life, life does not go as planned. Buster developed heart trouble and died before his mother, Mrs. Ruark.

The land in Buster's estate now with Mrs. Ruark still having the life estate interest was left in equal parts to Joann, Cindy, Randy, and Kevin. Joann listed the five hundred ninety acres with John Hausman Realtors in Tulsa. She got their name thru a referral that she or Cindy got from another Oklahoma City real estate broker. This broker was to get a referral fee from Hausman's. Things kind of fell apart from there. Joann was the only one to sign a listing agreement with John Sanford of the John Hausman Real Estate firm. I was to find out later that Joann's brother, Leon Thomas, wanted to buy the land for himself. He however, did not want to give the asking price.

Cindy called and asked me if I could sell the land. I was to learn that I should have made sure I had a signed listing agreement before proceeding. However, I was dealing with old friends and I almost immediately had a chance to sell the property to Steve Bryan and his brother Dr. Bryan who owned land together and Steve operated nearby. They wanted to expand their operation and the Ruark land would fit nicely into their plans. I decided the best way to handle the offer was to call John Sanford with Housman Real Estate and offer to split the commission since he did have a listing with Joann. He said sure, bring me down a signed contract and the proper down money and we will work together. I promptly got the contract and down money from the Bryans and headed to Tulsa. Mr. Sanford took both and thanked me very much. I left for my one-and-one-half-hour drive home. As I was walking in the door, the phone was ringing. It was Cindy, and Mr. Sanford had just called with a new higher offer on the land from Leon Thomas, Joann's brother. Boy, did I feel used. I knew that Leon or "Booge" as we all call him wanted the property, but thought he had given it up as too high a price. The Ruark kids did not want Booge to have it since they were not getting along too well with Joann.

I was fast getting myself into a pickle of a mess. Booge was a friend and customer. I did not want any hard feelings with any of the factions. I also had a responsibility to my clients, the Bryans. It seems that Booge was lying back wanting to steal the property when I thought he had given the idea up when I was contacted to seek a buyer. The Bryans agreed to better Booge's latest offer by just a few dollars. Mrs. Ruark and the Ruark kids wanted this deal to go through. I was not sure what to do next and certainly did not want to get my self in a jam with the Oklahoma Real Estate Commission where I knew that the Hausman firm would carry more weight than a kid from the "sticks." I called John Wallace, one of the Security Bank owners in Miami, who happened to be a partner in the largest law firm in Miami. I met Mr. Wallace at the appointed hour in his office and told him what was going on. He thought a while and said "You have got a bona fide offer from qualified buyers and you have an oral listing from four out of five of the owners. This will work out for a deal with your buyer, the Bryans." He laid out the plan of attack I should take. He said go to Bartlesville and get Mrs. Ruark to sign your listing and the contract offered by the Bryans. Then meet Cindy and her husband J.D. who live in Edmond and have them sign. The next step would be to fly to Houston and get Randy and Kevin to sign. I started the deal in motion with a call to Cindy, who arranged to meet me in Tulsa for her and J.D. to sign after I had first traveled to Bartlesville for Mrs. Ruark to sign. I stayed all night in Tulsa after our near midnight signing. I caught the early flight to Houston where Randy and Kevin were living at the time. I would meet and get them signed and then with four of the five on the line, I would stop in Dallas on the return flight and call Joann who lived in Dallas and see if she then would sign also. Mr. Wallace, the attorney, was sure that Joann would agree to go with the deal since all the others were signed and it was for more money. Wrong! Joann would not budge. Things were getting sticky with people on all sides I had known all my life.

I need to stop and add something at this point. No matter how fast or furious business is, don't forget family. My juices were really flowing as this deal took each turn. However as I made the plans for this marathon run to Bartlesville, Tulsa, and Houston I turned to then twelve-year-old daughter Jodee and asked her if she would like to come along. Jodee had never been on a commercial airliner and she always enjoyed our flights in our own little single engine airplane. Even though this was a fast trip, she would not be in the way and we would have several hours just to be together. This is one example of many different times Jodee and I would mix my business with pleasure for the two of us. We have always been very close and remain so to this day. You can work the hours I put in and still have a family life, you just have to be creative and work harder at it. We had a great time. In Houston, we had a five-hour wait for our flight back. We decided to ride the city bus across town and see the Astrodome, which was relatively new at the time and supposedly quite a ballpark. The bus went on and on through all the slums of Houston and the dirty part of down town. I guess it was an educational experience of how some people have to live for Jodee, but it was not pretty. The bus line ended about a mile from the Astrodome. We could see it in the distance. However by this time it was getting late as the bus took a lot more time to go across town that I thought it would. We decided we did not have time to take a taxi the rest of the way or to tour the stadium once we would have got there. We just stayed on the bus, which now was reversing its route back to the airport. I wasn't sure how Jodee remembered this trip with Dad, but just last week out of the blue she asks if I remembered our trip to Houston and the bus ride to the Astrodome. Little did she know then, but I was in fact writing my business history book. This was a chapter I might have forgotten had she not brought it up unknowingly. I had not told anyone of my project at the time.

Well, back to the Ruarks' land deal. Joann would not give when we called her on our Dallas stop. We came home and I called Mr. Wallace and asked what now. He was amazed as I that Joann would not sign. We remained stalemated several days. Finally the Bryan brothers called and said to forget them and let Booge have the land. By this time I felt a sense of duty to the Bryans for getting them in this mess. Steve Bryan is a very good man and remains a friend and customer today. He bought his doctor brother out several years later and became a chicken grower for Tyson along with his cow operation. I still like to tease Steve about his chickens since cattle is my thing. With Steve's permission, I called John Sanford and told him that if he still wanted to co-broker the deal I would get my four clients to sign his contract. He promised to do so and I talked the Ruarks into signing. This would be better than a court fight with Joann, who after all was their stepmother. I thought this is finally over. Now all we have to do is get the paper work finished and have closing with the lawyers and lenders.

Wrong again, closing day was set to be held in the law offices of Logan, Lowery Attorneys in Vinita with a firm attorney, Charles West, handling the closing for the lenders. We got to the commission check for Hausman and myself, which was agreed to be a fifty-fifty split. Well, Mr. Sanford threw another wrench into the works when he announced that I would also have to pay half of his finder fee he owed to the Oklahoma City broker who gave him the lead on Joann and his listing. I said I did not need a referral for my four out of five owner listing and that he could pay his finder fee out of his half. I had put up with Mr. Sanford's antics all I was going to. The city slicker had constantly tried to pull a fast one on the country kid. I told Mr. West to not hold up closing with our clients, just make a joint check to Hausman and Neill Real Estate companies. After the closing we would then set down and iron out our differences. We closed the deal with all concerned and the property was now Booge's.

Mr. Sanford would not budge on the split. We argued in Mr. West's office for quite some time. Finally, I took the check form Mr. West and tore it in two. The half that said Hausman I gave to John Sanford, the half that said Neill I put in my own pocket. I said, "I'm going home. When you are ready to settle my way, call and we will meet and put our check back together and cash it fifty-fifty as we were supposed to." Days turned into weeks and no call. Finally Red West, as Charles was known, called and said isn't it about time to settle this commission check. I told him I was ready, but would not budge on the split. He called John Hausman and he said settle this thing the way Neill has said all along. I was thrilled! It had become a game by now to beat the city slicker out -to snooker the kid. I got my full half of the hard earned check with each of us covering our own expenses and referral fee in Hausman's case.

The Bryans were not bitter over missing the deal and were very gracious as they always are. Steve and his wife Judy are just great people. I was angry with Booge for messing up my deal. Then I thought he just wanted to get the land as cheap as possible and Joann wanted her brother to have it even if it cost her a few dollars. The Ruarks got over their hostility toward Booge and were glad to get their money. I have learned to never have hard feelings over business deals. Today, Booge is a good customer and does all of our hay baling, as he is now in the custom hay baling business. The land brought five hundred fifty dollars per acre in 1979. My commission check was close to ten thousand dollars. We used it to build a swimming pool in 1981. Jodee after all had helped on this deal and she was at the age to really enjoy a pool. With my limited time off, this would be a real family treat not having to drive somewhere to swim, as there is not a public pool in Welch. We all enjoyed the pool very much. I enjoyed providing it without having to tap my cattle investment money.

As for Booge, we all never know just how things will turn out. Booge was the largest farmer in our area. Farm prices tanked in the early eighties and many farmers went broke. Booge did also. The $550 acre land went up for a short while that Booge owned it to a value of about $700 per acre had he tried to sell and found a buyer. The farm crisis had its effect and national land values plummeted. The lender sold the farm in 1986 for $219 per acre to another local farmer couple, Bill and Helen Mount. They had watched how they spent their money during the farm crisis and Bill had an off farm job with the Goodrich tire plant that had paid his bills during the bad times.

Timing means so much in business and life. Booge was a good farmer, but poor timing, bad crop prices, and declining land values cost him his beloved farm. The Mounts are also good managers who also had a sixth sense to not expand just before the bottom dropped out of everything in agriculture. They bought on the bottom of the land market. Today, this same land would bring over a thousand dollars per acre just a few over twenty years later. Is this a good buy or the top of another bust? It will be interesting to watch.

I learned at an early age to not be intimidated by anyone. Just because someone is older, seemingly wiser, a giant in the business world, or whatever does not give them the right to walk all over you. One should always treat others in their business and life dealings fairly and as you would like to be treated. When mistreated, stand up for your own rights. When the situation calls for firmness, act accordingly, but not without passion. Remember to act fairly and treat others as you would like to be treated in all your business dealings.

The eighties would bring much change to our community. The next chapter will look at how it would change Welch.

7

The Eighties Boom to Bust

The cattle business had gone through very tough times in the mid seventies as we discussed earlier. The early eighties would be just as challenging to farmers in our community just as Booge would experience in the previous chapter. Land values went to almost a third of their former high prices. This was hard on our agriculture community.

Dee Ann and I purchased our first land in about 1980 just a couple of years before the bust. We paid five hundred dollars per acre for two hundred ten acres. It had been overgrazed very badly by the former renters and needed some attention. With access to nutrient rich cattle manure from the feedlot, we knew how to build up the land. We also hired a bulldozer and put him to work building a pond, and clearing brush. We spread manure all over the land and then planted it to a new fescue grass variety called Kenhy. With the new fertilizer our grass took off and grew very well. We were very proud of our purchase and had in the deal assumed a very reasonable interest rate loan from the Oklahoma School Land Commission, an eight percent rate at a time most long term rates were 11 and 12 percent. Even though our land would fall in value by half for the next few years, I have always been glad I bought this ground. The cattle market had already experienced its horror years and I felt I had made enough profit off the extra cattle I could run on this new land to pay for the loss in value. Of course, we did not sell this land and thus its value really did not matter on paper at the time. Twenty some years later now its value would be close to one thousand dollars per acre. We paid the School Land loan off years ago and are proud we took the chance many years ago. Life is full of choices. In business most of these choices involve an element of risk. The trick is to manage some risk without betting everything you have at each turn. This is a very fine line, not well mastered by many folks.

The coal business was booming in our community in the seventies and at the start of the eighties. The coal mining in our area is all strip mining. The miners would dig with bulldozers and giant track hoes to a depth of sixty to eighty feet for a seam of twelve to twenty inches of coal. It is a very high quality coal that is in demand to blend with the large seams of lower quality coal from Wyoming. During this time from the Kansas state line and fifty miles south into Oklahoma up to thirty different companies were operating. Today there is one. Energy cost did not rise on the value received for the coal to offset higher fuel cost to mine the coal. Also, the land had to be restored to a productive nature and the rules regarding how this is done have became stricter. The margin left after expenses to dig for such a small seam of coal is just not there now. In the hey day of coal mining however there was a great many of our local people employed in the industry.

Our other large employer in the area was the B.F. Goodrich tire plant in nearby Miami, Oklahoma. It employed about twenty-four hundred people. It also fell on hard times in the eighties that we will discuss later. We employed about ten to twelve people during this period at our feedlot. The coal mining jobs and the tire jobs both paid very well. Both were far above anything else in the area and it made for a nice standard of living for several blue-collar families. The area is certainly different today without either industry or nothing comparable to replace them in the wage scale accustomed to. We had trouble hiring people during this time and were fortunate that our people chose their job because they liked what they did and liked how they were treated. While most thought the tire company would always be around, several wondered how many years the coal jobs would last. Nevertheless it was a struggle to keep help.

I remember one incident with George, a young farm boy who I liked and appreciated having for an employee. George, while liking his job, wanted to get ahead and decided he could make several more dollars working at the tire plant. He was kind enough to tell me what he was doing when he applied. Most did not and you learned only if they got the job. George went for his interview and like most eager young men would have poured a bucket of paint over his head if that was what it would take to get the job. Goodrich called me for a reference on George's work habits. I gave him a good report. The application and interview process took place over about one month. I did not try to replace George during this time because it still was not a sure thing that he would get the new job. Had I replaced him in the mean time and he did not get the job, he would have been out in the cold or else I would have had too many employees. Anyway, I assumed that I would get two weeks notice before he would leave if hired. Wrong, Goodrich hired him one afternoon and told him to report for work the next morning. Now, I was the one on the short end of the stick. We were short right on the spot one employee during a very busy time for us. I called the personnel person at Goodrich who had called me as a reference on George. I asked how Goodrich thought they could be a good corporate citizen to our area and pull a stunt like they had just done with George? I got no response of course; George had to report the next morning, and my other employees paid the price by taking up George's duties along with their own. I would never ask a prospective employee to do this for me. I always figured that how they treated a former employer when coming to us would be how I would get treated if they ever left. What is right is right. We gave George the time to seek his new and better job wanting to see him do better and what was best for George. We, however, were due that same respect back in notice before leaving. Goodrich did not act in a responsible manner in their requirement. Keep this in mind when you deal with employees or an employer. Treat either like you would like to be treated.

I like to learn from other people's mistakes, not to look down on them, just to use their misfortune in a positive manner to try to avoid their pitfall. The next two stories I will always remember and look back at quite frequently just as I do with how the markets affected my friend Morris Barnes that I have already reported to you.

The first is about the Patch family. John Patch and his son Bill had been coal miners in Welch long before the boom hit. They had done all right but it was not an easy or get-rich business. Bill and his wife Sannie had a daughter my age, Fonna and a son a year younger than I, Danny. I have been a friend to Fonna my entire life. Danny and I were never close friends for some reason. Fonna would marry my lifelong friend Pat Guest after a courtship all thru high school and some college. They seemed perfect for each other. Keep this in mind as I tell the story.

During one of the lean times in the coal business, Bill had brought in the Burkdoll brothers from Kansas as partners. Bill and Sannie were a young, full of life couple as we kids were growing up. When it snowed, Bill had a huge sled and would take all the neighborhood kids for rides. When they moved to the country they built a very nice home that was open and real nice for entertaining, which they liked to do. They had the first home swimming pool in our little community. Bill, like his father was a pilot and flew his own small Piper airplane. Their car was never new in those days, but they went by air many places. The coal business suddenly boomed and Patch Burkdoll owned coal company flourished.

Pat and Fonna were married and had two sweet young girls now. They would also enjoy the good times, as Bill and Sannie were very generous. There were many trips, parties, and fun to be had by all. Soon Bill decided he needed a jet and lengthened his own private runway for it and hired two pilots to be on staff to fly it, as he did not have a jet rating. If they decided they would like to lunch in New Orleans, away they would go. They would have huge parties in their airplane hanger. For one birthday, Sannie hired singer Mel Tillis who was very popular at the time, to come and play for their friends. Johnny Cash was also a popular singer at the time and had a hit tune about the "One Piece at a Time Cadillac." Bill having a crew that did nothing but restore antique cars decided to build a car after Johnny's hit song. The car was certainly a work of art just as the song described. Bill decided to give it to Johnny Cash, whom he had never met. Now Mr. Cash would not meet Bill and Bill just drove the car to Nashville and waited for Johnny to show up at his office. He finally convinced Johnny that there were no strings attached and got him to take the car. Later, Johnny and his wife June Carter Cash would develop a friendship with the Patchs. Bill did not believe in going to church, but he was very civic minded. A very active member of the local Lion's Club, Bill would work his heart out for many a project the Lions had going. One project was a new civic center for Welch. Government grant money was obtained for a large portion of the new building, but the Lion's Club had to fund the balance. Johnny Cash heard of the town project from Bill and offered to come and do two live concerts with his band. Welch had a population then of about 700 people and our civic center could squeeze in 1,015 people for each concert. It was the biggest night Welch has before or after ever experienced. Seats were taken up long enough for the overhead door to be raised and allow Johnny to drive in the one-piece-at-a-time Cadillac to start the show. It was a night to be remembered by all. Johnny and June played and sang their hearts out for our community all-free of charge to the Lion's Club. We made enough off ticket sales to finish paying our part of the new civic center. The town was grateful to the Cashs and to our friends the Patchs for bringing them here. I was Lion President that year and was master of ceremonies for the show. I was charged with keeping the crowd in the building for fifteen minutes while Johnny and June had time to get out of town ahead of the crowd. This was the hardest task I had ever tried. No one wanted to hear Joe after listening to Johnny and June. I kept the applause going and thanked everyone on and on till my time was up. The crowd cooperated. It was a night for a small town to remember.

Success does funny things to people sometimes. I also think that success without being in step with God is many times fleeting and short lived. Such was to be for the Patchs. At one point they had told around town that they had so much money that they never could spend it all. This would not prove to be the case, as is so often true. Soon the coal boom became the coal bust. Bill and Sannie had partied too much and forgot each other. They divorced, Bill found a bar maid at a club in Tulsa and married Jeanne, who was younger than his daughter Fonna. Sannie and the Burkdoll brothers got the original coal company and Bill started a new company. In a short time the jet was gone. Before it was, though, Bill completely rebuilt the home and made it into a sixteen bedroom mansion with a dining hall as large as most houses. It also had an indoor pool with a hydraulic floor that came down over the pool to make a dance floor. The money was going fast however. Sannie and the Burkdolls' coal company filed bankruptcy. Sannie moved to Tulsa and still lives there in a high rise apartment building. I will admire this about Sannie, while heart broken over the parting of her and Bill she never lets the money loss get her down. She still is beautiful and a life of any party. A year or two later, Bill developed cancer. He tried every exotic remedy to be found except turning to God for a cure. It is sad to see someone you care about lose their fortune and then their health and not know the Lord. Bill passed away at fifty-five years of age.

Pat and Fonna had followed the good life too far also and drifted apart. They divorced. This would also have ramifications on their two beautiful daughters in years to come. I think as adults they have overcome their earlier problems. Both Fonna and Pat while going opposite directions and finding new mates years later are still friends. Pat's new wife Janet is as great a friend to us as Fonna was and still is. Bill's legacy left was in the neighborhood of twenty-five thousand dollars each to his two children. Jeanne got the mansion and its debt. She soon met a young up-and-coming country singer named Ronnie Dunn. They married in 1991 and auctioned off the mansion. The place had cost between two to three million dollars, but in Welch only sold for four hundred thousand dollars. It was overbuilt for the area and the house had no insulation, which made utility bills as high as five thousand dollars per month in the winter.

Jeanne and Ronnie paid off the bank note on the house and took the few thousand left over for their new start in Nashville. Ronnie met Kit Brooks and soon Brooks and Dunn were recording hit after hit. I am sure that they could afford the mansion in Welch now if they wanted to come back which they have not. Years later, they are still together.

The entire story of the Patchs is like a fairy tale or soap opera. I think of the good they did for Welch and hate that they missed experiencing God's goodness during these times. I feel fortunate that we did not fall in their party trap any harder and end up the same way. We attended many of the parties and enjoyed to a point. We should have been a better example for the Lord at the time however. It is sad to see how their story turned out. However, I do not think less of any of the Patch family. They were friends then and while I seldom see them, I think just as much of them today. I am sorry they had to experience the wild ride down. I do try to remember how money affected them and try to learn from their mistakes in a positive manner just like I do with Morris' mistakes.

Another couple in Welch at the time was Leon and Ann Walker. Leon had been foreman for Bill Patch in the coalmine. He knew the business and went out on his own. Leon was also successful and did quite well for a few years. They built a nice home on an acreage and having worked hard to get where they were, were also careful in handling their business. The fall of coal prices was hard on them. They had not "blown" their earnings but did not have enough to survive the crunch. I have heard Leon say that at one time he could have sold out and cleared around two million dollars. He did not and would soon be broke.

To try to save Leon's coal company a partner was brought in; Bob Hartley was a local rancher, banker, and investor. Bob had made many dollars in coal dealings with Peabody Coal Co. He decided to get in the business in a big way. For tax reasons, the partnership was not incorporated. Bob and Leon gave the business their all, but to no avail. When cashed in, Leon and Ann were broke and had to move from their nice new home to a small mobile home. Bob and his wife lost several thousand acres of ranch land that was mortgaged and his stock in two banks. He salvaged enough to keep their home and to start over both in cattle and the coal business, albeit in a smaller way. Neither Leon or Bob nor their wives ever looked back. They all were common good folks before they struck it rich, remained that way during their boom years, and are still that way today. I don't know enough about their business to know what brought them down. I suspect it was just the industry collapse in general. If Bob had not tried to save so much on taxes, the company would have incorporated and not cost him so much in personal assets. Theirs was just a couple of mistakes and an industry collapse beyond their control. This is part of the risk so many businessmen and their families take every day. There are many minefields out there in the field of business. Don't miss the challenge for fear of the minefields; just be aware that they are there when plotting your course.

We can all learn from the Patchs, Walkers, and Hartleys. All three families are great people. One or two wrong corners turned would bring them down. How we react to life's adversities shows much of our true character. These people are not bitter and have gone on with the next chapter of their lives. We should follow this example when rough times hit us in one way or the other. Many people who have adversity in their lives also lose their spirit of life. Nothing is worth this price. I have learned so much from my above examples and each has made me more conservative in my financial dealings, and closer to my own family and God.

Our community lost companies, their jobs, and several people moved as the coal industry suffered. In 1986 adversity would strike again. The B.F. Goodrich tire plant announced in August 1986 their intentions to shut the plant down by year end. Twenty-four hundred people with the highest paying jobs in the area would be out of work. I do not know what forced Goodrich out. I am sure there were many reasons including their mismanagement. I also for years had heard employees on the night shift brag about sleeping four or five hours of their eight hour shift. If this practice was as wide spread as bragged about, no company could stand to pay the wages they paid and have half or more of the time spent sleeping. The good hard workers with the proper work ethic I am sure did not do this, but it seemed to be too many that did take advantage of the company. The company was lax in letting this happen and I am sure it was only one of many problems. Whatever, the company closed, jobs were lost, the community suffered, and many people had to move or accept lower paying jobs. It was a tough time for our area. If you are a company leader, how you handle the affairs of your company affects many lives. People in these positions should not take this lightly.

The plight of the three families told of in this chapter has left me a far more conservative individual. The economic ramifications to them are still vivid in my mind over twenty years later. We all can learn lessons in life by observing others. I respect each family and thank them for the lesson I learned in each instance.

The next chapter will deal with the midget fighting the big corporation. Another lesson to be learned.

8

The Midget vs. The Giant

This chapter is but one short story on how a giant corporation tries to avoid payment no matter what is right or wrong. The business world needs to see itself in a completely new light. Too many times a path is taken not because of what should or should not be done, but what we can we get away with at no cost to the company.

On a hot summer day in August 1981, Dee Ann loaded up her elderly mother and aunt for a trip to Joplin. She had some errands to run and took the opportunity to get her mother and aunt out for a day. Instead of taking the usual route to Joplin on the four-lane turnpike, which would cost a quarter, she chose the country route on a narrow blacktop road that was quite scenic. Only a short distance outside Miami she popped over a hill to stare disaster in the face. In the valley was a narrow bridge over a deep dry creek bed. A semi tractor without a trailer had suddenly jack knifed sideways in the road at the bridge. In situations like this you do not have a lot of time to think nor would it have mattered much in this case. The choices were to hit the concrete bridge, go over the creek embankment and a resultant drop-off to the creek bed below several feet, or try to get stopped before hitting the truck in the road. Only going about fifty five, she opted for trying to get stopped before hitting the truck.

She got her car slowed down but hit the truck in the back dual wheels. The truck's wheels were elevated in the air as the front end of the truck had fallen off the side of the pavement. The car hood slid underneath the tires. The dual wheels and tires of the truck were fast coming toward the windshield. I am sure this was a very frightful few seconds. The duals stopped at the windshield, breaking it, but not coming on through. A very close call and a sure brush with death itself. Dee Ann, while very shaken, was fine and Mother was fine also. Aunt Audrey however was shaken more than the rest with severe bruises and a broken arm Not life threatening, but still a very concerning time for a frail eighty-plus-year-old lady.

Audrey had a short hospital stay and the car was a total loss. It was very clear that Dee Ann was not at fault with the truck sideways in the middle of a bridge on a narrow road. You would think setting insurance liability would have been a piece of cake. Not to be. The truck was a brand new Ford being transferred from an Arkansas dealer to my old boss at Kissee Ford in Miami. It was determined that the driver let his back tires fall off the ledge of the narrow black-top pavement. He lost control, applied his brakes, and went sideways in the road. Testing of the truck showed that the brakes had malfunctioned and locked on one side when applied. This caused him to lose complete control and end up sideways on the edge of the bridge. Kissee's insurance did not want to pay, as they had not yet taken delivery of the new unit. The transferring dealer did not think he was responsible because he had sent the truck on its way with a transfer driver not employed by him. Ford said that even though the brakes malfunctioned, the accident would have not happened if the driver had not let the tires fall off the blacktop roadway.

I talked to my insurance company who immediately said that they would take care of us. In questioning them however it came out that the payment to us for damage to the car and the hospital bills and cost of collection with the others involved would be instilled on our insurance record and would no doubt result in higher premiums in the future to us for our insurance. I thought how can this be? Dee Ann is in no way at fault, but yet our insurance is going to pay the bills and put it on our record. I said no way; I'll handle this myself.

Easier said than done. Ford had corporate staff lawyers who gave me the run around. Both dealers involved said we feel for you, but it is not our problem Darrell Kissee did loan us a car to drive while all this was going on. We paid the hospital and I set about calling the attorneys every day. August became September and then October. Finally in November the attorneys started getting tired of my constant calls. All we had asked for was value of our totaled out car and the hospital bills paid. Nothing was ask for pain, suffering, or my time to collect. Still they would not settle. I finally started talking lawsuit. I had not wanted to take this route even though I was certain that pain and suffering damages would also be forth coming from such a suit. I just do not believe in treating people in this manner and was not going to sue except as the very last resort. Finally seeing I was getting no where fast except for my daily talks, I started adding in for the suffering and pain Audrey had endured. I added car rental for my friend, Darrell even though he had not ask for any. Also I ask for money over the value of the car since we would have to add to its value to replace with a new one.

This finally started to sink in with the Ford legal team They realized that we had not filed a law suit even though they had told us to do just such at one point. I think they thought if I got in the court system they could out wait me. Ford has their own legal team so the attorney expense was not costing them any more than the salaries of the lawyers on staff. When I just kept calling and taking their time they finally decided to talk settlement. I still did not want to make money on something that could happen to anyone, after all it was just one of life's accidents.

Ford paid us our car value plus two thousand dollars and all hospital bills on Audrey. Audrey was also paid five thousand dollars to cover her extra expenses during her healing process. Kissee Ford was paid car rental from August to late November on the loaner car. None of these amounts added anything against the Ford bottom line. They had just played hardball with the midget against the giant. Ford should have settled and then went to their two dealers involved and determined which or both were responsible for the driver transferring the truck. They could have saved ten thousand dollars and countless phone calls and time by there staff attorney had they paid up front. I also had been a former Ford salesman remember and still held them in very high regard. After all it took to settle, I was disappointed in Ford and their dealers. Instead of buying a new Ford product, we took our settlement money and went to Chrysler. They knew they were in the wrong; had they done the right thing and paid the actual damages only up front and without hassle, they would have saved money for Ford and retained a customer for their new automobiles.

Why can't the corporate world learn to do unto others, as they would like done unto them? It is a good lesson for all of us to ponder on. Many situations are not about who can win but what is right.

Next we will talk of the lost generation.

9

The Lost Generation

Land values in the late seventies shot up, cattle were making money, and times were fairly good in cattle country. Good times did not last long. Interest rates skyrocketed in the eighties. Remember, I mentioned my friend Morris who was paying over twenty percent interest. Land values fell. Cattle prices suffered and while losses were not as great as the 1973/74 lean years, they were bad. The generation of farmers and cattlemen from thirty to forty years old was caught in a real crunch.

All cattlemen and especially those in the early stages of their own operation such as the thirty- to forty-year olds suffered during this time. Several did not make it financially. One young family, Frank and Beverly and their boys worked hard at their cattle business. They were in this bad timing generation. Their land was purchased not at the high, but still in a very high range to pay for when your product is selling low. They worked hard taking care of their cattle. Like many young folks at the time, they probably had over extended themselves with a new pickup and maybe more equipment for the farm than just had to be for the operation. It is a fine line in holding expenses in line. Frank was not extravagant and for most of us we would not notice anything at their home that was not needed. In agriculture there are so many things that make the job easier, that corporate industry would just buy, that will get you in financial trouble. People in agri-culture have had to do more with less than other sectors.

Frank and Beverly worked side by side taking care of their cattle. They worked long hours and took the young boys right along with them. They however, had no income other than from their cattle. With a favorable loan for the time we were in from the government Farmers Home Administration they should have been able to operate in this manner. So many times this will turn out to not be the case. I do not agree that this is right, just the facts. The majority of newcomers to the agriculture world have to have outside income to pay the bills while getting started. Many times, the husband or wife, and sometimes both will hold a full or part time job off the farm to have income from which to live. The chores are done on the farm before and after work. You have to be very dedicated to farm life to put in this kind of workday. Many do so every day. The extra income gives a cushion to pay the grocery and utility bills as well as provide health insurance for the family.

In times of low prices in agriculture and the resultant losses, it is hard to stay a float if you have to pay the living bills, the interest on the note, make up the loss incurred, and keep going all on only farm income. If the living does not have to come from the operation during these early years it is not quite as difficult to overcome the losses and interest payments till good times return.

Frank's cattle brand was registered as "FB" which stood for Frank and Beverly. The jokesters soon labeled it "Frank and the Bank." The loss from bad cattle years, high interest rates, and no outside income brought Frank and Beverly's operation down. They had worked hard and made every possible effort to do what it took to survive. In another decade, I am sure that they would have made it. If cattle prices for all had not gone down, had interest rates been less, if they had put off buying their land until cheaper, they might have survived. Remember too, that land had not ever gone down in price. The saying that they aren't making any more land and its value will always go up did not apply. The dream of Frank and Beverly to own their own operation was not to be. They lost it all.

Many times the hardships of dealing with losing your business will spill over into home life. Both are so intertwined in farming or small business. Some folks instead of taking solace in their mate, the one thing that the bank cannot repossess, instead lay fault on each other and blame. This never solves anything, but happens so many times anyway. Other times after going through this type of situation, families just loose their spirit to try. I see many languish on, never happy, drift from job to job, and just loose their zest for life. This type of life is especially hard on the children.

This was not to be the case for Frank and Beverly. Twenty years later they are with the same ranch company where they found a place after loosing theirs. They had to leave family and friends and move to a new location, which sometimes helps. They took the positive attitude that while they may have lost their dream of owning their own ranch they did not and could not loose their most important possession, each other and their kids. They helped each other through the difficult adjustment time instead of laying blame on each other. This approach is hard for some, but so much the high road to take. Put your trust in God, He will always help us through difficult times.

Another such family during this time was Mike and Sandy Jane. Mike had lost his father at an early age and a couple of the local ranchers had taken him under their wing and taught him the ranch life. Mike was a great guy and tried hard. He married a beautiful, vibrant Sandy Jane. They worked hard and did well for a few years. While times were good, they also bought ranch land. One farm was purchased when land was selling very reasonable. However more land was bought not at the high time but still a high price to pay for with farm income only.

Sandy Jane also liked nice things, very nice things, and Mike being a loving husband wanted to provide her with some of the nicer things of life. They soon built a new house, not out of reason, but new. Times stayed good and they needed a car so a new Cadillac was purchased. Things kept on going and come summer they thought a boat would be a treat for the kids and the family to enjoy. The boat was also purchased. They were a nice couple that you could just not help but like. Credit was easy for them to obtain, too easy. Soon they had too much credit. Several dollars owed were also on possessions that did not add anything to their ranching business: the new car, the boat, and the new house with its new furnishings.

Times were uncertain in the cattle business. One particular year we saw losses on cattle go as high as one hundred dollars per head and before the year was over cattle made profits as high as two hundred twenty-five dollars per head. With pressure on Mike, after a cattle loss in the early year, he decided he needed to sell a set of cattle instead of finishing them out himself, as had been his custom My dad thinking the market would be better the next turn, talked Mike into not selling the whole set at this time, but only a one half interest to us. This would eliminate part of his risk, but still give him half to make money on if the market reacted like Dad felt it would. Mike talked his banker into this plan. He retained one half ownership and sold Dad a fourth interest and myself a one fourth interest in the cattle. This very set was the pen that made two hundred twenty-five dollars per head profit. The most I have ever at the time or since made per animal. We were thrilled to death. Mike was so glad that he had at least taken Dad's advice and retained ownership in half of his cattle. His operation could have used the profits on all the cattle had he only known or been in position with his banker to take on more risk. He was already so extended that the bank was afraid for him to own all the cattle through the feedlot phase. After all we had just came through a period when feedlot cattle lost one hundred dollars per head.

Mike struggled, cattle prices languished, and soon all the payments caught up with Mike and Sandy Jane. First to go was the extra ranch land purchased. Of course, without it, he could not operate as big and did not have enough cash flow to make the payments on the Cadillac, boat, and new house. Over time, all were lost. The reach-for-all-you-want era in their lives would cost a huge sum. Had the "extras" of life been put off until better afforded they might well have made it. They also had no off farm income. They lost their farm and of course the new house, boat, and car. Soon they were blaming each other for their fate. The happy go lucky Sandy Jane was now not a happy person. Mike could not provide for her as he thought he should and had for a while. They divorced. Mike went on, but has never been able to get back the start he had at one time. I am not sure what happened to Sandy Jane. It is a sad story of a very fine couple with a wonderful family.

The 650 acre farm that we almost bought with the Carters and Stoners sold sometime later to Joe and Trudy. They were a nice couple, but did not have a farm background. Joe had been involved in some type of job involving investments like stocks or bonds. He was a swell guy and we became friends. Trudy came from the city and did not help Joe on the ranch, which was about ten miles from where they lived. Remember I said this farm was very poor and we had intended to develop with the use of our feedlot manure. Joe did not have this so it remained a poor productive ranch. It also was sadly, just not large enough to make a family living on and pay for at the same time. Trudy's part time job helped, but did not pay enough to cover the family living expenses. Joe would work hard, but not having too much experience at what he was doing sometimes did things the hard way and did not accomplish much. Joe liked to take a break from work in the afternoon and come by our feedlot office for a Coke. He would check the markets on our market news Teletype and pick up needed supplies, which we sold from our feedlot inventory to many of the neighbors. We would always get into a deep discussion about the markets or state of the industry or some other topic of the day. I truly enjoyed taking my break with Joe and his visits.

Success was not to be for Joe however. He lacked the expertise needed at the time to survive. His place was not real productive and not large enough to support his family and make payments on at the same time. He gave it his best shot. He nor his family ever lived beyond a simple means. It just was not the right timing, right place, or enough expertise in a tough business to survive. Joe and his family left our area. They tried Florida for a while and then moved to a retirement city in Arkansas with Joe working in an A. G. Edwards Investment Co. office. He should have the skills to be successful in this venture. People liked him, he was honest, and knew this business. I never knew how his career went, as he never came back to see us. I stopped by where he had worked one time on a trip in Arkansas and thought we could have another one of our "Coke" breaks. The receptionist however said that Joe was no longer there and she did not know where he had moved to. I heard later that he and Trudy had divorced, but have never caught up with my friend again. It sounds like he lost his spark, the extra edge so necessary to succeed when he lost the farm I hope he has found it again. He is deserving and truly a nice man I was glad to know at one point in my life.

Knowing how to manage money is an art. In agriculture, many dollars are handled for just a few you get to keep. Many people never learn how to handle this cash. At times when you have just sold something and not paid the bank note, you seem to be rich. It is easy to fall in the trap to spend this money that is really not yours or is needed for the next crop or cattle purchase. Then there are the times that luck or timing is just not right and you lose money instead of making money that seemed so sure. In agriculture you are in a constant battle with Mother Nature for the rain and the course of the markets, which is often not just. It is a good life, but not easy, as the examples told testify to.

Do not be afraid of risk in starting your own farm or business. Just be aware of the pitfalls that can be had. Take things in stride and do not try to have everything you want at once. This is hard because you see so many of your friends with the new cars and boats or taking the nice trips. You have to remember that while they have a good job and salary they are not building up a lasting equity like you can in your business or land. What your friends many times spend are purchases on credit that will depreciate and be gone in a matter of time. They will make the payments and seem to have the good life. However, they are not building net worth. This is what you are building, doing without many of life's extras in order to funnel money to your business or farm. Hopefully, you will make the right choices and have equity and a nice net worth for your years of sacrifice. It is certainly not easy but well worth the effort it takes. In the end you will be rewarded with a greater net worth and able to afford many things in cash payment that you have forgone earlier in life on credit.

I am not sure how Dee Ann and I survived these times. Some of the reasons were we only bought a few acres of land, we had living income from our feedlot jobs, we did not have to buy equipment because I worked for a low salary but could use Dad's equipment free of charge. We did pay markup on feed purchased the same as all our customers did. We did not have to pay the smaller yardage fee however which helped some. Dad was also a good teacher and I had the opportunity to be around some of the best operators and minds in the industry. I could take what I learned about the markets from each and apply to our operation. We also, as we discussed earlier in this book, lived modest and paid for our home with outside income that was extra income earned not from our salaries at our jobs or from our cattle profits. Some good points to remember.

In the next chapter I will talk about developing a friend and customer, seeing him do well, and then seeing him turn on me over a false hood. Take heed from this chapter as I have watched since and see many families and friendships ruined over false rumors. Believe and trust in those close to you are a good traits to remember.

10

A Friend Thinks
He Has Been Had

Little things that do not amount to anything or wrongful perceptions by us can cause useless grief and heartache between family, friends, and even customers. Some little something taken out of context or a false rumor or lie can cause quite an uncalled for stir. This chapter is about how this can happen between a businessman and his customer and as is so many times the case in small business, the customer is also a friend.

I had such a customer in the eighties. Larry had got everything the hard way. His family could not help him get a start. While I am not sure, I don't think that Larry ever finished high school. I imagine that he had had his share of wild times in his youth. On his own he got life's act together and worked hard. Jean Ann, his wife, has been a wonderful influence on Larry and I am sure helped steer him in the right directions. Larry liked cattle and had saved enough to get a small start in the business. When he came to us, he had a new Farmers Home Administration government loan, which was popular then for young families trying to get a start in agriculture. Farmers Home would make a loan with a low interest to people with a good plan, honesty, and work skills, but short on down payment cash. Many to get their start in the business used it. Larry fit their mold very nicely and was an excellent candidate for this type of funding.

At the time, not many feedlots would accept small pens of fifty head. We had not in the past, but did for Larry and later found that we could serve numerous customers in this category no one else wanted to serve. I will talk more about this in future chapters. Larry would go to the sales and sit for hours waiting for just the right bargain price for a calf that would upgrade on feed. He was a very astute buyer on the plainer kind of cattle. After he got his fifty head put together he would bring them to us to feed. I took an instant liking to Larry and always gave him one hundred ten percent on his pen. We watched them very close and when ready to sell I put extra time in selling his herd because I knew it meant so much to him. Many times I would use Larry's pen to sell to local locker plants one at a time for a higher price than the major packers might give on the same day for the same calf.

Larry did well and prospered. He grew his business very fast. Unlike the folks in the last chapter he was in during a time of prosperity in the business. With his natural ability and good markets he plowed his earnings into more cattle. In just a few short years and an excellent credit source he built his number of cattle on feed with us up to one thousand head. This brings up a good point for a businessperson to file. Remember I said that Larry could only handle a small number; a number most commercial feed yards would not take. You never know where tomorrow's large customer might come from. We went the extra mile for Larry at the time because he was kind of like the underdog that everyone likes to see win. As it turned out, Larry did win for a while and we ended up with one of our larger customers as a result.

Larry and I soon became friends. I went to a cattle auction sale every Saturday for about fifteen years in my career. It was a way for me to keep in tune with the feeder cattle markets first hand. I enjoyed the day at the sale and always felt I made money by doing this. Larry also went to the Saturday sale and before long we decided to ride together. We would meet and drive to Coffeyville, Kansas for the noon auction. We always stopped and ate a roast beef sandwich at Hardees on the way and many nights the sale would last late and we would stop for a steak on the way home. I had a good time and enjoyed Larry's company very much.

My friend Stu that I have mentioned also fed about one thousand head of cattle at a time during this period. Stu was always a family friend my entire life until he died. I also took good care of Stu's account. Now, don't get the idea that we played favorites with our customers, you just cannot do that. All customers paid us the same and we took care of them the same. When Larry only had fifty head I probably bent that rule some, but did not break it. Nonetheless, we were blessed to have two large accounts and both friends. Though neither ever mentioned the fact, I think that Larry and Stu were both somewhat jealous of our friendship of the other. Both liked to be the top dog of the feedlot. That was fine and I could see how it happened. It never directly caused a big problem, but I could see it coming.

We had a buyer named Danny that I had let buy Bobby Bauer's cattle for him as I told you in chapter three. This had worked well for quite some time. Danny became good friends with Larry. We had Danny and Larry and their wives over to the house once or twice and had fun. Danny did play favorites. Many times he would not bid on Stu's cattle or another customer's for Bobby because Larry had some not quite as finished but close enough. We always tried to sell the most finished first, but of course the buyer still had the last say. I handled this pretty well for quite some time, but I knew the problem was growing and I needed to find a solution before someone got his or her feelings hurt.

My other large local buyer at the time was Canadian Valley Packing Company in Oklahoma City. I had worked hard to get this account and it had not been easy. It really became a good account through a stroke of bad luck for Canadian Valley. Their long time head cattle buyer had open-heart surgery and did not survive the operation. Mr. Wright, the owner, bought cattle for a while but he was up in years and his own health was failing. Mr. Wright's two boys took over the operation and although they knew the lunchmeat and sausage end of Canadian's business they knew nothing about cattle. They turned over the cattle buying to Tommy Scroggins, their long time head of the cattle kill operation. Tommy knew how to skin cattle from A to Z but had never bought cattle. He made no bones about it when he came to see me. He said that if I would help him procure the kind of cattle his plant needed, he would always buy some cattle from me. He made a similar offer to Steve Smola, my friend who managed Wheeler Brothers feedlot at Watonga, Oklahoma. Steve and I both tried to help Tommy all we could in picking the right kind and while we always got the market for the cattle sold to him, we neither took advantage in trying to get more than the market would bare. We could have got by with this in the short term, but both of us wanted a good long-term relationship with Tommy and Canadian Valley. It proved to be the right course for all of us. Tommy had two primary sources of cattle and Steve and I each had a good fair buyer. Some weeks I would be short of cattle and Steve would take up the slack, other weeks Steve was short and we would sell more to Tommy. This went on until Canadian Valley quit the business. Tommy moved to Paris, Texas and started a barbeque business. I stopped to see him one time on a business trip. It was quite a place. We still call each other on occasion.

Back to the original story, Danny, the buyer for Bauer Pack did not like Canadian Valley getting into his play nest. Danny also used fifteen cattle per week for his own operation. He got to where he would buy a pen of cattle, pick the best fifteen out for him, and let Bobby Bauer have the rest at the same price. I did not think this was quite fair, but I was in an award position to do anything about it. Later, I would say enough is enough and tell Bobby, who as you recall in Chapter 3 was run off by Dad for bad business practices that he could come back or send Tommy, his son, to buy again. I must have handled things all right. Bobby bought for several years without messing up again, Danny kept buying his fifteen per week for himself, and my friend Tommy Scroggins of Canadian Valley also bought. I was always proud of how I handled this situation without offending anyone especially Danny, who lost his commission on the Bauer cattle he had been buying.

I was not so lucky with my friend Larry. While Danny was still buying Bobby's cattle, I sold him a load of Larry's cattle. The deal called for him to sort one load of the best, most finished cattle and leave the second load in the pen. I knew the second load would be lesser quality and would bring less money, but I thought that I had got enough premium on Danny's load to make the pen sell where it should on the average. I told Tommy at Canadian what I had and that while the cattle were all right, they would not be as good as the sorted load nor would they cost as much. I thought this was fair for all concerned. I don't think that Danny started out to cause trouble, but he kind of liked to tell stories and of course he wanted his competitor Canadian Valley to look bad. He might have wanted me to look bad to Larry, but I do not think so especially since I had as of yet not told Bobby that he could buy his own cattle at our lot again and thus cut Danny out. Danny and I always have got along and he always knew that how I treated the cattle buying with Bobby and him was right. Although Danny quit the finished cattle business several years later, we traded every week for another fifteen years and he still stops to see me from time to time. Whatever the reason or however it turned out, Danny supposedly told Larry that I had gave Canadian Valley a cheaper deal than Danny had received and that I was in cahoots with Canadian at Larry's expense. Nothing could have been farther from the truth. Canadian's cattle cost less, but were the poorer quality end of the pen. If anything, I would imagine that the meat cost of Canadian's cattle was actually higher because of fewer figures in dressing. For a planned reason or just how he said it came out, Danny made my friend Larry think I had betrayed him. Larry got very mad and threatened to take all his cattle out of our feedlot that very day. I finally got him to see that that would not make any sense because it would set the cattle back moving them and the cost of moving would be a huge cost to Larry. We finished each pen and sold them as hard as the first time he brought the first fifty head. Larry never saw through what had happened and I don't know if Danny tried or not to set him straight. I never ask Danny.

We lost a large feeding account when Larry left. I more importantly lost a good friend. He would not listen to any explanation I gave. When we meet on the street, he looks the other way and goes right on without acknowledging he knows I am alive. I lost several nights sleep over this. I had never in my life lost a friend nor a customer in this type of situation. If I had felt the least bit guilty in how I had marketed his cattle, it probably would have been easier to accept Larry's attitude and turning on us. I knew in my heart that I had tried my very best for Larry in each and every trade on each pen of cattle he ever fed. He never realized this and to this day seventeen years later, he will not speak to me.

I don't know how I could have handled things any different. I did not get mad at Danny, what would that have accomplished? I just hid my disappointment and went on with my life. There was no use brooding over it any more and certainly no use in taking it out on Danny. Yes, I know that is what most people would have done in the same situation, but still it would not have solved anything. You are the bigger person, if you can learn to look beyond how they have harmed you and let bygones be bygones. Hard to do, but well worth the effort.

I did all I could to convince my friend Larry that I had not wronged him. Sometimes we have to realize that in spite of all we try to do to correct a wrong perception the other person will not listen. This is their problem. Hold your head high, be nice, take the high road in talking of another's actions toward us, and finally go on with your life. Just be sure to look yourself in the mirror and make sure you have done the right thing.

In the next chapter I will look at another big customer who quit because his relatives helping him in his operation were cheating him.

11

Raymond Betrayed by His Cousin / Cattle Buyer

During the late '70s and early '80s we fed cattle for close to ten years for Raymond Moorland of Tulsa. Raymond was the General Manager of Affiliated Foods in Tulsa, a large cooperative grocery warehouse that owned coop grocery stores and supplied many independent grocery stores with their products to sell. Raymond was a very astute businessman and had guided Affiliated Foods very well. He owned a ranch in Wagner, Oklahoma and somehow learned of our feedlot. He paid us a visit and before long decided to send us cattle from his ranch for us to feed and market for him. I learned a lot about the wholesale meat/grocery business from Raymond over the years. When Raymond took his morning, noon, and afternoon breaks at work, he would always call and visit about his cattle. We would have about a ten-minute conversation three times a day. Dad and Raymond were about the same age and hit it off well. Dad and I always enjoyed Raymond's calls and visits to the feedyard. Raymond would tell us how wholesale meat including turkey, chicken and beef were selling in their stores. We would tell him what we were learning from packer buyers, reading on our news wire, and of course how his cattle were doing in the feedlot. It was a good combination and helped us in many ways besides having a good customer to feed for.

Raymond was different than most of our customers in that in the ten years we did business, I never met his wife or any kids. I don't even know if he had any. He was strictly business and a good business friend, but never a social friend as many of our rural area customers became.

One of the first lessons learned with the relationship with Raymond was in the need for good communication by all involved in a deal. Raymond's ranch manager was a swell guy named Houston Parsons. He only saw Raymond on maybe a Saturday and pretty much handled the ranch and the cattle as if they were his own operation. He tried very hard for Raymond. Houston and Raymond visited the lot before sending cattle and Dad and I discussed with them the animal health program we thought should be used on the ranch for optimum cattle health at the feedlot. Unlike our other customers, Raymond wanted all his cattle vaccinated and processed at the ranch and after a proper backgrounding time sent to the feedlot where no further vaccinating against cattle disease would be done so as to save money by not duplicating these costly shots. All went well the first couple of pens, and then the third and fourth pens hit and several in each pen became sick soon after arrival. We thought the cattle acted like they had BVD, a cattle disease that was included in the vaccination program we had all agreed upon. We had our vet, Dr. Roger Parker, the son of Stu, and another long time family friend and our vet check the cattle. He agreed with us that the cattle had BVD. I called and arranged for Houston and Raymond to meet us the following Saturday morning at the lot to discuss the cattle. We went over the vaccination program again, and soon learned our problem. Houston had bought some new vaccine just out called Seven Way. Seven Way was a shot for seven different types of cattle blackleg disease and did not include vaccine for BVD. Houston had in error assumed that since the medicine was Seven Way, it must include everything you needed to vaccinate the cattle for. It was an expensive lesson learned by all. As soon as we vaccinated the cattle for BVD and the shots had had time to take effect, our cattle sickness stopped. After this we always made it a practice even on our own cattle to revaccinate cattle on arrival at the feedlot. It cost a few dollars more, but it made certain that the vaccine shots had truly been given and in the case of our own cattle we learned that a booster shot at the start of the feeding time would boost the immunity of the cattle and we would have even less stress and sickness in starting the cattle on feed. We continued this program our entire cattle career.

After a few years, Houston retired and Raymond turned his ranch management over to his brother Bob, who owned an adjoining ranch. Raymond had his cousin, Wayne buying the cattle at the local sale barns. Wayne did not have a very good reputation in the industry for being completely above board, but of course we did not tell Raymond of the rumors on his cousin. We thought that at least Wayne would be true and honest to Cousin Raymond. This did not prove to be the case. Raymond found Wayne giving false prices and weights on cattle bought for him in a few short years. Raymond lost all interest in feeding cattle after this. He did not want to start a family fuss by accusing Wayne of what he had found. Raymond just decided to quit his cattle-feeding sideline. After all he did not need the income because of his position at Affiliated Foods and he certainly did not need the extra aggravation of trying to keep his buyer honest. We lost a good customer through no fault of our own. Life plays out many situations that do not turn out as we hope for many different reasons. We just have to adjust and handle these situations. God will truly take care of us, if we will let him.

One lesson I think we can all learn from our customer Raymond is a situation we all find ourselves in from time to time. Case in point—about five years after Raymond quit his feeding venture with us my father suddenly past away of a heart attack, which I will tell you about in a later chapter. I called and told Raymond of Dad's death. Even though we did not talk regularly any more, I still considered Raymond a good business friend. He thanked me for the call and sent flowers, but did not attend the funeral. We all have times like this. Raymond was a busy man at Affiliated- and we were not social friends and not business friends for about five years. He was under no obligation to do anything further and maybe he wanted to, but could not because of his schedule. However, it would have meant so much to our family and me had he been at the funeral service or wrote a nice note. Flowers mean a lot and sometimes that is all we can do, but we never know when we can really comfort someone or make a difference in their life. A short note might mean more to many people than the prettiest flowers. A good lesson to think about.

Raymond called a few times a few years later thinking about feeding cattle again, but never did. He retired from his job at Affiliated and I have lost track of him completely. I will always remember the many years of those three-times-a-day phone calls. We had a special business relationship for those years.

Next, The Big Win.

1985 Lincoln Mark VII we won from Cutter Animal Health

12

The Big Win

This chapter has no business or life purpose other than to tell of a big windfall in our life. In 1984 Cutter Animal Health, now known as Bayer, conducted a national contest among animal health product dealers selling their products. They gave away five Caribbean cruises in a drawing among all their dealers, one from each of five districts in their company. Our long time friends at West Plains Vet Supply entered our name in the drawing. We won our district drawing and set sail with about seventy Cutter people who had earned their trip as a sales reward and the other four winners. Our cruise took us from Miami, Florida to the Grand Cayman Islands, Jamaica, and Cozumel, Mexico. It was a wonderful prize and trip. We enjoyed our Cutter friends very much.

One morning after enjoying a rather late night of "ship life," I awoke before Dee Ann and went to breakfast without her. About an hour later Dee Ann appeared on deck hunting me without fixing her hair or makeup as she usually would. I wondered what was up and she soon told me of her big scare. She awoke after I left and when she dropped her arm off the side of the narrow cot that was also close to the floor, she felt water on her hand. Quickly waking up she found our cabin had about six inches of water on the floor. Being half asleep and on the ocean she decided the ship was going down. She immediately put her life jacket on and tried to get out, but could not get the cabin door open. She banged on it till the cabin steward heard her and helped open the door. No, the ship was not going down, but a water main line in the wall of our cabin had broken and flooded about six cabins including ours. Our entire luggage on the floor was soaked. We were moved to the main deck with a cabin with a large window, a great upgrade from our flooded cabin. The ship laundered all our clothes and we continued to have a fun-filled time.

One night a storm came up and the waves were hitting the fourth deck windows. We were of course, told to stay inside the ship and off the decks. "Sick Sacks" were placed in the hallways of the ship for anyone getting seasick. We were fortunate to be in the middle of the ship and thus not as subject to the constant up and down felt in the cabins in the fore and aft sections. We got through the storm just fine and had another tale of our trip to tell.

The last night of the Cruise, Cutter was going to draw from among the five dealer winners for a new Lincoln automobile. They lined us up and numbered us in alphabetical order of our last names. Neill beginning with "N" was number two in our order of winners. The Cruise Director rolled a single dice to see who would win the Lincoln. He rolled the dice out about thirty feet on the floor. I could see more than the two spot, our number, and thought there goes one good car to someone else. To my surprise, the six spot had turned up and just being five of us, he had to re-roll the dice. This time there was no mistaking as good ol' snake eyes came up. You cannot know our excitement over this huge win. It was a thrill of a lifetime. We were allowed to order the Lincoln in our color choice and when it arrived we were hosted in March, 1985 to corporate headquarters in Kansas City for an award dinner and tour of the Cutter plant in Kansas City and delivery of our new Lincoln. Jodee and her friend Lori Garner joined us in Kansas City for the car delivery. Saturday morning we got up and Dee Ann and the girls drove the new car home. I drove the old car and stopped back in Nevada, Missouri for my weekly visit to the cattle sale in Nevada. Still had to make a living.

We kept the car nine years and enjoyed it very much. Quite a thrill to win both a cruise and a car. Dee Ann and I were very thankful for our windfall.

The next chapter will deal with how a sudden death would turn our life upside down.

13

Sudden Death

In about eighteen months time during 1984-85 we had three wonderful one week vacations.

The first was a family trip Dee Ann, Jodee, and I took to Cancun, Mexico in summer of 1984. Jodee was between her sophomore and junior years in high school. We spent a week on the beach at Cancun and had a grand time. The next was the cruise Dee Ann and I won and talked about in the previous chapter. The third in the summer of 1985 was a trip to Hawaii which I had won as part of a largest increase in purchases contest from one of our suppliers Tufts and Son of Oklahoma City. We won a trip for four and being three of us, Jodee invited two friends, one of whom we paid for. Three teenage girls in Hawaii was quite a trip in itself for us. We enjoyed seven days of wonderful Hawaii. Remember, even though we worked many hours a week and did real estate work on the side and participated in civic clubs and church, we always found time for family. Our vacations were never over one week at a time and many times less days. However, we always had fun and packed the most into the short time. We never spent huge amounts of money on vacation, but still had fun. Most of our family outings were camping on a river, canoeing, cooking out, and just enjoying family and sometimes friends that came along. Most of these camping trips included our friends Bob and Patricia Neil, their son Rob and their twin girls

Diana and Denise. The girls were a year older than our Jodee and grew up together. Bob and Patricia are great friends today. Patricia was the daughter of my old family friend Stu Parker we wrote of in an earlier chapter. Multigenerational friends are special. We need to take time to cultivate these relationships just as we do family. Anyway back to the three vacations in eighteen months, they proved to be God given and the last of far off vacations for years to come.

February 25, 1986 changed our lives forever. God will prepare us in His own way if you let Him lead the way. Dad had been very active in the feedlot business until early 1983. Mom had shoulder surgery and knee surgery about six months apart. She was pretty much laid up for nine months or so. Dad stayed home, did the cooking, kept house, and tended Mom all this time. He would ask about things at the feedlot, but rarely came out. I was in full charge of the business for the first time, but still had my father, partner, and advisor around to ask questions and bounce ideas off of. This proved to be excellent experience that would save me in the future. When Mom got back on her feet, Dad again returned to the feedlot. However most of his time now was spent going after the mail, visiting with customers while I worked, and dragging the gravel road with the big tractor and blade he loved to operate. Most business operations were left to me, but he would fill-in for me on Saturday so I could spend the morning at home before heading for the cattle sale.

During these years I look back and see that he planned things like having Richard Smith cross fence the home ranch west of Welch so it would be easier to manage the cattle and grass. He would think of projects to try to make our faster paced life easier. Our small business feedlot now was of about 9000-head capacity. The business was turning more complex. He told me several times in these years that when I had been at the feedlot thirty years to get out—either sell, get a manager, or something, but quite clearly I had to get out. I said, but I will only be fifty years old by then. He countered with the age did not matter, it was the years of stress that would take its toll and thirty years was enough. I did not agree then, but as most always, he proved to be right. Dad had so many positive qualities.

He could put someone down and make him or her like it if they had it coming. He had a way with people and employees in particular that I could never match. I was the one who found a way to add health insurance, retirement profit sharing plan, most raises for employees, and better time off for them. However, I never achieved the respect of the employees that Dad could. He just had a special way with people.

February 25 about midnight, I got one of those dreaded phone calls in the night. Dad had suffered a massive heart attack. Not knowing at the time what was happening, Mom had driven Dad to Vinita, fifteen miles away to the hospital. Even though we lived a short distance away they had not bothered us until the nurse at the ER told Mom she had better call us as the situation was bad. Dee Ann and I flew to Vinita after the call and we stayed close to his room for the next three days. Now, Dad had always taught me that one of us had to be at work to manage the feedyard, so I spent the night at the hospital and then went to work while Dad was stable. The Vinita hospital was quite small, but Drs. Allensworth and Dehart were long time family doctors and very well respected, as was the small hospital. They talked of moving Dad to Tulsa, but did not think he could stand the move, so elected to continue treatment in Vinita. The second night at the hospital that kept only five people on staff during the night hours was quite traumatic. During the middle of the night, another patient at the end of the hall suffered a code blue. All five nurses rushed to his room. I went to Dad's ICU room to be with him while this was happening. St. Francis Hospital in Tulsa was monitoring him but I was not sure how this worked at the time. Anyway his heart screen in his room suddenly went wild with the lines going every which way, I looked at Dad and he looked at me. Both of us were scared, but would not tell the other. I ask Dad if he felt all right and he said he did. Fifteen or twenty minutes went by before the nurses stabilized the other patient and the ICU nurse returned. It turned out one of the chest leads on the monitor had come loose and caused the erratic movement on the screen. I was sure glad God was with us during these minutes when I did not know whether to call for help when I knew the nurses had their hands full with the other patient, or wait as we did and hope for the best. It was a hard and draining night, but we made it ok. I spoke to Dad early in the morning and he seemed fine and I went to work. About eight a.m., only an hour or so after leaving the hospital, I got the call to rush back as Dad was having another attack. I rushed in the ICU only to be turned back by Dr. Dehart. In a few short minutes he came out and said that Dad was gone. What a shock! I had not even thought that he would not make it. God takes us in His time and place. I thought later that at sixty-nine years, Dad had hit his prime and his personality would not have made him a good patient for a long-term illness. The three days started my preparation for life without my friend, partner, and Dad. Dad did not suffer or have to go through a long illness and left at his prime. Not an all bad way if you are prepared to be with God as Dad was.

The funeral was on Sunday with a large crowd gathered with us. Dee Ann, Jodee, and I attended Sunday morning services before the funeral. That was hard to do and not the custom in our community for a bereaved family to be in Cchurch, but I thought what not a better time when hurting to turn to God for help in His house of worship. On yes in our true fashion, I went to the feedlot and weighted up a load of cattle for Bobby Bauers that I talked of earlier. He drove his own semi to the feedlot to pick up the cattle. He wanted to stay for the funeral, so I loaned him a company pickup to drive. At the end of the funeral, the casket bearing Dad was moved to the rear of the church for viewing by all that attended. Our family was seated at the front of the church. I decided what I needed to do was to stand by the casket and personally thank each one who came and for their influence on our lives. This was hard to do with all the emotions that come with a funeral, but I am so glad that I made it through this and greeted each one. I had at that time never saw this done in our community.

Life would certainly change for our family and me now. Mom never adjusted very well to being without Dad. She seemed to have several health problems, get scared a lot at night, and in general struggled to adjust. She never was bitter and in fact continued to serve the community in the best way she could. She played the organ for many weddings and funerals even though her hearing had been very badly damaged by a cordless telephone ring. She continued to teach a Sunday school class and a mid week Bible school for grade school age kids. When she could no longer do these things, she wrote a book "God's Hand in Mine" telling of her difficulties of having three children with Cystic Fibrosis. This book was completed only a few months before her death. Jodee stayed with Mom for awhile before getting married. We ate supper with her most nights and kept up things around the house for her. After two or three years we sold our home and moved in with Mom. This might not be the right approach for most families, but for Dee Ann and I it was the best way to make Mom's last years more comfortable. She was easy to live with, gave us our privacy, and I know this approach kept her out of the nursing home and prolonged her life.

Meanwhile back to Dad's funeral. As I said the funeral was on Sunday. It was a large funeral attended by so many of Dad's friends and business associates. He had left a large footprint on this earth. The next morning I was back to the feedyard trying to keep things going there, still numbed by all that had happened. After lunch I was surprised by a visit of several of his Miami bank partners. The next chapter will deal with their mouth-dropping request.

I learned that life on this earth can change so quickly. One must be ready at all times to meet our Maker. Those of us left behind must trust in the Lord and carry on as God and our loved one would have us to. I also learned that situations that seem impossible are not with God's help. We just have to ask and trust in Him.

14

The Bad Bank

I was surprised Monday afternoon when several of the partners and the president of a bank in Miami that Dad had invested walked into my office. As I have previously told you, Dad and I both were investors and directors in the Welch Bank. In 1983 a group of about twenty men approached Dad about investing in a bank in Miami. My old boss and friend, Darrell Kissee was the main contact of this group. I was also offered the opportunity to join this group. Each full investor was to invest two hundred thousand dollars with three or four investing half that amount for half the amount of shares. They would borrow the balance of the purchase price somewhere in the neighborhood of one million dollars. This seemed like a real deal at the time and Dad jumped on it. I wanted to, but thankfully decided that the investment would cut me too short of investment capital for my growing cattle business.

The group of men were all successful, two car dealers, a lawn mower distributor, a motor coach manufacturer, two farmers, a funeral home director, an ex-banker who would also serve as the first president, a cattlemen, and other diverse backgrounds. It looked like the area was ripe for a locally-owned group to take over a relatively new third bank in town. The lead bank in Miami, Security Bank was owned by law partners Ben Owens and John Wallace, and banker John Buford had sold to out of town interest and while still strong had lost much of its personal touch and lead direction for the city of Miami. John Robison, the ex-banker of the group, was a former president of the second largest bank in town, First National Bank. It looked like this group would have an easy time of growing the third bank to prominence in the area.

Miami National Bank, as it was named, did grow but in so many wrong ways. President Robison went out to get all his former customers to come to his new bank. It would turn out however that the ones that followed him were the very ones who would not or could not pay their loans. They did First National a big favor stealing these customers. The second problem was the second in command George made mostly small car and personal loans. Most of his customers would pay George, but they were a shady group that would not pay when George was let go. The third strike I am sad to say was all the bad loans shoved into the bank by my former boss, Darrell Kissee. I am sure that he did not purposely try to send bad loans to the bank, but as it turned out the bank suffered many losses on his relatives and customers who had loans at the bank. Banking regulators had caught up to the practices that the twenty-man board had overlooked. I always perceived the problem of the board was that each of their investments in this bank was not on the surface a large amount of money for each of these successful businessmen. No one paid enough attention to what was happening and listened to management who were literally giving the store away. After the Bank was placed on a Cease and Desist Order by the National Bank Comptroller of Currency, Mr. Robison was relieved of his job of president and Joe Allcorn was brought in to right things. Mr. Allcorn was a personable fellow, but did not have the skills needed to turn the bank around. I think Dad had finally realized the troubles of the bank and was wondering how to deal with it when his heart attack occurred. I do not know if this added stress contributed to his attack or not. I am sure it did not help. A couple of weeks before his death, he had finally shared with me some of the problems at this bank. Until then, I had no knowledge at all except that things were not going well. During this time, two or three partners had sold their stock for very little, the former president got rid of his shares and the motor coach maker was allowed to give his shares to George.

The day of the meeting in my office found only a fourth of the original group left. The Oklahoma City Bank that made the stock loan had let the directors that left off their stock note that all had pledged collectively to pay. This was done in error, but still done. The group wanted me to join them in Dad's place and they needed another two hundred thousand dollars by all to bring the bank capital back to standards because of all the money lost on bad loans. I was still reeling from Dad's sudden death, had a feedyard low on customers, and now this added problem. I told the group that I would come and do an examination of the bank loans and think about their proposal. I found out that Mom was still liable for the bank stock note and if all others would not or could not pay, she would be liable for the entire amount which had grown to about one and one half million dollars with accruing interest and short payments being made. I certainly did not have the experience to grade bank loans, but was familiar with loans from my involvement and directorship at the Welch Bank. I also just used good business sense and dived in to the loans every evening after work at the feedlot for about ten days. I determined that the bank loans were in much worse shape than everyone thought except the national bank examiners who had placed the bank on watch. To confirm my results of the loan review I next went to my old friend the half-wit, as we called each other in our twelve years of school we shared. We always said two half-wits made a whole and it usually did. Pat Guest and I studied, played, and grew up together in Welch. He was now a CPA with his own firm in Tulsa. I asked Pat to recommend a qualified auditor I could hire to review the bank loans. Pat introduced Clayton Woodrum to me and he quickly set in with the bank board approval to doing a review of the loans. I told the board that I would pay up front for the review and if the board wanted to see it after I shared the highlights, then the bank could in turn pay me back. This was fine and soon Clayton's audit confirmed my assessment of the loans. We were in very close agreement to the amount of potential loss still in the bank loan portfolio. I shared our findings with the board, which in turn paid for the audit. I then, to protect Mom's interest, rolled up my sleeves and joined the bank board. I did not however put up any additional money nor did the other director owners. Pat, Clayton, and I all studied both my and Clayton's loan reviews and decided that the million dollar capital infusion needed by the bank did not make good business sense.

Soon Darrell Kissee's troubles compounded and his own auto dealership, ranch holdings, and a race horse venture were in trouble. Darrell left the board. By now the board was down to Darrell's brother Jack, an auto dealer from Claremore; Bob Rasor, a lawn mower distributor and part owner of a chain of furniture stores and also an investor in Darrell's race horse; and myself. We dismissed President Allcorn and Vice President Couch and Jack Kissee introduced us to a friend of his, Ron Watkins. Ron was a former bank president that now specialized in cleaning up bad banks. Ron moved in for about six months, reduced staff to save money, worked on the bad loans, helped us with the regulators who were seeking more capital which we would not put in. When Ron thought we were stabilized, he brought in his friend, Bill Harvey and persuaded us to hire Bill to run the bank. Bill was a great guy, but had had a shady past at a former bank. He was as good as we could get at the time and place we were in. Bill worked hard for us for close to a year. On one occasion, Bill and I were in Dallas talking to the national bank comptroller of currency, our regulators. We decided to repossess a car with a past due loan while there. We found the address of a business where the borrower was to be. When we introduced ourselves to the receptionist, we heard a door in the back slam and knew our man was skipping out on us. We hopped in our small rental car and gave chase. We soon were on a rain-slickened freeway under construction going eighty-five miles an hour in chase. It was not to be; the guy slipped away and we lost him.

I worked at the feedyard until one every day, went home and donned my banker clothes and went to the bank till at least eight every night five days a week. We would go over past due loans and decide who to chase next. Our capital kept going down with the loan losses and as a result our loan limit for good customers continued to go down also. Bill saw the hand writing on the wall and got a job with Federal Land Bank who Ron had gone to work for as their system was also full of bad loans at the time. B.F. Goodrich announced their plant closure in August of 1986 and closed four months later. The largest and highest paying employer in the area seemed to settle our fate, as more bad loans showed up this time through no one's fault except for the bad local economy. Lloyd Lamb replaced Bill as president. Ron had also hired a young, hotshot attorney named Darrin Rudy to work in loan cleanup. We all did the best we could. I would set the tone and decide who we would work on next and Lloyd and Darrin worked hard at my direction. I spent hours working on our plan to survive, deciding how to work each past due loan, and keeping morale up among the employees. I seldom ever spoke to a customer. I left that to our staff.

We certainly weren't the only bad bank in Oklahoma during these times. There was one to five bank closings by regulators throughout Oklahoma every week during these months. The Federal Government put together a program called the 13C which would help a new investment group buy banks by taking out many of the bad loans so that the new group could start fresh. I was allowed to put a new group of investors together to apply for the 13C program. This group included myself, Larry Smith who owned a chain of Sonic drive-ins, Dennis Watson my attorney would own half of the new venture, Rudy Farber a very conservative banker from Neosho, Missouri, and two of his right hand men would own the other half. My fellow directors, Jack and Bob were not allowed to apply for this program because they were there when the problem was created. I was viewed as the good guy who was not there when the bad loans were being made, but was now the one trying to save the bank. The 13C application ultimately did not work. My partners at the good Welch Bank wanted to look at a bid on the bad bank, which I was in favor of. I did not, however, want to get these partners into a bad deal. Art and Charles of the Welch group reviewed the loans and wanted to try for a deal. In my opinion, however, they were overly harsh on an already bad deal. I knew the proposal they wanted would not fly with the feds. Art was a vice-president of the Security Bank in Miami even though he was an owner-director of our Welch bank. All types of conflicts were potential and I did not push our group to change their appraisal of the Miami bank. I just told them that while I wanted the deal to work with them, I knew it would not fly with the feds, and I still had to try to salvage as much as I could out of this bad deal. I would learn years later from Stoner how he and Art thought I should have let them take over for me and seek the direction they wanted in trying to gain the Miami bank with federal help. I was trying not to force my bad deal on them and at the same time trying to do the best I could for Mom's interest. They never understood this and resented me for this and the fact that I was even invited to join the Welch group when it purchased the Welch Bank from Security Bank. Sometimes you never know how your friends and alleys are really thinking.

I finally cut a deal with the Oklahoma City Bank that held our stock loan. They had as I said, let many of the former directors off the note without the other's permission and left themselves open. I made a deal that Jack, Bob, and I would pay one million dollars, two thirds of what was owed, for cancellation of the entire debt. I felt bad not paying the whole amount that all had agreed to do. However, I knew, for my own survival, I had to drive a hard a bargain as I could. Our share of the one million was well over what our share would have been had everyone originally involved paid their share. While not proud of this deal, as I was taught to always do the total right thing, it needed to be done. The bankers accepted our offer and we soon had a new problem. Jack could not come up with the last sixty thousand dollars of his share. Bob and I each loaned half of it to him with a note for thirty thousand. Months later fearing Jack was going to go down completely I pushed him to let Mom have a new Lincoln for note payment. This he did and later also with Bob. Jack had to look at all the loans many of his relatives had in the bank unpaid. I know it worked on him. He got a little hard to get along with toward the end, but I can't claim I did not understand why. He really was a gentleman and wanted to do right. About two years after our demise, Jack had a heart attack and died. I believe his age was around fifty-eight, much too young to die this way. He left a wife and son in the business much as I had been left. Steve Kissee, Jack's son, took over their auto dealership and continues to operate it to this day.

My other friend and partner, Bob Rasor, is now my million dollar friend. I learned you might as well make the best of things that
you can, no matter what hand in life you are dealt. Bob had been
Dad's friend at the bank. Bob was about twelve years younger than
Dad and about fifteen years older than I. Strange the friends we
make. Bob, Jack and I spent a lot of hours together at the bank.
While Jack and I had a strained but ok relationship, Bob and I grew
closer every day. We soon were going to dinner with Ruth, Bob's
wife, and my Dee Ann. We even took a few trips together when
things got settled where we could be gone. My million-dollar friend
is still that great friend today. So many times in these situations, you
find partners mad at each other and the blame flying. This was never
the case with Bob and I. Much better to have a million-dollar friend
than a million-dollar enemy.

We also were blessed at the bank with a wonderful staff of support people, who had no fault in the situation. The secretaries, tellers,
and cashier were solid folks who tried hard to salvage their bank. The
strong will of this group of employees made me try harder to save this
bank. The bank crew bounced back time and again from one disappointment to another as we went through the process. They always
cheered me up after a disappointment and we just went on trying
harder. I have never seen such a dedicated group of employees.

The bank got down to a loan limit of less than twenty thousand
dollars because of our now very low capital. Any overdraft paid for
a customer, good or not, counted against that customer's loan limit
and if we allowed anyone's loan limit to exceed the limit amount we
could be held personally liable as directors of the bank. It so happens the bank examiners were at the bank one day when a local
doctor was called that his account was overdrawn. He promised to
bring in a deposit and one of the bookkeepers allowed his check to
clear. Well, the doctor did bring the check in, but it was after the two
p.m. deadline to count on that day's business. Technically, he was
overdrawn for the day the examiners were there and thus over the
loan limit. The girls had paid a check against policy, but it was still
our neck on the line even though the check was there and the
account not overdrawn on the next day's business. The head exam-

iner looked at Jack, Bob, and I and asked what we were going to do about this described situation. I called for a short recess and huddled with Bob and Jack in the hall. I told them enough was enough and it was time to fold. I was going to quit and go back to the feedlot. Jack and Bob quickly said that if I was out they were too. We went back into the room and once again the examiner asked what our plan was. I reached into my pocket and got my bank keys and threw them across the table to her and said I'm turning the bank over to you and going home. She quickly said that I could not do this, and I in turn replied, "Watch me." This conversation went back and forth awhile and it was getting late on a Friday afternoon. I finally suggested she call our FDIC contact in Dallas that I had come to know quite well. I got him on the phone and explained the situation. He replied that for all the failed banks in the country he had never heard of one calling it quits on its own. It was always the regulators coming in and shutting the banks down. He got our examiner on the phone and told her she had better listen to me and get ready to assume control of the bank. She finally did and at four-thirty that Friday afternoon in November of 1988, I left the bank.

The auction for the remnants of the failed bank was held early the next week in Oklahoma City. The FDIC would take the best acceptable bid for a takeover of the bank with the FDIC insurance making up the loss in the bank and difference in the winning bid. Another first, I was allowed to make a bid with my former 13C group on the bank. When I walked into the bid room in Oklahoma City, you could have heard a pin drop. Everyone was stunned that a former director of a failed bank was being allowed to bid on his own bank. As I said earlier, the FDIC people did not view me as the problem, but as help in the solution. Our group came in second in bidding and thus ended my Miami banking career. The economy of Miami has not to this day recovered from the Goodrich closing and the people that had the high bid on the bank operated it about eight years and sold it to First National Bank in town. I am sure they never made any money on the bank. God was watching over me once again throughout this venture. I got out without losing my own business and He saved me from probably a bad deal had we won the bid.

March 1986 to November 1988 was a long time in my life. In February of 1988 I was at the feedlot early one morning and outside sorting a pen of cattle to market. It was a cold February day, but I got hot working the cattle. I was called to the phone to talk to our IBP cattle buyer, Larry Haley. I went upstairs to my office and Larry and I started trading on the pen of cattle. Soon I was feeling dizzy, in a cold sweat, and having chest pain. I quickly told Larry I had to get to a doctor and hung up the phone. I called for Dee Ann down stairs to come help me. She flew up the steps to see what was up. We decided she would take me to the doctor in Miami. I had started going to Dr. Ray after Dad's death at the Vinita hospital. I did not blame them; I just did not want to go back there. I also had to fit doctor appointments in as could and Miami was now where I spent so much time and my long time friend, Patricia Neil, was the doctor's Girl Friday. She would always get me right in, as she knew the constraints on my time were so great. That day she got me immediately in and Dr. Ray very shortly sent me to the hospital for admittance. This turned out to not be a heart attack, but the first of about six such episodes over the next fifteen years. I was finally told I had Chronic Fatigue Syndrome. The days of 7-1 at the feedlot and 1-8 at the bank along with working weekends and still going to the cattle sale had caught up with me. I will talk more of the Chronic Fatigue as we go along.

We can make out of life whatever we want. My experience in this failed bank left me with health problems years later. Our family lost many dollars. I failed in my attempt to turn the bank around. I also gained so much experience in business and life. I worked with a wonderful group of people and have my million dollar friend. The experience taught me so much at a young age. I have never been the least bit bitter at having failed to turn the situation around. It was beyond repair when I stepped in. I knew I had done my best. I wish it would have turned out different, but I am still blessed by all I learned and my friends.

This chapter dealt with the bank during the 1986-88 timeframe. The next will deal with turning the feedyard around during the same time.

15

Turning the Feedlot Around

The last chapter went through the bank turmoil from March 1986 to November 1988. That was just one part of my life, I also had to restructure the feedlot and get it profitable. With all the turmoil of Dad's death I did not put any of my own cattle on feed for two or three months. This would prove to be one more way God was looking over me. The summer of 1986 found the U.S. Government conducting a buyout of dairy cows. The milk price had gotten really low and the dairy people were in trouble. Uncle Sam decided to buy the excess amount of dairy cows in the country and turn them into hamburger. They had not realized that people eating tons of cheap hamburgers were not going to eat much steak. Soon finished cattle in the feedlot fell in price every week until about ten dollars per hundred pounds had came off the price. Our customers were losing money and quit putting cattle back on feed as they sold their finished cattle. I missed most of this loss because I had not had the time to get cattle on feed for my own account. Late summer however found me with a feedlot fast becoming empty. You could have shot a rifle anywhere through the pens and not hit an animal. I had to fast stabilize this situation. I had to generate profits to keep the bad bank afloat and to meet our overhead at the feedlot. Many of our customers had gotten old and retired or passed on. Some left me when Dad died thinking I could not handle the yard by myself. I was thirty-seven at the time and while I knew I could handle things much as I had been the past few years, I knew I had to prove myself.

Feeder cattle were getting cheap with all the losses being taken on finished cattle. I would toss and turn all night and wonder what to do. It came to me one night. I started buying the cheap feeders and every time I had a pen of two hundred put together, I would find someone to partner with me and sell them a half interest in the pen. Then I would start buying another pen and do the same thing. I soon had about four thousand head in my own inventory, over twice the amount Dad and I usually owned together. I also filled the lot by selling an equal number of cattle to investors such as my friend at the bank, Bob Rasor or Sam Morrow, a retired feed supplement manufacturer who had sold feed supplements to Dad for years. Sam believed in my cattle ability and had me buy several cattle for us to feed for his account. God watched over us; all these cattle made over one hundred dollars per head. I kept the lot making money and made money on the cattle so that I could pay our share of the bank note on the Miami bank. It proved to be the best time of profits in my entire career over these months. Quite a relief.

I turned to Bill Helming Consulting Group of Kansas City to help me formulate my plans to turn the feedlot around for good. The Helming Group was a livestock and meat advisory service. Dub Berry, who I had met when he was CEO of National Cattlemen's Association, was now with the Helming Group. Dub and I got along well and I respected his wisdom. I used their group a lot in the late eighties for consultation and to bounce ideas off of. I stayed with this consulting group until 2001.Dub retired in the nineties and I never had the same relationship with the Helming Group. They did help me a lot when I needed it most. They helped me decide to hold feeding seminars with their group and extension service university speakers giving cattle seminars in Welch that we sponsored. We did one a year for several years. Purina Mills came on as a helper at these seminars by 1990.I had brochures made and developed a trade show display and started doing four or five trade shows a year promoting the feedlot. I also attended seminars at Oklahoma State University as I have my entire career. It would have been easy to have skipped the annual OSU seminar during my 86-88 years at the Miami Bank, but I did not. It would prove to be to my benefit that I did continue going. Besides the great program the OSU fellows put together, I got to mingle with some of the best minds in the business during the breaks. One night after the last speaker of the day, four or five cattlemen were visiting including myself and Bill Haw, the CEO of National Farms Feedlots owned by the famous Bass Brothers. National owned a lot at Parsons, Kansas about forty five miles from us and was one of our competitors for cattle customers. We always got along good, but in those days were competitors. Well, Bill told us of his plan to take National customer pens to a minimum of three hundred head and charge a chute fee every time they doctored a sick animal. I went home and the next day started the welders splitting our two hundred size pens into two one hundred head pens. The following year we split several of these pens into fifty head pens. We bought a new thirty thousand-dollar computer system and software to be able to track and bill these smaller groups of cattle. This would prove to be our found niche in the feedyard business. In those days no one wanted to mess with the small groups of cattle and being from eastern Oklahoma most of my customers were smaller operators of Arkansas, Missouri, Kansas, and soon Tennessee, Kentucky, Florida, Alabama, Georgia and several eastern states. I created a business model that was a lot more work than the old days when I had seventeen customers that fed cattle year round and kept our then nine thousand head yard full. When I quit the feedlot business in 2001 we had grown to a fourteen thousand-head capacity and it was not at all unusual to have one hundred fifty different customers with cattle on feed at any one time.

All businesses need "their signature." We found ours quite by accident. Our feed mill could be seen for miles from its hill top location. The original blue color did not last long, nor did the next painting of a different shade of blue. I turned to a local paint company for advice on a color that would stand out and last. Yellow would be best I was told. The new yellow mill drew several comments and everyone noticed it. Soon I was painting all the fences yellow. I told my customers and prospects alike that while the cattle business could see days of poor markets or lousy weather, or both at the same time, I could always look out my window and have a bright outlook. My philosophy of making the best we can of every situation was relayed in this manner of my bright outlook to all. We soon were buying our semi-trucks in our signature yellow. We had several calls each week it seemed from someone having seen one of our trucks go through their town and reminding them to call us about cattle feeding or selling their corn crop. My friend from Tennessee, Bob Schmidt has told me numerous times of how his father, upon returning from a tour to our bright outlook yellow feedlot in Oklahoma, asked him how come all his fences were painted black. Our signature and trademark had by chance been one that portrayed my own philosophy of life and was so evident in our brochures, trucks, and facility.

I also started doing cattle talks to different groups of cattlemen. I had never done this before and did not do much of this until things got settled down at the bank. During the decade of the nineties I probably averaged eight to ten of these talks a year. I developed a slide show and one program per year, which I gave over and over again. By 1989 I had bought an airplane and would fly to these cattle meetings, many in Arkansas. Often I would not get home till midnight and be back at the lot at seven the next morning. I usually took Perry Knight, my flight instructor, with me in case I got too tired after such long days. We made a lot of fun out of these ventures and flew several trips to Arkansas, but also longer trips to Kentucky, Tennessee, and Texas drumming up business. I always found a way to make work fun since I put in so many hours on the job. Dub Berry and I also added to our feedlot promotion trade shows at farm shows or state cattlemen's conventions. I had some of my feedlot pictures I had taken enlarged to show off our facility when displayed on the trade show booth I purchased. The booth was three large cases on wheels that set up to an eight foot by eight foot display with a counter-high table for brochures. It was brown with a large amount of our now signature yellow mixed in to show off the display. We added yellow director's chairs for the booth. We had a professional company design a four-page color brochure of our company to pass out to future customer prospects. We always had a drawing signup at the trade shows so that we could obtain a good address list of prospects. A thank you letter for visiting us at a trade show or perhaps a visit to the feedyard was always sent to customer prospects. We developed a scrap book of pictures of our crew, facility, and a broad segment of the different types of cattle we fed for our customers. We also ran timely placed ads in target market area cattlemen magazines. We managed our cost very effectively. You have to manage your ad budget carefully when targeting a small audience. We also worked at forming relationships with agriculture extension agents in our target areas. The agents would not favor us over other feedlots, but did pass our name along to several new customers because they knew us and thought we would treat the ranchers from their areas well. Our different approaches that Dub and I plotted out and I executed worked well for us.

Working with county extension agents across the country and with our own Craig County agent Roy Ball, we hosted many cattlemen tours. One such tour was a group of cattlemen from Tennessee. Roy Ball had set this tour up with his counterpart in Tennessee. They wanted to see a feedlot and also ranches of interest in the area. Roy set up Neal and Christi Schou's Limousin ranch as one stop on the tour after our feedlot. Bud Mitchum, one of the Tennesseans, on the tour liked the Schou ranch bull genetics. He soon had made a deal to buy ten of their bulls. Now he had to find a way to get them home. Bud decided to feed a pen of his cattle with us. He could load a local truck from his area with feeder cattle to come to us and the truck could take his ten bulls back on the return trip. You never know how you will meet your next great customer, but this is how we met Bud. He continued to feed three to four pens at one time year round with us until we closed. He soon turned the marketing of his cattle completely over to me. I would call with a bid and the housekeeper would answer the phone. She always would say "Mr. Bud is busy out in the fields. You know he would tell you to do whatever you would if they were yours." I would do just that. I always appreciated the loyalty and trust Mr. Bud placed in me.

Another tour from Tennessee came by and while we did not get any new business directly from it, a few months later the county agent from Nashville who was on the tour told the agent from Knoxville about the Oklahoma feedlot he had visited. The Knoxville agent called and set up a meeting with his producers for me to give a presentation to in Knoxville. This was a long trip and I probably would not have made it, but my operations manager, Mike Day had promised I would, so I did. To my surprise we ended up feeding cattle for Charlie Riddle and Janet Green, Danny Stooksbury, Milus Stooksbury, Tim George, M.J. Reynolds, Tommy Irwin, and one or two more. The one trip to Tennessee that I had not wanted to take resulted in several new customers and several loads of cattle coming to us. I learned you never know just where that next customer will come from or who might refer him to us.

Back to the 86-88 years, things were still not easy even with the cattle profits coming in. Don't get me wrong here, Dad and I both paid taxes faithfully, but also always prepaid a lot of expenses such as corn and other needed supplies for the feedyard. Under cash accounting rules this was perfectly legal and Dad always said we needed a cushion in case of a bad year in the business we could let this prepaid catch up and thus let Uncle Sam shoulder some of the loss. Well, I had got probably somewhat carried away before Dad died and had got to buying up to one million dollars worth of corn ahead at the end of the year for delivery the next year. It usually made good business price sense and we always knew where our corn supply was coming from during the bad winter months when the roads could get bad. We always made our deals with people who would get the corn delivered on time no matter the weather. Prior to 1986, banking laws allowed Dad to borrow money on Neill Cattle Co., a corporation and also as an individual cattle feeder using different assets on each statement, but still borrowing at our Welch Bank up to one million dollars and I would also borrow on my line of personnel credit up to the five hundred thousand dollar limit. Well in 1986 banking laws changed with all the bad banks in country and in essence the law would only allow one credit limit per person no matter that he had another corporation and different assets in it. I would not let Mom borrow money after Dad died and thus to do what our family had been borrowing to the tune of one and one half million dollars I was now limited to five hundred thousand dollars. I went bank hunting fast. I did not think I should be borrowing from the competitors of our Welch or Miami bank interest so I looked elsewhere. Dad's old friend Art Graves suggested I try two banks in Coffeyville, Kansas where he banked. The first I talked to turned me down. I was only thirty-seven, unproven, and had this huge bank note liability hanging over the family head. I went to the other, Condon National Bank, and talked to Pat Marso, the president. Pat and I hit it off and soon I went away with a five hundred thousand-dollar loan. This with my Welch limit got me to one million dollars two thirds of what was needed. I did not try the Miami bank because it was already in hot water and had too low of a loan limit to help much anyway. I was still short of cash I needed to buy goods to postpone taxes and did not have enough cash to pay the tax when it would come due February 28. We had to file early because as qualified farmers we paid no estimate ahead and thus our file date was February 28. I forgot to relate during the last chapter that after Dad passed away on February 28 before we made funeral arrangements I had to go to our accountants, Gayle Edmondson, and pick up our return to file. I had the money in place already this year and did not have the problem of cash flow till paying the 1986 tax in February 1987. Anyway, I called Gayle and told him that Dad had passed away and could he get us an extension on our tax filing. He said sorry, but it was too late for the extension to be filed. We had not waited until the last day on purpose, but it always was hard for Gayle to have ready any earlier this early in the year that our tax was due. This gave new meaning to "Death and Taxes" to me for sure. I will never forget paying the tax before making the funeral arrangements.

Back to December 1986, I realized I would be short of cash to pay for cattle, prepay feed for tax purposes, and have cash for the tax return come February with my lessened loan limit. My friend Pat Guest, told me that Oppenheimer Investments was selling a tax deferral deal by loaning one million dollars to a customer for buying Treasury Bonds. You paid the interest on December 31 and sold the bonds in January. It was complicated and you ran the risk of interest rate loss if rates went up while you owned the bonds they could lose face value. It still looked like a way out for me. I decided it was legal, but risky because of the interest rate floatation. To make the deal work for me I needed to do not one million, but four million dollars worth. Pat Guest never realized I would go this far, but I did. The next year my new banker, Pat Marso, said I sure like to do business with you, but wish you would not do the T-bill deal again. I said, don't worry I have had enough of that and am not in the corner this year. I will not do that again. I lost about fifteen thousand dollars on the T-bill straddle with Oppenheimer, but it did get me over the hump on my tax problem that year. By 1988 tax year I was in a new trap. Being on cash accounting, we always rat-holed cattle and feed checks starting in November and did not cash many checks until January to postpone the income off the checks if they were deposited. Well, late December 88, I wrote a check for two hundred fifty thousand dollars for corn. The corn dealer insisted he had to have the check in hand on December 31 not just postmarked then. I thought ok, I will mail the check to Nebraska on December 29, they won't receive it till December 30 or 31 and no way the check will make it back to my bank before January 2 when I had my rat holed checks ready to deposit and thus cover the check. You guessed it, the check got to Nebraska overnight, a rarity then. The Fed flew big checks every night to the Central Bank and ours got back to Welch on the 31st. I was over all the loan limits and really had to scramble to cover the check, but did so with some of the rat holed money, but it sure messed up my tax planning.

God was sure with me in these years. Besides all the money funneled to the bad bank, paying the tax, doubling my cattle numbers, buying a new computer system, I also had to spend fifty thousand dollars in the summer of 1988 on cleaning the feedlot lagoons. I would have liked to postpone this, but Dad and I had been trying for five years to get the dry weather needed to get the water off the top and get heavy equipment in to get out the build up of manure. I had to do this, as we would soon be in trouble with the EPA if our lagoons ran over in the coming rainy season. So with the weather and lagoon conditions right, I spent more money and got them cleaned.

There was certainly a lot of financial juggling during this time. I also juggled my time at the feedlot, hunting customers, at the Miami bank, and of course I spent about a day each month in meetings at the Welch bank. It was hard, a challenge, the Miami bank failed, but I enjoyed it all and leaned very fast how to run a fast-changing business. Dad had taught me well.

Several of Dad's friends had sons, most a little older than I who also lost their fathers and work-mate about this same time. Most all of these men lost their ranches within five years or less time. It was not that they were lazy and did not like to work. They had only been taught to work and not taught to manage. Their fathers always did the business and the boys worked. Mine, thank goodness, taught me both to work and manage. I was prepared to do what I had to do to survive. This is an important lesson to remember if you have children in the family business.

I learned very important lessons in money management during these years. I paid off the bad bank obligations, cleaned lagoons, and upgraded our computer system. You sometimes have to spend money in the business to succeed. There is also a fine line in over spending and not spending where it will count the most. God blessed me in making the right decisions for us during this time. It would have been so easy without God's help to have managed everything so much different that would have resulted in failure.

The next chapter will deal with the Chronic Fatigue Syndrome I developed from all the long hours and stress involved.

Cattle pens

Feeding the cattle

16

Chronic Fatigue Syndrome

The last paragraph in Chapter 14 told of my start with a very frustrating illness known as chronic fatigue syndrome. A close cousin to this illness is fibromyalgia. In February 1988 I told of Dee Ann rushing me to Dr. Ray's office and on to the hospital with heart attack symptoms. My heart checked out fine. Chronic Fatigue Syndrome is an illness that is diagnosed more by the process of elimination than any one test that says you have Chronic Fatigue Syndrome. I was tested on the treadmill and an echo cardiogram for the heart, then a neurologist was consulted. The neurologist studied my family history of cystic fibrosis to see if there could be a link from my ailment to the family disease. None was found. I was tested for Lyme disease, Multiple Scrosis, Lupus, and several other autoimmune deficient diseases. Pesticide poisoning was looked at with my many years of being around a wide variety of agricultural chemicals. Nothing was found to pinpoint the cause of my ailment.

I lost twenty pounds in the weeks and months following that first trip to the hospital. I stopped losing weight at one hundred fifty pounds which left me very thin on my six foot frame. For months I could not walk straight and tall. My muscles and joints were weak and left me walking stooped over in a very slow and unsteady manner. My left arm would quiver for ten to fifteen minutes and when it stopped my body would be drained of any energy. I used the hand rail on the steps to my upstairs office to pull myself up the stairs. I had to really work to keep my mind concentrating on anything. This caused a real challenge in my business life. I had trouble sleeping nights and this compounded all the other problems.

This condition stayed with me in the above stated form for about six months. Since this first bout in 1988 I have been on a roller-coaster with periods of three to nine months of fairly normal times with only limited flare ups after periods of too much work or recreational activity. Then the old symptoms will appear again out of the blue and stay with me for three to six months. Some periods of the renewed bouts see varying degrees of the severity of the symptoms. It is frustrating to say the least.

I have some of the ever-smiling-take-whatever-happens-in stride attitude my mother was so blessed with. I have never felt sorry for myself. Depression goes with Chronic Fatigue Syndrome in many victims. Many doctors wonder if the depression is a cause or an effect of the illness. My impression would be it is an effect. If you do not have a strong resolve and will, the illness will definitely depress you. The only time I have ever become depressed was in November 2003. I had closed our feeding operation down as I will relate in a future chapter. I guess I had always thought that if I shut down the feedlot, the long hours, and the stress of business I would get over the illness. I had done all of the before mentioned and still came down with one of the prolonged times of the illness. This was the end of the straw in my mind for a few weeks. I worked this depression out on my own and soon was back to my old self. I would come to the conclusion after this round that I probably would never be able to work the long hours sometimes required in the cattle business. This was in a regular ranch operation I had going after closing the much more demanding feedyard business. I could neither take the long hours sometimes required nor the physical work I now needed to do to help my now small crew of cowboys.

In the early years of the illness I still sorted all the finished cattle for shipment myself as I always had. It was hard to do and probably not too safe to be in the alley full of cattle no faster than I could move. I tried to stay in as good of shape as possible by helping walk the cattle pens if at all possible. At times it was easier than others. I could be feeling very good and be working, playing during off hours or whatever when just like pulling a light switch my joints and muscles would weaken and I would have trouble walking. It is hard to understand how you can feel so good one second and then the next have a multitude of problems.

Dee Ann has stood by me and helped so much during these many years of this life altering illness. There have been many times though when I knew she was wondering if I was faking this illness or had some kind of an emotional problem. This bothered me more than any other aspect of the illness. I knew in my own mind that what I was going on was real and that it was not emotional. This part is the most frustrating part of the whole ordeal. At times I would also suffer from a "brain fog." It will make thinking extremely difficult. In the cattle business I had to be on my toes when trading the customer's cattle to get each customer the most I could for their cattle. I always managed to get my trades accomplished with the best price on the market. I just had to work extra hard to concentrate on what I needed to do. One of my doctors Dr. Stanley Schwartz in Tulsa has worked with several patients with Chronic Fatigue Syndrome and experimented with many vitamins and supplements that help to varying degrees. One tried without much success was taking Vitamin B12 shots three times per week. I was trained to give myself these shots much as diabetics give themselves insulin shots. I have a much greater respect for those that do this for a lifetime. I tried the shots for about four or five months. They did not seem to help and Dr. Schwartz discontinued having me do this. I was sure glad. The more times I gave myself the shots the worse I hated them.

One supplement that seemed to help the "brain fog" a great deal is called NADH. I don't know what it is, but tried it on Dr. Schwartz's orders. It works very well in helping me think clearly again. I take several other vitamins and supplements that seem to help the symptoms somewhat.

In 1988, Chronic Fatigue Syndrome was sometimes called "yuppie flu" as it seemed to affect many young up-and-coming people who ran a fast-paced schedule. It was thought at one time to have something to do with mononucleosis but most of this thinking is no longer considered to be valid. I was the first in our community of five hundred I know of to have this illness. It is not thought to be contagious. Over the years there have been several in our town develop the illness. At one time there were eight to ten from Welch going to Dr. Schwartz. From the Welch bank I was involved with, four out of about twenty-five employees and directors have developed the disease. This has made me question the non-contagious theory, but Dr. Schwartz could never find any link that would prove otherwise.

Cindy Layton developed the fibromyalgia form about seven years ago. Hers came after a period of much stress and short nights of sleep while dealing with a very complicated broken leg suffered by her son, Rowdy. Cindy has had a very much harder experience than I have. She took disability from work and has few things she is able to do with any vigor. Teresa went to the hospital for tests. The day she got out, I saw her stop by her place of employment at the bank before going home. Watching her walk into the bank, I immediately knew she would be diagnosed with the Chronic Fatigue which I later found to be true when I talked to her. One of the partners and directors in the bank was Art Cousatte. Art was working himself at both ends of the candle much as I had done when I spent so many hours at the Miami bank and the feedlot. Art was a full time banker at the time with Security Bank in Miami. He also was a director at the Welch bank. He owned a plastics company and also a trucking company. He would go by the plastics or trucking companies each morning before his bank job and end the day at the other. His days started on the job at six in the morning and lasted till late in the evening. He has also had more trouble so it seems than I. Maybe I underestimate my own problems over the years, but I do not think so. Others in Welch have also dealt with this illness. No cure or cause has been found to this date.

Since my first bout in 1988 with that first trip to the hospital, I have been admitted around four more times through the years. Each time but one I would go in with heart-attack-type symptoms. The one time I did not, I went in with extreme stomach pain. It was thought but never determined that I might have suffered from an ulcer attack. Perforated stomach ulcers killed my mother's father in his forties and my own mother in her early seventies. I was admitted this particular time in the middle of the night. There are things in life we never forget and marvel at. One of these occurred that night. As I was being wheeled to my room, we met Paul Ingram Thomas, a local funeral director taking a body out. The body was of his grandfather, W.C. Thomas. W.C. or "Buss," as he was called, was the funeral director in Welch, a career he started late in life after an early career in farming and custom hay baling. The thing I will always remember about that night that "Buss" passed away was Paul Ingram in the middle of the night was at the hospital in his crisp white shirt and tie just like he would be for a funeral. I wondered if he slept in a white shirt. He must not have slept in this one, as it was fresh and crisp.

On one of the visits to the hospital, I had been trading cattle with my friend the IBP buyer, Larry Haley. As soon as I was tucked in the bed and put on an IV of morphine for the pain I was in, I got a phone and called Larry to finish the trade. The morphine already was taking effect. I was feeling no pain. I traded with Larry and suddenly realized I had no idea whether I knew what I was doing or not. I quickly told Larry to call the feedlot and ask my staff if I had done the right thing or not. Larry did not try to take advantage of my situation and I had traded the right cattle at the right price. Jeri Harden is a nurse at our hospital and a long time friend from church. She walked in my room to check on me and was amazed that I was trading cattle so soon after coming in. She teases me about this years later.

I am sure that stress and long hours caused my own Chronic Fatigue Syndrome. However, even during the years of managing the feedlot and the bad Miami bank with such long hours I never felt the stress. Early on, I would not sleep well wondering how I was going to pay for the losses at the bank and keep the feedlot business solvent. When I finally came to my plan to fill the lot with the now cheap cattle and the profits they would soon see coming in, I never worried much again. I enjoyed the challenges presented and the opportunity to prove myself in my new roles. The long hours however had their effect and through the years I have had the Syndrome flair up while playing as much as working. When I overdo it at either work or play, I suffer.

Along life's way you many times see a side of someone you have not seen. Sometimes this new side is good and sometimes it is bad. I saw a great side to my friend, Frank Robson one day as I was leaving a seminar at Oklahoma State University Stillwater. Frank is a brother to Mrs. Sam Walton and has done very well in life. He is known as a shrewd and hard trader on whatever he is working on. Frank is heavily involved in property rentals, ranching, and banking among other things. He would feed a few of his cattle with us, but never a large amount. He was always, however, very supportive of me and when at a meeting would hunt me up and visit awhile about the cattle industry. Anyway as I was leaving our Stillwater meeting, my fatigue syndrome had really kicked in full force. We had spent several hours sitting during the conference and my joints were so stiff and muscles so weak I could hardly walk. I was having extreme difficulty getting to my car for the trip home. Frank saw my problem and immediately stopped the conversation he was having with another gentleman and came to see if he could help. I explained my problem and told him I would be fine as soon as I got to my car and got started home. I thanked Frank for his interest and offer to help and made my way on. I did fine as soon as I got to the car and got home fine. The next morning was Saturday and Frank called my office early to check on me. I was not there yet, but Diane had spoken to me on the phone. She told him I seemed fine. I returned Frank's call and again thanked him for his interest. The following Monday and again on Wednesday Frank called and related that he had visited with one of his bank presidents who seemed to have a similar problem about me. He asked me to call his man and visit about how the Mayo Clinic had helped him. I did so on more than one occasion. I could not get scheduled into Mayo and never went there, but I always will appreciate the extra mile my friend Frank took out of concern for me. I saw a side of Frank that I had not known. He is a very caring man who even as busy as he is will take time for others. I think Frank showed a great deal of character and has a trait we should all strive for in our lives.

I have dealt with the Chronic Fatigue Syndrome in a positive way. I managed to carry on and expand our business for so many years while dealing with the illness. Many other suffers are not as fortunate as I, some of which I told you about in this chapter. I hope and pray that medical science one day will find a cause and cure for this illness. The key to dealing with an illness such as mine has to be a faith in God and help from friends and family, especially your spouse. Remember to rest all you can, keep a positive attitude, and don't quit doing your job if at all possible.

If you know someone with this type of illness take a minute to offer them a positive comment. Do not look down on their situation. Comments about mental state, laziness, or a faked illness sure have no place in talking with or about someone with this type of illness. Your support will help more than you can ever imagine.

I thank God for my drive to carry on and for the ability to accomplish all that He has allowed me to do so far in my life on this earth. We all should learn to count our blessings and remember no matter what the situation we may face, there is someone that is much worse off. God will see us through our struggles in this life, if we only turn to Him. Remember this as you go down your own life's path.

The next chapter will deal with family and work.

17

Family and Work

I have talked at length about the importance of remembering family, nurturing them, spending time, and instilling values in your kids. My folks managed to have time with me even though growing up I always had a sick brother that took their attention. Cystic Fibrosis is a very trying disease.

Thirty-five years ago most Cystic Fibrosis patients died very young as did my two brothers, Eddie at six months and Tommy at two years. My older brother Steve lived to twenty-three, graduated from college, and was married. This was very rare then. Today modern medicine has extended many lives to teens and twenties with some to the thirties. Hopefully, we are closer to a cure for this terrible disease. Steve took close to fifty pills per day, slept in a mist tent with antibiotics, and had twice a day inhaling treatments with cupping treatments on his back to loosen the thick mucus that goes with the disease. I was taught to always look out for Steve when we were doing things together. I would ride along sometimes with him after he learned to drive in case of car trouble I could go for help. We had normal fights like kids do, but were always close. I often wondered how I was the one to escape the awful disease when my only other three brothers had the disease. We never know why we receive this or that blessing. Even though healthy, my raising was not easy for Mom, I missed over thirty days of school in the first grade. Every sore throat, measles, mumps I had. I have often wondered if I was born with a poor immune system considering I have the chronic fatigue syndrome now for sixteen years. Doctors have looked at different links but never found anything. There is so much about medicine that modern doctors still do not know. One good that came out of my having the mumps in the first grade was giving them to Dad. What, how can that be good giving the mumps to a grown man? Well, you see in those days, Dad smoked as most of his generation did at the time. He had wanted to quit, but never could. His mumps were so bad, he could not smoke for a week and when well he never did again. Quite a cure, but at least it worked for him.

Growing up, Dad took me on several business trips and after I finished the seventh grade I always went to work in the summers and did something with Dad. My first job on my own with him was to pick up rocks from an area he was developing into a housing addition. I took the old pickup or a tractor and trailer and picked up rocks now and again all one summer. I never left the then still pasture land with the pickup so I was all right driving. Seemed real fun to be driving at about twelve-years old. At fifteen years of age, Dad and I would go out every morning in the summer to cut "green chop," a tall sorghum crop we chopped standing and green in the field and fed to the cattle as soon as chopped. It would not keep chopped green, so we only chopped the amount needed for the cattle that day. Dad would drive the tractor and cutter and I would follow at his side in a two ton feed truck. The cutter would blow the chopped feed into the truck if I drove the same speed and within about two feet of the cutter. It would be a real challenge when the field was slick after a rain, or if the cutter balled up and Dad had to slow down or stop. We always had fun doing things like this together.

When our own daughter, Jodee came along, I remembered the fun times I had with Dad on work trips and doing things together. We did not begin to raise Jodee to work cattle, pick up rocks, or drive the feed truck. Some families do this and it works for them. We decided however to limit Jodee to more lady-like work. This did not keep her from doing things with me like going to the Saturday cattle sale and keeping track of the cattle I bought. I have related the real estate trip to Houston she shared with me. She also went to Garden

City with me to obtain and drive home a new feed truck. One New Year's Eve when about sixteen, Jodee stayed out a little later than she was supposed to. I think this must have been the only time this ever happened, but the way I cured it was to simply get her up early on New Year's Day and take her with me to the feedlot. I had recently gone to a cash raising sale a troubled animal health supplier had conducted. I had bought a whole wall of cattle identification tags for one hundred dollars. I had no idea how many tags I had bought, but Jodee's job that day was to count and organize the tags by color and number. We ended up with about thirteen thousand tags. She still talks of tag counting day. I made my point on being late without belittling her, but made a very big point.

Being an only grandchild and daughter could have made for one spoiled daughter, but not for Jodee. My Mother worked with Jodee and taught her a lot growing up. The Christmas before what would be Jodee's sixteenth birthday, Dad wanted to order her a new Ford from our friend Darrell Kissee and have it come in for delivery on her April birth date. I would not allow this and this was one of the few disagreements Dad and I had. I told him she needed to start with an old car she could fix up. He was afraid she would have car trouble somewhere if driving an old junker. That argument didn't fly when shortly after her new driver's license was obtained, Mom sent Jodee to Miami on an errand in her brand new Lincoln. While driving down the street in Miami, the new Lincoln stalled. It seems that through no fault of Jodee's the car's transmission had gone out with only six thousand miles on it. No more said about being stranded by the old car.

Jodee got a job at the Miami McDonald's. What a learning experience. She would tell of people coming through the line at the drive up window and breaking into tears if something was wrong on their order or chewing them out. People tend to take out their frustrations on who ever is close at the time. She saved her money and soon could afford a car. We looked and looked for a 1965-67 Mustang to restore. In 1983 we finally found a 66 Mustang in pretty good shape for thirteen hundred dollars. She saved more and had the car painted and the interior redone. We bought accessories for her birthday and

Christmas gifts such as tires, chrome wheels, and a stereo radio. She had a grand time seeing the car come to new life. Even though she hired all this work done, it was a great sense of accomplishment that she saw in the fruit of her earnings from work. I had had similar fun in my youth with my Model A Ford I started out with.

After one year of college and just a few months after Dad's death Jodee came home one day with her steady, Doug. They wanted to get married and continue college together at OSU. Doug was a year older and ready to transfer from the NEO junior college at Miami they both had been attending. They met on the job at the McDonald's where both worked. I told them I thought they were right for each other and old enough if they could figure out how to support each other. Dee Ann and I would pay for the school tuition as planned, but nothing toward living expenses if married. They saved from their jobs, got married just before the start of the new school year and moved to Stillwater. Both worked through school and Jodee went to summer school while working so as to catch Doug and graduate at the same time.

After graduation both went to work for Halliburton in Duncan, Oklahoma which is about two hundred fifty miles from Welch. This was in the days of the fifty-five mile an hour speed limit and a trip to Duncan would take five hours at best. How was I to see my only daughter with the schedule I had? I decided it was time to sharpen up my flying skills again. We had owned a plane for a short while in the early seventies and had sold it when our first house was built. Sixteen years had passed since flying, but soon Perry Knight of the local airport had me up and flying again. I decided to buy a plane that could get to Duncan in two hours instead of the five hour trip by car. This was in 1989 and the bank nightmare was over, and things were going well once again at the feedlot. I found a nice 1975 Piper Archer for twenty-six thousand dollars in Covington, Georgia through an ad in the "Trade a Plane" magazine. Perry, an airplane mechanic, and I flew to Georgia and checked the plane out. It checked out fine and a deal was struck and I returned home in the new buy with Perry following behind in the rental plane we used to fly down in. I now had a way to see Jodee and Doug and still be at work the next day without upsetting the fatigue syndrome with too long of a time on the road. The plane would be very useful in recruiting customers for the feedlot. We kept that plane from 1988 to 2001 when I sold it and closed the feedlot. The kids were now living close to home and the fatigue syndrome was bothering me to the point I no longer felt safe flying very far from home.

Your family pillar is so very important. Plan how you raise your children in God's way. Instill the proper values and work ethic in them. All of this does not happen by itself. You have to set the example and plan the effort to instill these values.

I will talk more about family and business as we go through the book. Also if you have not already read my mother's book *God's Hand In Mine*, it deals with many more details of family than I have in this short chapter.

The next chapter will talk of things that could have been.

We made a lot of business trips in this plane.

N180CC

18

What Could Have Been

The one area Dad and I both were out of tune with today's business practices even for a small business was the fact we thought one of us had to be at the feedlot every day if work was going on. In those days we only fed once on holiday and weekends instead of twice a day in the week. One or both of us would always be at work until the cattle were fed and checked and the help was ready to leave. We did have a night watchman that spent the night at the yard and unloaded cattle coming in. At least we did not have to be with him all the time, even though the night man always called if he had trouble with a heifer calving or a water tank running over. I have been back to help him many a time on a night after work or Sunday afternoon or a holiday evening. It was just part of the job. In Dad's day and my early days we only had ten employees, so we had to do more of the actual work. When I quit, we had about twenty-two employees. I did little of the physical labor then, but still stayed late if the crew was having trouble.

Most of today's large cattle ranch or feedlot owners simply hire a manager to take care of things and they go about their daily business without worrying about the cattle care details. This is fine and works for most. I however, could never treat my employees this way. We were still a small business and if they had to work Christmas, I should too and did. We did go to weekend shifts so as to feed the cattle twice a day on weekends as through the week. I knew I could not always be there every hour, but always kept a pager and cell phone on me so I could be reached if help was needed.

We recently sold our feedlot property. The new owners were to have employees move in on a Sunday and take over their cattle care that we had been providing on Monday morning. I was at the office packing out the last of our personnel boxes on late Sunday afternoon. The new people arrived having got up at 4:30 in the morning to make the long trip from western Kansas to eastern Oklahoma. They brought all their possessions in stock trailers pulled behind their pickup. They arrived at about three in the afternoon to houses that had not been lived in for five months where the water and heat had been shut off. The new owners came by and stayed about five minutes and left for their motel saying they would see us at the closing the next day. I thought sure they were putting up their employees in the motel that first night till they could get the water turned on and furniture unloaded. This was not to be, nor did they stay to help the two employees unload their things. I guess if I could treat people this way, I would still own and operate the feedlot, but I could not and would not. I believed in treating employees fairly and not asking to do something I would not do myself. I would have helped the employees unload their trailers and then put them up in a motel for the night till they could get settled. This is a big difference in today's generation of new owners. In years past, most small business people would have operated as I, today many do not. I think there is always a happy medium in most things, but probably we need to pay more attention to those that help us.

When Dad died suddenly, I was my own foreman, corn buyer, cattle seller, personnel manager, and most everything else that had to do with management. I had one lead man that I looked to for the mechanical workings of the yard and one man in charge of feeding. I should have changed this management during the time I was spending every afternoon at the bank. However, I did not think this would be fair to a new assistant to give him duties I was doing and then take them back when I was back at the feedlot full time. At the time I did not know the bank ordeal would last thirty-three months. Money was short at the time also, so I just stretched further. I did teach my secretary and store clerk to be the grain and supply buyer. I would set a price I was willing to pay and she would talk to the farmers or elevators until someone agreed to sell to her at the agreed upon price. Early on, Diane Cox, my right hand, would not know anything about corn or trading, but she listened well and believed I knew a price that would work. She saved me hours of phone time and soon learned to trade with the farmers as good as I. Mike Fitzpatrick was my man in charge of the mechanic workings of the lot and also lived on the property and served as night man. One lesson I finally learned was that I allowed my employees to work their day off for extra pay if they wanted to. This worked well for me and in the short term for the employee. However for the long term, it was bad because the employee would burn out. Mike stayed about ten years and did just that. He came in one day and said he was leaving right then to operate a service station. He did not seem mad about anything, just wanted a change. That was fine, but I sure wish he would have given some notice. I relied on him and he was gone in five minutes. This is one practice as an employee you should remember: leave on good terms and that means giving notice when leaving. I always missed Mike after he left and although I never said anything I thought he had done me wrong in the manner he left. Those feelings are long gone now and I enjoy seeing him when the opportunity arises. After he left, he moved only two miles away, so he was still a neighbor. Best to get along with everyone, but especially neighbors.

I learned early on that I needed consultant help after my consultant, Dad had died. I mentioned the Helming Group that I used for long term company direction. Another early consultant I needed was a feed nutritionist. I called long time university friend, Don Gill, an extension nutritionist at OSU and ask his opinion of whom in the industry would be a good fit for me to use. He recommended Gary Tibbetts of Farr Better Feeds of Guymon, Oklahoma. I called Gary and he agreed to come over and see our operation. We hit it off almost immediately. We agreed that he would do our work and come for a monthly visit to the feedyard to check things out. He wanted to sell us our feed supplement since that was part of his job at Farr. We agreed that I would put his supplement formula out for bid against Farr and other companies we had used in past. If he was the low bidder, his services for the nutrition work would cost nothing, but if not the low bidder, I would pay him for his work. He always managed to be the low bidder and things went well till one visit he reported that Farr was moving him to Greeley, Colorado and he would have to give us up. I laughed and said that it would be easier to get to Welch from nearby Denver airport then to drive ten hours from Guymon. This made sense and the plane ticket to Tulsa was only ninety-nine dollars plus a rental car charge for Tulsa to Welch. This made a much more pleasant trip for Gary and he continued to do our monthly visits. Gary and his wife had six kids and Shannon, his wife, home schooled the kids. They were the neatest, best mannered kids I have ever met. Gary on many occasions brought one child with him for his visit. They never caused any trouble and of course I believed in this philosophy, as I have told you of trips I took with my Dad and likewise Jodee with me. This relationship with Gary was great for our consultant work until Gary got transferred to Nebraska, this time to be a plant manager. Farr would no longer allow him to do our work so I had to look elsewhere. We continued to be good friends though and he would bring the whole family by to see us on the way to his in-laws in Arkansas.

In about 1990 Farr was sold to Cargill, a large privately owned company. Gary did not want to work for this large company and was trying to decide his next direction. I had the bank problem behind me now and was fast changing our company to one who would service the little feeder no one else wanted. This was taking a lot of customer development time and I was still having seemingly constant problems with the chronic fatigue. It would get so bad during this time that I would have to pull myself up the stairs by the handrail. I called Gary and ask if he would be interested in joining our business as a partner. I was willing to let him earn a stake in the company through his sweat equity because I knew we could work so well together. Gary and Shannon and family came and visited and looked the situation and town over. They thought long and hard and I just knew he would take me up on my offer. In the end another small mineral company called Zinpro offered Gary a territory of Colorado and Nebraska. They could live in Greeley again and Gary would travel his two states. It paid a better salary than I could offer, but of course had no ownership. They took the Zinpro job and Gary is still there today. However, he is without Shannon. Something happened between the two and they had a bitter divorce. Gary never said what happened. I often wondered if they had moved to Welch, where Gary would have been at home every night instead of on the road much of the week, if things would have been different for them. On the other hand, if he had become my partner, what would the divorce have done to company financial stability?

What could have been did not happen. There are corners of our lives where major decisions have many lasting results good or bad. If Gary had came and continued with a stable family life I am sure we would have been a wonderful team. It was not to be. I saw my friend so sad for many years after the divorce. It caused problems with his spending time with his precious kids. He has now found new happiness with wife, Joyce. She has put the sparkle back in Gary's eyes. The kids are growing up and doing well. It's sad his family split, but I am so glad Gary has found new happiness with Joyce.

Major life corners need to be studied and well thought out to seek the best solution. Sometimes things may not work out as we would like, but trust in God and He will guide us around every curve and corner presented in this life's path.

Many small business owners venture into other side businesses. I was no different. The next chapter will tell my side ventures.

19

Side Ventures

Small business people are accustomed to wearing many hats and many own more than one business. I have already told of my real estate company and house building activities. Another venture we sort of backed into was the retail selling of cattle working supplies. In the seventies there were not too many local places that ranchers could buy their cattle supply needs such as vaccine, wormers, antibiotics for sick cattle, fence post, barbed wire, and gates. We kept a pretty good supply of these needs for our own use and neighbors were always coming by and we would sell them what they needed out of this inventory. By the late seventies, we had a thriving little side business selling these supplies out of our little 16x30 one room office. In 1981 we built a new office and had a showroom for these cattle products. We added a few items of inventory that we would not use, but most was still cattle working supplies we would eventually use if not sold. Buying larger quantities got us better prices, which helped the bottom line on our cattle as well as our customers. We never marked the products up a lot, but would manage enough profit at the end of the year to have paid for the office help that had so many other duties. Most years we would sell about eight hundred thousand dollars in this side line business.

For seventeen years or so, we held an annual spring open house and sold the cattle products to people who came from far and wide. We would sell booth space to our vendors, usually fifteen to twenty companies, who would send their rep to the show to help us sell their products. The booth space paid for advertising in paper and radio, a meal, door prizes given away, and usually a local band for entertainment. Some years we rented the local civic center for the event. Other years we would rent a large tent and have it at the feedyard. A few times the event was held in a new barn or shop just built at the feedlot before it was put to use for its intended purpose. People came to these sales from about a sixty-mile radius each year and most came back to us throughout the year for the products they needed.

The way we operated the store was not a great burden to our time for the extra income we received. The cowboy crew would unload the large loads of inventory and the office help would sell off and on though the day as people filtered through. We also would pick up a new feedlot customer from these people every once in a while.

In 1985, I was addressing my annual tax problem with my accountant, Gayle Edmondson. We were talking of different ideas to save on our taxes. Gayle also had side interest, one being a fuel distributorship. We had investment tax credit that year and bought quite abit of new feedlot equipment. This time Gayle suggested that I buy a semi-truck to haul grain to the feedlot. He also mentioned that he could supply the fuel for the new venture. I laughed at his way of getting new business for the fuel bulk plant, but did go shopping. Another point, I can not say enough, is our long time practice of not replacing a supplier that took good care of our account and had fair prices just because someone new came along trying to sell the same thing. I have always tried to stick by this principal and it has served me well. In the fuel case, we bought all of our feedlot fuel from Maple Oil of Vinita and continued from 1970 to the mid '90s when they went out of business. Frank Maple had taken care of our fuel needs without a snag in the 1973 fuel shortage and we never forgot how he always managed to have fuel for us and even our custom silage cutters when fuel was so hard to come by. I also knew if I was to be in the trucking business, it should be in a separate corporation for liability issues. We wanted different fuel tanks for this operation so friend Gayle, got the new account and kept it till he sold his oil company. Frank Maple retained his large account with the feedyard and everyone was happy.

I went shopping on New Year's Eve for the new truck purchase. I checked with two or three dealers and ended up at the Freightliner Dealership in Joplin late in the day. We negotiated three or four hours, but in the end, Carl Evans sold me a new Freightliner that would start my trucking career. I also bought a Guthrie grain trailer from their factory in west central Kansas. Carl Evans eventually moved to the local Peterbilt dealership and I became a friend with his boss, Clair Larson and his sons. The Larsons ended up feeding several pens of cattle with us and of course I bought several Peterbilts from their salesmen and my old friend Carl Evans. You learn to get ahead by trading with those who trade with you first, those who treat your account right and finally and least a good deal.

My first driver hired was my old friend from the car lot days. The same Jerry Garroutte, who had taken me home for lunch on my first day of work there years ago, was now in the truck driving force. I made a deal with Jerry to drive for me. I am sorry to say he was not happy driving the longer distance we went than his old job had required and he only made three loads and quit. Sometimes things do not work out, but we remained friends. My next driver was Dale Charles. Dale started in March 1986 and stayed with me until we closed out the trucking operation in July 2001. Yes, the March 1986 startup date with Dale came after Jerry's three loads when the new truck and trailer bought on New Year's Eve 1985 came in from the factory in early March. This all happened in the same time frame as Dad's death and my new duties at the Miami bank as well as the added load at the feedlot. I never missed a beat and took all in stride at the time. I had purchased seventy-five loads of corn from Harold at the Hopkins, Missouri elevator a round trip of five hundred eighty-two miles for our driver. Anyway, many loads of corn awaited Dale, and when he ran out there, Diane Cox, my new corn buyer had him some more lined up and did for all those years we hauled corn. The corn truck never made over about ten thousand dollars a year after the driver and all expenses were paid, but it gave us a lot of leverage buying corn for the best price for the feedlot. We hauled about one third of what we would use and bought the rest from elevators or farmers who owned trucks and could deliver corn. Many of our good corn suppliers were managed by people we seldom or never met in person, just a voice on the phone who treated us right.

While on corn, I want to pause to tell you of the Sorenson Feed and Grain of Cumberland, Iowa. Marion Sorenson and his son Kevin were in the elevator and trucking business. We got a call one-day in the early eighties I think. They had two loads of corn sitting in Anderson, Missouri that had been turned down because the Anderson people claimed it had too much moisture in it. Corn is bought and sold on a fifteen and one half- percent moisture basis. The Anderson plant was for chickens and they would not take any moisture above the fifteen and one half percent at all. We would buy corn carrying one or two percent extra moisture for the cattle at a discount and get along fine in cattle feeding. Someone had told Marion that we might buy his corn. He called and told me the story that he was turned down, but thought the moisture was real close to fifteen and a half. I made a deal for the two loads and when checked at our elevator, we found them to be just fifteen and one half, thus no dock from us. I had learned over the years that several of the chicken plants would get overbought on corn and out of room so they would find excuses such as too much moisture and turn the corn down. We found a good supplier in Marion and Kevin and bought six to eight loads a week from them for over twenty years. I met Marion in person only once in all this time. Kevin, we met more often in the early years, as he would sometimes drive a truck delivering to us.

We built many long-term relationships with suppliers over the years. Marion had a brother Roger who learned of us and also called to sell us corn. We soon found out Roger would not shoot as straight as Marion on the grade and condition of the corn Soon, the only time corn was purchased from Roger was when we were really desperate and had to have some corn from about anyone. However, Roger could have sold us corn week after week like Marion had he played straighter with us instead of two or three times a year when we were in trouble.

Our own corn truck was working well and did not require much of my time, so the next year I added another semi-tractor and this time a cattle hauling trailer. This worked well both in regard to service for our customers and also financially for us. We soon were hauling all of IBP's cattle for them to their Emporia, Kansas plant 173 miles away. They usually bought about ten loads of cattle a week from us and had us haul them all. We added a second driver and one would take the morning load and come back in about seven or eight hours and we would load up the next load and start a new driver to Emporia. Several times when we had extra cattle and IBP was short of cattle we would make three turns in twenty-four hours. Everything had to keep running just right to make this work, but we did it with the first load driver sleeping in between loads. We also hauled Saturday and Sunday loads to them occasionally. When we could, we backhauled customer cattle loaded at their ranch on our way home from Emporia and hauled them back to the feedlot. These loads we hauled cheaper for the rancher bringing cattle back to us and still made extra money for us.

The only down side to owning our own cattle hauling rig and hauling so many loads for IBP was it cut out the loads that old friends Bill Bailey and Joe Lewis had formerly had. I had not thought about us getting all their IBP loads, but always felt bad about losing their haul. It was only good business for us and added to our bottom line. However I never liked being the one who cost them loads. We still used them when we needed extra trucks and continued to get along. Several years later I was a pall-bearer at my friend Joe Lewis's funeral. He died after a battle with cancer.

Most small business people have some sort of side venture as I have described in this chapter. In our case, the good bank trade propelled my net worth greatly. The supply store and the trucking corporation added dollars to the bottom line and kept money in our pocket that would have gone to someone else. The early years in real estate paid for the house. In short, it lets you get ahead in a way you never would in one business alone. None of the side ventures required very much risk or a great deal of extra capital. A little extra earned here and there if it does not distract you from your main business is certainly something I would recommend every business person look at. However, as said, you cannot divert too much time and resources to the neglect of the cash cow.

Next chapter deals with estate issues.

Joe Neill Trucking

Dale Charles a great truck driver

20

Estate Tax Issues

Most small family businesses have at one time or the other had to face the tax issues in estates when an owner dies. Some families are well prepared for this event, both emotionally and financially. Many are not. I was caught kind of in between. Knowing God has a better place for us when we leave this earth if we have obeyed His commands and obeyed and followed The Lord's teachings in His Word is of great comfort to the Christian family left behind. The most important estate plan we need to make on this earth is to prepare for Life after Death. I don't know about you, but I sure do not want to spend eternity in hell, so I am doing my best to follow the teaching set forth in the Bible so that I will spend eternity in heaven. This essential planning for yourself is also of utmost importance for your family and friends. Our example in life to the people in our family, friends, and those we come in contact with in our daily personal and business life may just be the stumbling block to someone else's salvation or more hopefully be the example that leads someone else to the Christian life. This is true estate planning.

After this is in order, the next step is to have our earthly life in order. I would hate to leave things in a mess business wise when I left this earth and of course none of us know the hour or place of our demise. My father was ready to meet the Lord and while I hated to lose him, knew he was going to a better place. While most affairs were in order and I was here to look after Mom, nothing had been done as far as estate planning. Dad had a total of twenty thousand dollars in life insurance. The Feedlot Corporation was eighty-nine percent owned by Dad, ten percent by Mom, and one percent by myself. Of course Dad's ownership would go to Mom without any tax consequence. We had a corporation in place and I could sign checks and continue to do business. I had a window of opportunity while Mom was still here to do some planning. I was the only child, so there were no family feuds or fusses to contend with as Dad had had with his brothers and sisters when his own father died in 1968.

Early on I purchased a life insurance policy on Mom with my funds in the amount $250,000 to cover her death and give me some tax protection until things could be rearranged. Dad's death came at a time of low land values. Remember in the real estate chapter I told of land falling from a $700 per acre high to $200 on the low. We were close to the low at his death. This gave an opportunity for Mom to transfer land to me and I in turn paid on the debt we owed to get the Miami Bank settled. This got the land to me at lower values and kept us under the then $600,000 exemptions in the estate laws on what was passed on from Mom. I traded and bought other ground in the bank trade. When we got figured out where we stood Mom wanted to transfer all she could to me while the tax rate would be low. We left her money to live on for her life span and her home and car. Everything else was put in my name. I in turn took out a $400,000 life insurance policy on myself with Mom as first beneficiary and Dee Ann as second. This was in case I was to die before Mom; she would have peace of mind even though we both knew Dee Ann was the one to take care of her whether I was still around or not. This served us well and when Mom died we were in as good a shape tax wise as we could have done without leaving Mom with anything which I would not do. We ended up paying about $30,000 in taxes and in the neighborhood of $20,000 in fees for the attorney and accountants.

What could have been a nightmare, turned out fine. I have seen families spend half of what their loved one worked hard for and give this to Uncle Sam. I know the government needs funds and we have always paid more than our share of the income tax. However death tax seems unfair and like paying twice. Today, in 2004 we see reduced rates until 2009 when we have no tax for one year and then in 2010 the tax goes back to the old high rate. This is absolutely absurd! Most will do no planning with this type of situation when the Congress should have this settled this issue one way or the other and then left it alone. We certainly cannot in good conscience plan the year of our death to avoid taxes.

I have tried to do better planning since I did not have a son or daughter coming after me in the family business. I will talk in a future chapter of helping our daughter and son in law get a business start. I have bought a large amount of permanent life insurance years ago that is still building cash value. Some say this is not a good investment, but I have had years of peace of mind and the cash value has not been that bad in these past years of poor stock market return and low interest. Permanent life insurance belongs in one segment of your financial planning. I also elected to close out our family feed-yard at an early age. Even though my health problem is not life threatening, I realized from dealing with it, what could happen if I had passed suddenly and left a feedyard to be closed by someone unfamiliar with selling customer cattle and taking care of their inter-est. The harder thing to do without experience would be to close the lagoons and get out from under the EPA laws feedyards deal with every day. Today, I have things very uncomplicated and I will do something fun, hopefully productive for mankind and the Lord the rest of my days. I sleep well at night knowing my financial affairs and business dealings will not burden anyone. I hope you will heed this lesson soon if you have problem areas in your business life. We never know when our time is coming.

In the next chapter I will discuss land deals in our life. Some are quite interesting.

21

The Land Deals

Land is a tool of the trade in the cattle business. Like most ranching families, our land started with land purchased by my grandfather in the early 1900s. My father added to this land base during his time and the family land holdings also included land passed on to my mother from her mother. This is the way ranching families hold on to a land base that would be hard to establish without a base to grow with. This does not mean that it is always prudent to hold land just for the sake of owning land. Times change and we have to change with the times and the needs and desires of the next generation.

The original family ranch was located fifteen miles west of our hometown, Welch, Oklahoma. I do not know why my grandfather chose to settle here when he moved from Indiana with his family, but it was good black land and the bluestem pastures were in a limestone rock area that is known for wonderful native pasture. In his day, the ranch was located on a gravel road twelve miles from Welch to where his house was. The road was not very good and is the main reason my Dad moved the feeding operation to Welch because it was so hard to get grain and cattle trucks to the ranch in muddy times. Fortunately the road was paved in the mid '50s and the travel to town was much easier. Consolidation has been taking place in the agriculture community for at least fifty years, maybe more. In the early days, my Grandfather had many neighbors close by, within a half-mile or so. This has changed so much during my lifetime. Today the ranches are mostly large operations with owners who live in town or maybe even in Tulsa. Very few owners of the land are left living in the area. The ranches will have cowboys living on them, but they are still scattered far and wide. When I was growing up, my uncle, Dad's brother, ran a country store. It was fifteen miles back to Welch and eighteen miles to the next town on west Lenapah, Oklahoma. Floyd Neill kept this store open seven days a week and he was always there to greet his customers. He had the first of today's quick stop stores where you could purchase gas, groceries, and get a sandwich on the spot for lunch. He had a booming business through the fifties and into the sixties. When he died in 1966, the area was seeing a fast consolidation to fewer families in the area and the larger ranches. His family ran the store a few more years and sold it, but by the seventies the business was just not there and the store closed for good. It was the end of an era. Times change and we have to change with the times.

In the early '60s the local community church decided to build a new building. They saved and soon the new construction was under way. The last Sunday in the old wooden building came and many in the congregation were wondering what to do with the old building. It would be expensive to tear down and was in disrepair. Granddad always went early Sunday morning and lit the old coal stove so it would be warm when everyone arrived. The week before this last Sunday in the old building had found Granddad in his eighties at the time burning old houses in his pasture that had been abandoned and on land he had purchased as part of the early consolidation of the area ranches. Back to church on the last Sunday in the building, Granddad lit the fire as he had so many times, but something happened this time. The stove blew up for some reason, burning his arms pretty bad and setting the building on fire. The fire completely destroyed the old structure by the time the fire truck could make the journey from Welch. Luckily the new building was of concrete block construction and while the fire blackened the roof on the new building, it basically was not hurt. Granddad recovered from his burn. Everyone praised him for practicing all week in his pasture in the art of burning down a building. Of course this was not the case, but he took a lot of good-natured ribbing about burning the church down. The Lord can work in funny ways at times. You see the old building was still insured and the congregation collected the insurance, which paid the note off on the new building.

Dad bought about a thousand acres in this area and ranched with Granddad. When Granddad died in 1966 part of this land went to Dad and the rest to his brothers and sisters. Dad and later I, bought some of this land from the family members. We would end up 2,350 acres of good bluestem grass. This may sound like a large ranch to many readers, but in the new twenty-first century it is not enough to make a good living for a family alone without outside income. This ranch would run about 300 cows, which we never did. We ran yearling steers through the summer and it would take about 500 steers from April to early October when they would go to the feedlot or in later years I would do what is known as a double stock program, 900 to 1,000 steers from April 15 to July 15. This was double the amount and left half the time. This did not hurt the grass and while the gain per steer was less than grazing till fall, the total pounds produced on the ranch was more than the smaller set left till fall. This, in most years, is not enough for a complete living in today's world. It would be a good supplement to our total operation when managed with the property we would acquire closer to Welch.

Dad and Granddad's first feedlot was on land they purchased from Mom's stepfather when he had a mill that he used to produce feed for his hog operation go up in flames. He decided to retire and sell the land, as his health was poor. A new mill was built and pens for cattle were added. About 4,000 cattle would eventually be fed out at this facility. They had made one mistake. The numbers on feed were never meant to be that high, but neighbors such as Dad's old sale barn partners would ask if they would feed a pen for them, they did, and before long the custom feeding business was off and running. The location was adjoining the Welch city limits and proved to not be a good choice. The smell would have some town's people complaining and the land was too flat over much of the area and the pens would get muddy in the winter. Dad went looking for a new location. He found 160 acres about four miles south of town. Its rolling hills would provide the drainage for a great feedlot. Mrs. Plott, the widow and owner of the land, did not want to sell, but Dad kept going back and finally offered an amount that sounded good to her. In 1960 construction was started on the new property. In 1964 another 160 acres was acquired from neighbor Len Ethington and his wife when they retired. A couple of years later another 120 acres was bought from the Reavis estate when both Mr. and Mrs. Reavis passed away. This property was across the road from the original track. In 1968, Mom's mother passed away and she inherited 290 acres about a mile West and across the highway and another sixty-six acres three miles on south. This would give Dad's operation 876 acres close to Welch.

Granddad died in 1966 and Dad was on his own till I joined him full time in 1969. I had planned, as told in an early chapter to be an automobile dealer, but after my older brother Steve's death in 1968 and Dad's back and stomach problems ,I felt it was best for me to come home and help him. I graduated from the junior college and did not continue my education, except under a very good teacher, Dad. We worked well together and grew the feedlot to about 9,000-head one time capacity. Shortly before Dad's death in 1986 we bought 110 acres from neighbor Otis Kay's estate. I had tried to buy Otis's entire ranch of 460 acres. When cow calf pairs sold for $700, Otis would tell me an acre of land was worth the same as a pair. At the time land was selling for $400 not $700 an acre. This went on till Otis's death. I tried to buy his land from his estate in about 1982. Land was selling higher now and interest rates on land loans was about 10 percent. I finally offered the Kays $675 an acre if they would finance the purchase at 8 percent, about what a CD at the bank would bring them at the time. They would not do this and I would not give any more.

Don Kirby, from west central Oklahoma, near a town called Pond Creek decided to invest in some land in our country and came to look at the Kay property. Across the road on the Reavis property we had the best corn crop we ever raised growing on land we had built up with manure from the feedlot. We always figured Mr. Kirby thought all the land would grow corn like ours, which was not the case in this area without the nutrient buildup the manure provided. He bought 350 acres of the best part of the Kay land for about $750 an acre. I had bid on the entire ranch, which included 110 acres, and the Kay house that the Kirbys did not buy. The 110 acres where the house was included a hill covered with brush and was the worst land on the place. The house was a small frame house built in the fifties and did not add a tremendous lot to the land as a whole. The family ended up keeping this land till late 1985 when Dad and I made a deal for it. By this time, land values had started falling from the highs when the Kirbys purchased their part of the Kay land. We bought the 110 acres for $375 dollars an acre. We planned to use it to run a twelve inch irrigation line under the highway along a fifteen acre tract we owned that was part of the Reavis land that the highway when built had cut off from the other land and then cross a county gravel road, go across the Kay 110 acres to the adjoining two hundred ninety acres that Mom had inherited. This would give us an area for three center pivot irrigators with each covering about one hundred ten acres. In turn this would give us a place to pump water from the now required lagoons to catch the run off water from the feedlot. The EPA requirements for feedlots were fast becoming a big part of the operation we had to deal with. In the early days, this was not a factor. I think we need to take care of the environmental, but I also think the regulations have caused much more rapid consolidation in the feeding industry. I am sure regulations have hastened consolidation in other industries where economy of scale helps to pay for the regulations passed. Our irrigation project cost $200,000 for the three center pivots and the close to 12,000 feet of underground lines we ran from the lagoons to the pivots including the cost of going under the highway. This was a huge sum for us at the time and a big step in keeping the operation viable.

We bought the land in 1985 and soon had purchased the irrigation system from S & H Farm Supply of Lockwood, Missouri and Eddie Thomas their sales rep. We prepaid the amount to S & H for tax purposes and the system was to be installed in early spring 1986. It turned out that Dad passed away before construction would start. He would have enjoyed the labor saving large pivots so much had he lived to see them. Before having them, we used traveling guns that had to be moved every day by moving temporary aluminum pipe carrying the water to a gun that traveled along a cable to a stake one quarter mile from the start. Each run of the traveling gun covered less than ten acres, so it took many trips of moving this gun to match what the new center pivot would do in one pass without any labor to move over the hundred acre plus system of each center pivot. With the feedlot expansion and stiffer laws from the EPA we had got to a point where the old traveler had to be ran twenty four hours a day to keep the lagoons down during the summer pumping season. I would get up many nights in these days at two a.m. to go out to check that these guns hadn't got stuck. If stuck the big gun could keep pumping waste water in one place where it would soon run off across the neighbor's property and could eventually get to the creek a couple of miles away. I remember getting lost one night in the maze of some tall sorghum we had grown with the water to graze cattle on. It was a dark night and the six foot tall crop with lanes where the traveling gun had run soon seemed all alike and suddenly a forty acre place I knew like the back of my hand was a wilderness I was lost in. I never missed going out in the middle of the night to check the guns.

Our second irrigator after the traveling guns and before the large center pivots was a thirty three acre center pivot we purchased from S & H to irrigate the Reavis land. Eight thousand feet of six and eight inch line was ran underground to it, but because the land was of an irregular shape it would handle only the smaller pivot with four places to move it too. Some of the four would not do a full circle sweep because of the highway or a ditch and trees along another side. We would pull this about 500 feet long machine like a long snake from pivot point to another with a tractor. It had about five towers with each having a set of tires to move it along. It would get out of shape if not careful moving it along from pivot point to another. It was a lot of work, but much better than the old traveling gun. The problem with the small pivot where it would not make a complete circle was we had to watch and be careful not let it run through the fence. I remember one call I received from Jim Ratcliff, one of the first in the area to have a cell phone in his pickup. He was driving toward Welch and had just ran under one of the towers of the still running irrigator which someone had forgot to watch. It had ran through the fence and on the highway still pumping waste water. I was sure glad it had not caused an accident or sprayed someone's car with the lagoon water that wouldn't see the light side of this calamity. Jim just laughed and we got up there and moved it very quickly. Another time our help forgot it and it ended up in the trees on the south end of this property. We had a few thousand dollars in damages to the machine this time. I was sure glad when we would get the large, one circle pivots up and running. They were nice but also presented challenges at times. We would pump and pump at times when the rain came faster than we could get the lagoons pumped out. One year we had thirty-three inches of rain in ninety days from April 4 to July 4. We pumped and pumped more that we should have. The water would run off through the grass, but that was better that the lagoon running over as at least this way, the water was spread over a larger area and filtered through the grass. Our problem was that the rain soaked ground made ruts where the pivot tires ran as much as two feet deep. When it dried up we spent $30,000 filling in these ruts with limestone crushed rock to make a solid base for future rainy times.

Another year we had huge amounts of rain during a week around the New Year holiday. We had the lagoons pumped down for the winter and had winterized the pump motors. With the unusual large amount of rain for the time of year we had to prepare to pump again. We got a warm spell in mid-January and the weather forecast was for the temperature to not drop below forty degrees at night. We could pump at a temperature above thirty-six degrees just fine. We ran the water pumps all day and all night pumping the waste water through the center pivot irrigators. We were pumping water through the pivot at the rate of 700 gallons per minute. Everything went fine the first day, night, and the next day. Again, we ran all night with a warm weather forecast. Alas, the wind came up the second night and dropped the wind chill down to thirty degrees.

The pivots pumped water out that in the thirty degree wind chill soon started icing the overhead water pipes. The weight of the ice was too much for the pipes and collapsed the entire system. It cost $17,000 to repair the damage and our insurance policy did not cover ice damage. We had taken a chance on the weather and lost. We were under pressure to get the lagoons down before January temperatures prevented pumping or we had more rain that might have caused the too full lagoons to run over. Just another business pressure we had to deal with on an on going basis.

Chapter seven told you of our first land purchase and seeing the value go down soon after even though we made money on the cattle ran on the land. I have always heard that they aren't making any more land and it will never go down. It sure ignored this rule in the eighties and fell in half or more over time. Land did not get back to its earlier hey day till the late nineties and early twenty-first century.

The land to the east of the feedlot belonged to neighbor Sam Martin. Sam was a bachelor until he was nearly seventy years old and he married a neighbor widow lady. Like many old set in their way bachelors who had no one at home to take his frustrations out on, Sam from time to time would get a little cantankerous, but all and all was a good neighbor. I had always hoped that when the time came for Sam to sell that I would be in a position to buy his land. Timing is everything as I have said and you might know Sam called one day in early 1988 and thought he was ready to sell his land. Alas, I had to tell him I could not do anything until I got the Miami Bank problem solved and the note paid on it. I was afraid to get in too deep even though I sure wanted that land. Better judgment kept me from biting off more than I could handle. I am sure God always watched over me and helped me to make the right decisions. Later that year when the bank was turned back to the Feds and the bank note paid, I approached Sam about buying the land, but he was feeling better and decided he wanted to keep it awhile. Sam moved to town with his new wife, Jeannie, but still came out to his old farm house from time to time to just get off to himself. We got to be pretty good friends during this time. He had retired and rented his land to Cliff Wilkins. Sam passed away in, I think, 1991. His heirs decided to auction the 900 acre ranch instead of a private treaty sale. They knew I needed the land very badly for our expanding operation and the continuing stiffer EPA regulations on feedlots. A niece came and asks if I would leave her alone at the auction and let her buy the 160 acres where Sam had his house. She wanted to build a new house there. I told her she did not want a new home so close to our feedlot. That with the best we could do, it would still be closer than a city raised girl would want for her family. I told her I would help her get another 160 about a mile away, but she did not want it. The land was advertised for the auction in several tracts and after each tract had sold, the entire 900 acres would be auctioned as a whole and which ever way brought the most total money would be the winning bid or combination of bids. Cliff Wilkins, the renter, also was a feeding customer of ours, and he also wanted to buy the land. He came to talk to me about it. I told him for our feedlot to survive and continue to provide a place for him to feed and the twenty plus jobs we now had for our community that I had to have the land adjoining us to keep up with the stiffer regulations regarding feedlots. Cliff did not listen to this and left in a huff. I got wind that he was going to join forces with the niece and go together to out bid me on all the land with the niece getting her 160 acres and Cliff the rest. The niece was willing, so I had heard, to pay quite a bit over the current land market for the one tract she wanted. I sure hated to have to buck them at the auction, but also knew for our company's future I had to own at least 500 acres of the land closest to us. Another neighbor and customer, Teddy Linthicum, came to see me about us joining together to buy the land as Cliff and the niece were told to be doing. Teddy wanted 240 acres across the road from us. I agreed to this thinking I didn't want all the neighbors mad at me and I really hated to stretch for the entire 900 acres anyway. This would give me the leverage Cliff had when they put all the tracts together for bid. A third neighbor, Butch Langley, came to see if I would let him have ten acres joining his land if I got the land bought. I would have liked to have kept this ten acres if I made the purchase, but again agreed to this to get along with a good neighbor. Sale day came and it was to be held outside Sam's old farm house. Greg Highsmith, a local real estate agent and auctioneer who I had known forever conducted the auction. Greg would start the bid on each tract of land and I would make sure I bid first each time and then quit bidding. He would start the land at $375 an acre. After about three tracts being started with me bidding first and quitting, everyone was looking at me like, "what kind of a fool is this?" My plan was to bid first so that later, a neighbor could not say I bid against him at the auction and thus feel bad toward me. By bidding first, anyone else had to bid against me instead of the other way around. I also had decided to go for the entire place with me bidding for what I wanted and the acreage Teddy and also Butch wanted and I had agreed to bid for us all. There was no use to run up the individual tracts of land. I would simply wait and bid till no one else did on the entire ranch. The auction day found the weather bitter cold with a strong wind that made things worse. I was as nervous as a cat on a hot tin roof. Cliff and the niece were huddled together and got the winning bid on each individual tract. When they put the land together, I started the bidding again and this time after Cliff bid, I would raise each bid till he stopped. Greg and owners went into the house to figure the total value of the individual tracts versus my total bid. Dee Ann and I had a calculator and had being trying to add up the values to make sure we were ahead of the individual totals in our bid. We felt we were over the hump, but still very nervous and very cold. Greg figured inside for about fifteen minutes and came back out and announced that our bid was the winning bid for all. We gave $445 an acre for the land. Teddy took his 240 and Butch his ten and we kept the balance, 650 acres. It had been quite a process, but I felt good about it.

Another neighbor, Bill Fansler, was farming the 200 acres of farm ground for the Martins. He knew it was going up for auction in November and the family had told him not to plan on the land for farming the next spring. Bill did not want to lose this nice farm ground he was renting so about sale day he went ahead and plowed the ground for the next spring's crop. I told the family and Greg, the auctioneer, that it was their place to see that Bill did not force the land renting issue, as I wanted to farm my new land with our crew and equipment. They did not help me in this and I could have just walked away from the deal, but of course I did not want to do this. I also did not want a fuss with a neighbor so I told Bill he could farm the land one more year with me getting the landlord owner share of his crop. This was not right, as I had purchased the land under the clear announcement that the renter had been notified that their rent land was not being renewed for the following crop year. Bill should not have pushed this falsely as he did, but I also knew that the Fanslers were old friends and neighbors and life is too short to have a neighbor mad at you right or wrong. I could not help bidding against Cliff as the future of our company and the jobs it provided were at stake. I could help this and told Bill to farm it the next year with written notice from me that it was to be his last. We had no further trouble and Bill and his family get along well with us today. He just made one wrong mistake and we have all done things we wished we hadn't. I am sure this was the case with Bill although he never told me.

As for Cliff, he fed with us for three or four more years and his cattle always sold on the rail for three to four dollars over the live market at the time. He was never happy with us for one reason or the other, even though we went out of our way to do right with his business. He finally left us and went to feeding at another feedlot in western Kansas. The way he treated us hurt very much, but it is a part of business that you have to live with from time to time. We knew we had done a good job of feeding and marketing his cattle even though he liked to tell the opposite around town. I never said anything and always treated him nice when we would meet in the café or on the street. We put another 160 acre pivot and more underground pipe from the lagoons to the Martin land that we needed to dewater our larger lagoons from our expanding feedlot. We now were up to about 12,000-head capacity.

In 1995 another neighbor, Don Floyd decided to sell his land. He had 319 acres that joined us on the south. He contacted Greg like the Martins and I'm sure they planned their auction with us in mind. Don also owned some land two miles away and some down the road a mile. About eight different tracts were advertised and the auction drew another big crowd. This time the plan was to auction to high bid with the winning bidder getting the tracts of his choice, one or all. This put a new wrinkle on things and once again I was very nervous. I needed one more pivot and three of the tracts totaling 239 acres would be just right to put another 160-acre pivot on and leave a tree belt with about sixty acres of pasture between it and the other eighty-one acres where Don's house sat. I knew I could not afford the house place, but needed the other three. The house tract had eighty-one acres because Don had built a swimming pool in the corner next to his house and it needed an acre out of the adjoining eighty for the pool. The bidding started and several people bid after my first bid including Ted Dixon, a local real estate broker and land investor. I knew I had better win the first bid this time so I kept bidding. As the bidding got higher everyone dropped out, but one gentleman I did not know. I figured, but never knew that he wanted the forty acres two miles away, but I could not afford to find out. If he took the eighty in the middle of what I needed I would not be able to put up the pivot I so desperately needed as we were expanding again. I did not really like having to expand, as it put more pressure on my chronic fatigue syndrome and more work on me. However we knew we had to take care of our customers or they would go elsewhere and ever more importantly we had to feed more cattle with the same equipment and people to remain viable. The industry competition would not let us raise our rates, so we had to feed more with the same people and equipment to stay in the industry. I bid $665 dollars an acre as the winning bid and took the three tracts I wanted. I figured I had given about $18,000 over the land market for this property and probably could have got it bought cheaper had I quit and the man behind had took the forty I suspected he wanted. I never knew for sure and I am glad I handled the sale as I did.

We let a new earth moving construction business owned by neighbors Troy Merit and Tracy Kelly have the job of clearing the brush off this purchase. This was new business for me and thus I did not feel obligated to let my friends, the Mullers, who did all of our lagoon work have this job. Troy and Tracy were young and neighbors and I wanted to help get them started. They kept a small dozer busy on the property for three months. Troy and Tracy always did a good job for us and I used them where I could without cutting into the Mullers' longstanding job with us in the annual lagoon cleaning. Troy and Tracy expanded as they did well and before long they employed forty people and had leased or bought a lot of equipment. Things did not go as well as when they had eight or ten guys and they worked with the crew every day themselves. Nothing wrong with getting bigger, but they did it much too fast. Before long, they were in trouble and into drugs. I don't know if they took drugs to keep them going the long hours they worked or if they started selling to finance their struggling business. Before long the business went down, the law had them for the drug pushing, and Tracy lost his wife and kids. They were such a bright and hard working pair that had so much ability. Somewhere the wrong turn cost them their business and family. Years later they are still struggling. I so hate this, as they were good boys before they took their wrong turn.

About a year later I next bought 120 acres west of the feedlot from the Sprowles estate, a local family who had moved years before. They had rented this land for years to Larry Gross. I never tried to buy it as long as Larry was feeding with us, but after he left me as told in an earlier chapter I called Nevada where the family now lived and inquired about purchasing this land. I soon had a deal for $400 an acre. On paper this sounded much cheaper that my other deal, but it was not as nice a property. It would work well for me though as one of our large center pivots put up in 1986 liked about twenty acres being able to make a full circle. This purchase would allow this to happen as soon as I got the fences moved. Every land purchase we made got the brush cleared, new fences put up by neighbor Richard Smith, the local custom fence builder. Richard would also built a pipe corral where needed. We would apply feedlot manure and before long the place would not look the same. This all cost money, but we could cash flow the money out of our feeding business.

About five years after the Martin auction, Teddy the neighbor who bought 240 acres with me in that auction had gotten into a financial bind. He owed me for feed as well as several other people. Teddy and I always worked well together, even though I had to get tough with him several times to collect large sums he owed me for feeding some of his bulls. I wanted Teddy to succeed and offered him a lot of fatherly advice some of which he would listen to. Teddy offered to sell eighty acres of the Martin land and soon another 200 behind the eighty he had previously bought. I bought both tracts giving him a profit on the Martin land and $500 an acre for the poor 200 acres joining it. I got my bill paid and now had 400 in this section across from our other land instead of just the 160 I had purchased as part of the Martin auction. We started hauling manure to this land and built new fences all around. The next year we limed the ground and tore it up and planted the before native and fescue pasture that was poor to a new Bermuda variety called Jackpot. We also cleared several acres of this land and it soon was much more productive.

In about 1998, Don Kirby from pond creek called and wanted to sell me the Kay land he had beat me to back in 1982. He had never done very well renting it out and had had it in the soil bank program of the USDA for several years. It was coming out of this contract and he wanted to sell. I finally gave him $750 an acre; the same price he had given back in 82. We immediately started Richard Smith fencing again. Mullers cleaned the ponds out. We fertilized and limed the ground and soon it was productive again. I have found you have to spend money to make money and then care for your investment by not overgrazing and abusing the land. It will pay better dividends in the long run with proper management.

Our next purchase came in 1997. This time I bought 216 acres from Lloyd Johnston that joined our home place on the edge of Welch. Dad had turned this property down at $95 an acre in the early sixties thinking it was too high. Lloyd Johnston's father bought it and left it to Lloyd when he died. Our house sat very close to this property and was overbuilt for the town. I thought I had better try to buy it so that we would have more acres to sell with the house if the time to sell it ever came. I also did not want a chicken house or something else that would hurt our house valve built close to the property line. It would be best if I could buy it. Several people had tried in the past, without success. This time though, Lloyd decided he might sell and do better investing the money in the now booming stock market. He did not live nearby and had rented the land for years to his brother, Lymon. I gave $675 dollars an acre for this land, which seemed high at the time, but I was glad to get it. Part of the land joined the city sewer lagoon and a creek going through it caught the sometimes green water from the sewer lagoon. I really did not want this. I also wanted a long stretch of land to make a runway for my airplane. Neighbor Leon Fansler had the land south of my new purchase and already dealt with the creek. We made a deal in Leon's favor, but what I wanted. Leon got forty acres by the creek and lagoon and I got twenty acres of good flat ground. This would give me with my adjoining Johnston land a long nice site for a grass runway for the airplane. I practiced and practiced landing in this pasture, sitting the plane down till about ten feet above the ground and then going back up. It would make a good site. I called Larry Nichols who had about twenty acres on the north side of this property. I wanted to buy this so that no houses would be built in my landing pattern. Larry did not want to sell. He wanted to turn the land into a housing development and I wrote this ground off and did not build the runway. Larry got the first house sold on his new project and started a second. He never got it sold. The financial bind also put a strain on his marriage. Larry called one day to see if I would still buy the land where no houses had yet been built. The local economic development group bought the unsold house and a row of lots on the north side of the street Larry had put in. I gave $15,000 for the rest of the lots that joined my Johnston purchase. I could now feel good about building the runway there. Alas, I never did as my chronic fatigue was acting up more now, and I was getting to where I did not feel comfortable flying the plane except local joy riding on a good day. It was a pretty expensive toy to just joy ride in, so the project never went forward.

In 2000, Mom's brother Craig Campbell died. Craig did not have any kids of his own and left his estate to a step son and his wife and my cousin, Terry. He wanted me to have his farm ground that I had farmed for him the past several years and his house went to Chet and Pat the step son and daughter in law and his mutual funds to Terry. His land was eighty acres west of town that was a very poor eighty. I sold this land a year or so later to a young man trying to get started in the ranching business. I thought this was good for him, as he was going to put it to grass for his cows and it did not really fit our operation being several miles from anything else we had. The other tract was 200 acres at the east edge of Welch. It also was pretty sorry farm ground, but we soon limed and fertilized it and sowed it to a new fescue variety called Max Q. My friend the fence builder Richard Smith built a corral and new fence around it. Two ponds were build and it now is a very productive pasture land.

The most enjoyment in my entire career has been cleaning up places I had bought and making them productive. A real sense of satisfaction can be had seeing something get better and more productive. I wish health and industry changes had allowed me to enjoy the land more years. I will tell in future chapters about the big decision to sell the land I had worked so hard for.

I learned early on in my career to plan, take risk in appropriate amounts and time, and look to God when making big decisions. All of this action can culminate with very satisfying results.

The next chapter will deal with the fast changing industry.

Neill Cattle Co. 2000–14000 custom cattle feedlot

22

The Changing Industry

The cattle packing industry started changing at a pretty fast pace in the '80s and by the early '90s most of the small packers that processed from one to five loads of cattle per week were being replaced by the big packers that processed 3,000 or more per day. They were much more efficient and could sell everything about the calf except his "beller."

In the seventies we had for several years sold 5,000 to 6,000 head of cattle to Akin and Fincannon Packers of Tulsa. Mr. Shanholster or "Shannie" as we called him was their buyer. Shannie lived in Girard, Kansas about fifty miles north of us. He bought all the cattle for the plant for several years. While we did not get to sell near all the cattle they used, it was a big account for us to sell over 5,000 head a year to one plant. The cattle they liked were calf feds finished at 750 to 800 pounds. In the early eighties this plant closed after one of the owners died and the other retired.

Herrod Pack of Joplin, Missouri was another small packer we sold several cattle to. Bob Woodrow was their buyer. Bob was a tuff trader, but we sold him several cattle for a number of years. They too, sold when with changing markets and older owners they chose to sell to owners who would kill nothing but non-fed cull cows.

Coffeyville Packing Co. in Coffeyville, Kansas was another small, local who bought several cattle in the seventies. Dick Fisher was their buyer till seeing the hand writing on the wall, he left to join the large IBP. CoPac as they were referred to was struggling. John Nunnley took over the buyer's job and we got along well until one day I sent a load of cattle to them and did not get the check the next day per the agreement of paying. I called and learned that John was in jail over some kind of charge involving cattle and that the plant did not have the money to pay. I found out how to get hold of the Jewish plant owner who lived in Florida and gave him a call demanding my customers' money. He told me I should not sell cattle to them and offered no help. I called the Federal Packers and Stockyard's administration in Kansas City after a visit to my attorney friend, John Wallace of Wallace and Owens in Miami. Mr. Wallace got a Kansas attorney to help me in this matter. In a matter of hours the P & S had the cooler at CoPac locked and a hold put on the cattle carcasses. We got the Florida owner's attention and he paid for the cattle. We sold them a few more loads with cash paid before the cattle left our yard, but before long they were gone for good. The next group to try this plant was a couple of real nice men who had ran a locker plant but never a packing plant. They too were soon in trouble and owed us for just a handful of cattle, about five thousand dollars worth. I was about three years collecting this, but finally did.

Wilson and Co. was another buyer for a few years. They had a plant in Oklahoma City and were the last of the original big four packers of the early twenties. The other three originals had gone by the way side over the years and Wilson would too. They just did not change with the times and learn the new methods of the packing industry. Wayne Yocum was their buyer and we got along great. In the spring when the crappie fish were biting on Oolagah Lake he liked to plan a cattle-buying visit to our feedlot. Dad and Stu Parker would go early to the lake and get the boat in the water. Wayne would come to the feedlot and I would show him the cattle and trade on a few while he was there and others later on the telephone. As soon as we could finish, he would make a mad dash to the lake to meet Dad and Stu and enjoy a day of fishing. He continued this practice until Wilson shut down. Wayne was of retirement age and soon I lost track of him. I always missed my old friends who left the industry. This would make it hard for me in turn to leave the industry years later.

Another small plant in Pryor, Oklahoma was trying to make a go. They too had trouble and gave me a bad check for a load of customer cattle. My old friend Stu Parker and I went to Pryor and stayed till we came home with the money.

A group of men built a large locker plant type operation near Grand Lake. They would purchase about fifteen cattle a week from us. Bill Breeden ran the plant and knew what he was doing. His two partners, the Farrier brothers had been in the grocery business for years and I had at one time approached them and Mr. Breeden about selling our beef in their store. They did not bite on my plan then, but a few years later put in this plant called Beef City and did just what I had suggested. They sold part of the fed beef they bought from us at their grocery store in Grove and the rest at the meat counter at the plant. The plant was doing well, but apparently the grocery store was not. Soon the Farriers were taking more out of the plant than it would make even though it was doing very well at the time. Bill Breeden did not like what he saw happening and being the minority partner insisted the Farriers buy his interest in the plant out. They did and Bill moved to Iowa. The Farriers could not run the plant and turned to a young man who had ran a locker plant nearby. Jerry Taylor was a good man and tried hard, but the business was different without Bill Breeden. The last five head I sold Jerry, the check for bounced. It took Jerry three years, but he paid all the money owed to us. I have always admired his grit to do what was right even in adversity. The plant shut down for good in the early eighties and a Miami bank foreclosed on it from the Farriers. For one reason or the other it never sold and sits in shambles today, twenty years later. It was a nice, small plant when shut down that just ruined through no use. Such a waste of capital.

Pete Tankersley owned a small plant in Ft.Smith, Arkansas and bought a good many of his cattle from us. He also ran an ice cream plant and sold frozen food. I forget how many coolers and freezers he had to keep running in the summer and year round, but I always thought that if would be a nightmare if he had an extended power outage or breakdown in these coolers. I did not meet Pete for seven or eight years after I had started our weekly cattle trades. He finally came and visited the feedlot one time. Until then all our business was over the phone with me describing the cattle I thought best for him and he in turn bidding me. Poor health overcame Pete and he closed down, as he could not find a buyer in this fast-changing industry.

Joe Brown also had a Ft. Smith plant and I also sold him cattle over the phone for years. Like Pete I did not meet Joe for several years. Near the end of his career Joe fed some cattle with us in addition to buying cattle from us. He also closed without a buyer when old age and bad health caught up with him.

The Canadian Valley plant I talked of earlier could not make the change in the industry under Tom Wright's sons. Canadian Valley at one time had five top-notch managers for the different sections of the small profitable company. My friend Tommy Scroggins ran the kill floor and later bought the cattle. The rest of the five including Tom Wright suffered from the same old age and health problems. Mr. Greenhaw, the original cattle buyer had open heart surgery and did not survive the operation. Mr. Wright suffered from senility and had to quit. The boys both bright had never been taught how to operate the entire operation. They only knew the sausage making end of the plant where none of the original five had worked. I always felt sorry for these two brothers. They were thrown in a fast changing industry without the training needed to survive and survive they did not. In the early nineties the plant sold and before too long had quit processing live cattle, but buying only carcass beef from other packers. We lost another good outlet.

Excel bought cattle once in awhile from us over the years, but was never a strong player. One of their buyers was Don Sealey. Don was a nice guy, but would get real mad if the trade did not go his way or if Excel would not let him buy. On more than one occasion he left, throwing gravel all over our office porch with his car tires. J. D. Bales replaced Don in our territory for Excel. J. D. was super nice and told good stories, but bought very few cattle from us. Excel left our territory for years. For a short while in the mid nineties, John Jeffery the son of Duane Jeffrey, one of our customers who I partnered with on cattle from time to time traveled to the lot from his Western Kansas territory on the urging of his father. John bought a few loads, but never did a great deal. I probably never tried as hard with Excel. In 1986 I had sold a load of Stu Parker's cattle to Excel on a flat meat-hanging price which was based on the carcass weight at the plant harvest. I did not know on the day scheduled that Western Kansas was having a bad snowstorm. We loaded the cattle on Bill Bailey just a few weeks before we started hauling most of the cattle. Bill got to Dodge City at the Excel plant at 5:30 p.m. just as scheduled. Excel wanted them there between 5 and 6 p.m. for harvest on the evening shift. Bill unloaded and left and got back home late that night. The storm was bad in Dodge City and Excel cancelled the second shift and did not start the plant back up for three days. Stu's load of cattle sat at the plant without feed the entire time. We all agreed that the cattle were in no shape to harvest now, so they were sent to recoup at a local feedlot for three weeks during which time they got in another storm. Finally they were harvested and Excel called to see how I wanted to settle. I said that whatever was fair for their other customers was fair to us. We agreed that the load did not kill as expected and we knew the feed cost at the Kansas feedyard. All total the loss was estimated at $3,100. We all agreed on the loss. I thought Excel should pay the entire amount since we got the cattle to them on time and unloaded in good shape. Ours was the only cattle in the plant that night bought on the rail. They offered to pay one third of the loss. Stu and I did not agree with this, but decided to settle with them and not make waves. We thought this would be better for the future. I just never trusted Excel after that. Treating people right goes along way in the way our integrity is perceived in life. Excel failed this test with me.

Kenny Bowland of the Monfort plant in Garden City called on us for awhile, but Kenny never was very aggressive in his cattle buying and when National started coming every week, Kenny quit coming. The Garden City plant burned a few years later and Kenny lost his cattle-buying job, as the plant did not rebuild. I don't know where he ever landed.

Kenny's old boss, Mark Foss left Monfort and went to Packerland in Hospers, Iowa. We sold him a few loads of Holsteins that the Packerland plant specialized in. This continued until the

Hospers plant was closed and Mark left the company. Mark and I had become friends when both of us was on a program at the Arkansas Cattlemen's Convention.

My old buyer at Frosty Morn in Montgomery, Alabama showed up years after that plant had closed at a plant in DesMoines, Iowa. We traded on a few loads from time to time.

In about 1992, a new modern chance for us came along. Jot Hartley of the local Spur Ranch and son of the earlier told story of his father, Bob Hartley came to us with a plan he was pursuing. He was working with a Japanese company, Itoham, the second largest grocery company in Japan. Jot was making a deal with the Itoham unit called Calco International to raise half Angus/half Wagyu Cattle. The Wagyu was a Japanese breed. Spur would raise the calves to 400 pounds and then ship them to us to grow to 775 pounds. The live cattle would then be trucked to Tulsa International Airport and "FedEx" to Japan on a 747 airplane. This was quite a site to see the cattle loaded in crates of seven or eight head and loaded on the huge airplane for the flight to an island off Japan where they would have to go through a quarantine period before being barged to the mainland. We did several pens of these cattle the next few years. Twice they fed them out at our feedlot. They wanted them slow fed to gain 1.68 pounds per day till the cattle weighed 1,700 pounds. This would take twenty-three months. Of course, this was very different that our usual American feeding of 120 to 180 days with the average daily gain of three pounds or more per day. Mr. Wada, the local Calco rep, was Japanese and spoke English, but was hard to understand on the phone, so he usually faxed us instead of calling if he could not come up. He started each fax with "This is my request" and went on to the subject at hand. I really enjoyed working with him. Our very first meeting had a lesson to be learned. He asks if we could feed different feeds than we normally fed such as soy lees or cotton lees. Everything ended in lee. I had no idea what he was asking for, but said sure, I would get right on figuring out how to do so. I called our current feed nutritionist, Steve Armbruster, a very talented feed consultant. He too could not figure out what a cotton lee and so on was. I finally very sheepishly had to back to Mr. Wada and ask him what a lee was. What a surprise I got, Mr. Wada did not know either. We both had been smoking one another. We had a good laugh and Mr. Wada said he would call Tokyo and find out. It turned out a lee is a name for a by-product. Thus a cotton lee was a cottonseed hull, a by-product of cotton production. We fed the cattle as asked and weighed them one at a time every thirty days to see how we were doing. At the end of the twenty-three months the cattle had gained exactly 1.68 pounds a day at a cost of seventy-three cents a pound per gain verses the projected cost of seventy-one cents per pound of gain. Steve Armbruster had guided the nutrition work very well. Calco and myself were both very pleased. The Japanese economy was faltering very badly in the early to mid nineties. The high cost to produce the type of beef the Japanese wanted was simply too high for their depressed economy and they could buy American type beef much cheaper. The Japanese closed their deal with Spur Ranch and our company and moved their operation to New Zealand. Mr. Wada moved to their hog division in Indiana. We received a lot of recognition in the industry for our foreign experience and it helped us in our customer development for years. Jot's cattle operation had struggled to cash flow land payments and cost of production in years after the Japanese deal fell through. I knew it had hurt him financially and even though I had to get somewhat tough with him at times to collect the feed bill he owed for our growing his breeding stock to sale weight, I never forgot the fact that he helped us when we were down and needing customers by bringing Mr. Wada and Calco to us. I always found a way to deal with Jot even when he was struggling because he had been good to me. We continued to feed breeding stock for Jot and his Spur Ranch till we closed the feedyard. One needs to always remember those who have helped us in one way or the other.

The cattle market by 1993 had developed into selling to one of four major packing companies. The four were IBP, Excel, Monfort, or National. We sold ninety percent or more of ours to IBP. Their Emporia plant did not have feed lots close by, as did their Garden City, Kansas, Amarillo, Texas, or Lexington, Nebraska plants. We certainly needed them more than they needed us, but it was still a good deal for both of us. Larry Haley was my IBP buyer, my entire career. He started buying for IBP in February 1969 and I came back to the feedlot in August 1969. I learned to trade with him watching Dad and him trade over a nickel per hundred at times. Larry would walk round and round the little 16×30 office in the old days. I swore he would wear a rut in the concrete floor going round and round during these trades. The tuff years for the feeding industry in 1973 and 74 were probably also tuff for Larry Haley. He gets paid a salary and a bonus based on his cattle purchases profits. During those bad years I sold most of the cattle over the phone to plants in Alabama, North Carolina, Florida, Louisiana, Arkansas and our locals from Joplin to Oklahoma City. There were probably thirty choices to sell to then. In 1993 the four mentioned above was all that was left for all practical purposes. The cattle finished at 750 to 800 pounds in the '70s were now all sold at a more efficient weight for the entire industry at 1,000 to 1,300 pounds. The nation's cow herd shrank from 130 million head in the '70s to a little over 100 million in the end of the '90s. More beef was produced from fewer head with the larger weights cattle were fed to.

In April of 1994 IBP entered into an agreement with about a dozen central Kansas feedlots soon known as the Kansas Cartel. They would buy cattle from these lots at the top of the week's market and early on give them till the middle of the week to decide whether to sell or not. If the market looked weak on Tuesday morning they would turn in more cattle than if it looked strong. The Cartel was soon causing myself and other small feeders selling to the Emporia plant fits. I would get a good market bid from Larry about every third week when they seemingly would be short of Cartel cattle. On the weeks they had plenty of Cartel cattle, Larry's orders were always three dollars under the market. I always sold on a biweekly show list instead of a weekly list that most feedlots used. I liked this method in that I could play more games in my trading with the packer. I would put the cattle on the list a little early or green and if they did not sell for two or three weeks it did not matter, because I always got them sold by their real appointed time in the end. My customers never knew the weeks I was being bid so low by IBP. This went on for weeks and soon months, April till August being the worst time that year. I called Larry's boss, Bruce Bass every other day telling him I could not survive under these marketing conditions. On the days I was not calling, I would write a letter. I was also talking to my friend Bill Helming and trying to figure out what to do. Helming arranged some phone meetings with other feeders in the same boat as I. Some were getting kind of radical for me and threatening to sue IBP. While none of the ones I talked with did, there was a group that sued IBP. The lawsuit was in the courts from the mid nineties until judgment was announced by the Alabama court in February 2004 in favor of the ones suing. The presiding judge threw out the jury verdict. The plaintiffs are now appealing this verdict by the judge. It will be in the court several more years. I think they were justified in their suit against IBP, but I could never join it. I felt like even though I was done wrong, I had to get along with the few players left in the industry and you did not make friends suing. I just did not believe in going this route. It will be interesting to see the final outcome of this decade long suit. Some tried other plans, but none seemed like a good solution to me. Larry Haley was as frustrated as I. This after all was affecting his paycheck as he did not have the Cartel yards in his territory. I tried in vain to get included in the Cartel type deal to no avail. Bruce did finally tell me he would try to help when I was in a real corner if I would tell Larry so and not abuse this offer. This would help some.

In the mean time before this offer was made I had called National Beef. They had recently been bought by Farmland Industries and their home office was in Kansas City. Their plants were in Dodge City and Liberal, Kansas. The new head buyer for Farmland National was Al Walker. I did not know till a couple of years later, but Al was the son of IBP's first head buyer, Russ Walker. I never met Russ, but felt I knew him from all the times Larry would talk about him or call him while trading on our cattle. Al had also at one time worked as a buyer under his Dad at IBP. He knew who we were and how our cattle would do from what he had heard from Russ in the early years. Al told me he would have a buyer in our yard before the end of the week. He did and continued to do so till he left the company a few years later. Al sent Craig Swafford over to buy cattle from us from his home at Liberal. We immediately hit it off well. I sold Craig several loads that first visit and every week there after. It made life much easier for me; I was back to getting the market for our customer's cattle. National would subsidize the extra freight it took to get our cattle to Dodge City or Liberal over the local cattle in nearby feedlots. We gave them a larger territory in case of short numbers of ready cattle or bad weather in their area. I am sure Al also liked gigging his old friends at IBP a little. Craig came over every week for about a year and a half. It was working so well, that Al decided to hire a new buyer Gary Marcus and have him live in Eastern Kansas and buy from others and us in the area for the National plants. Gary was more cautious in his buying than Craig being the new buyer in the company. I did not blame him, but missed Craig for months and would call and visit him once in awhile for old time's sake. Al left National when U.S. Premium Beef bought 30 percent of the company and the thrust was put on buying more cattle in the beef rather than live. Al did not want to change the way he had operated for so many years, so he left. He became a commodity broker in Phoenix, AZ. When I learned what he was doing, I called and opened an account with him. I kept this account with Al till I left the business. I did not do a lot of hedging so I was not a big account for Al, but it kept us in touch with each other. Art Wagner was the new head buyer. Art always treated me well, but things were not the same as when Al was in charge. Gary and Al did not early on work as well together and this hurt some. We still sold close to 40 percent of the cattle to Gary for quite some time. Art got a promotion and brought in Denny McDougal whom I had sold cattle to over the phone when he was at Monfort in Dumas, Texas. I always liked to trade with Denny and he would buy my plainer cattle that were hard to sell. The last load I sold him at Monfort was a load for my good friend and customer Wayne Chidester. Wayne had a commission company on the Tulsa Stockyards and later ran a sale barn on his own at Pryor. He liked to feed big rough late cut bulls. Many would also have long horns. I had sold Denny several loads of Wayne's cattle over the years and got along all right. The last load had a few more horns than usual and I guess got Denny in trouble with the plant manager because they slowed production. The cattle sold on the rail did not pay back as well to Wayne either. Wayne quit feeding with me after this load and Denny never bought any more while he was at Dumas. Neither got mad at me, just quit without a word. It hurt to lose good accounts and in Wayne's case a good friend to boot. Things beyond our control just happen at times in business. Life goes on. Denny was somewhat tough on us when he came to National, but Gary continued to buy as many as they would let him. Gary likes to come to Grand Lake on his off time and I enjoy seeing him or talking to him on the phone once in awhile since I have left the industry.

In the latter part of the nineties my good friend and customer Bill Stoner ask if we would like to feed his cattle on the Laura's Lean all natural program. Bill's limousin cattle had been bred closer to pure limousin over time and had lost a lot of their grading ability. We had been selling his cattle flat in the meat to Larry at IBP and the high yielding limousin cattle would net Bill back two to three dollars over the market. The number of choice cattle was less and less as the lean type of purer bred limousin cattle went to market. Larry threatened to only buy them grade and yield. Bill knew he would have to breed some quality grade in the cattle or change programs. The lean cattle he had would work well on Laura's Lean Program and bring Bill the premiums he was used to. Bill is one of my biggest mistakes. I will tell of this mistake in Chapter 23.

In the late nineties another packer appeared on the scene. Alex Fraibeg, a Canadian opened a remodeled old plant in Pleasant Hope, Missouri, just north of Springfield. His new plant was only about 130 miles from us. His buyer was old friend, Lonnie Littles. The new plant never found its niche in a hard market and industry. They tried Holsteins; lean cattle like the Limousins, Choice type Angus cattle, and finally went to feeding old heifers commonly called heiferetts in the industry. Every change involved us. They bought cattle from us every week of whatever type they were trying at the time. When the heiferetts were tried they fed 2,000 of these type cattle themselves with us and also fed in several other lots. Our capacity was up to 14,000 by now and they filled several pens. This helped us a lot especially in the summer when feeding numbers slowed down. Alas nothing worked for them. Alec had very deep pockets and never went broke even though the plant and at the last his heiferett project all lost tons of money. He just finally shut the plant down and quit. His business was good for us while it lasted. The only drawback was the heiferetts required a lot of attention by our crew and it hurt us in our over all operational efficiency.

We traded with the largest packer in the country, IBP and also sold many small mom and pop locker type packing operations. Some of these would process only two or three up to fifteen per week. The small plants were more trouble to service, but usually wanted a smaller size animal that the large packers did not want. Thus the extra effort helped our cattle marketing program. One of the larger of the small packers was Turner Meats of Nowata, Oklahoma. Andy Turner had run this operation since taking over from his father years before. Andy was now in his eighties and ran the operation with son, Don who himself was past sixty. The Turners liked a leaner type beef than the major packers. They dry aged their beef for fourteen days to have a great product. They also had a family café that used many pounds a week of their quality beef. I spent as much time with Andy on a trade for fifteen as I would with Larry Haley of IBP on maybe 500 head. I always felt a customer was a customer. The Turners liked a kind of beef that the large packers did not so it was worth the effort to us. We had another satisfied outlet for cattle. Alas, soon after I quit the feeding business, the Turners also quit the packing business. Time and no next generation caught up with them also. A changing industry and increased government regulation made selling their business nearly impossible so they merely shut it down. It is a shame to see such long viable business just go away without anyone to take over.

The late nineties were a time of fast trading in the cattle industry. Buyers would all wait on the first one to blink and then all buyers and feedlots would trade their week's show list in about fifteen minutes time. I kept a pager and cell phone with me at all times so as to not miss the trade. Cattlefax would call a recorded message of the starting trade to all their member feedyards and the race was on to get your cattle sold before the packer got filled up and quit buying. One week I was attending a hospital meeting in Ft. Worth, Texas as part of my duties as chairman of the local hospital board. The call for trade came and as I looked out of my borrowed office in the ninth floor of the downtown building I was in I traded cattle. Much different that looking out over the feedyard as I traded. If I was in the pickup on the road somewhere and got the trade call, I just pulled over and went to work. I had to be ready as I knew not the day nor hour of trade. Reminds me of how the Bible calls on us to be ready to meet the Lord as we know not the hour nor place we will.

In the end of my feeding career Larry Haley was still buying cattle for IBP/Tyson. Things had gotten better and they would buy about two-thirds of our cattle. The industry is still going through constant change. The old way of doing business is gone and a new way is struggling to find its niche. I know much of the change is good for the industry and I was never afraid of change. The part I do not like about change is the big getting bigger in all segments of the industry. It is harder and harder for the small operator to survive. The same thing is happening in many other industries also.

Most all industries and businesses change as the years go by. Many companies or business owners never learn to adapt to a changing world. For the past one hundred years our country has seen change nearly every decade with new technology being developed. The changes can completely alter a business plan. Consumer demand for our goods and services change with the advent of new products and services. An astute businessman must look ahead to see how technology and competition is changing the landscape of his business. So many times we get so wrapped up in the day to day operation of a business that we neglect to look out one, three, five, and ten years and chart our own course of business on our terms. This long range planning is essential to the survival of any business.

The next chapter will talk of employees over the years. I think you will enjoy it.

Larry Haley — IBP cattle buyer

Cowboy crew

23

Employees

Employees and customers are the two main ingredients of any business. You cannot have one without the other. None of the other essential parts of any business including cash flow, inventory, facilities, business model, or plan mean anything if you do not have key employees to represent you and of course the customer drives the business. Without good employees, customers will not stay with any company. Like wise, employees have to realize that ultimately customers pay them and the other bills of the business. The business owner has to treat employees with respect and dignity. I hope I have always filled this role properly. I certainly have tried. My philosophy has always been to treat employees as I would want to be treated. I tried to never chastise an employee in front of his or her peers. I tried to never raise my voice and shout or curse an employee for a blunder one had done. I am sure that these rules were not always followed, but for the most part my error would probably be letting things slide too easily. Employees can take advantage of an employer who is mild mannered and I am sure that I had this happen to me.

I never liked the drill-sergeant approach to employee dealings. I once had an assistant foreman who had been an Army man and wanted to be the drill sergeant. He was simply trained by the Army for this type of approach to employee dealings. It was not wrong, but it was not my method of operation. It is hard to have two methods of employee dealings in the same company, unless you want one to be the hatchet man. In our case the foreman was a great worker and a wonderful fellow. His method however, caused troubles with our troops because they were not trained to be directed this way. The foreman got hurt on the job and was disabled, to a point where he could not longer due many of his former duties. I tried everything for him to find a niche where he would fit in our group. What I thought would work, did not for one reason or the other. The foreman job could have been handled with his handicap, but he could not handle it in my fashion. I don't think I was right or he was wrong, just different style and we were not ever on the same page. The other employees soon caught on to this and took advantage of the situation. I finally helped him get another job that both of us thought would be easier with his new handicap. The first job played out though no fault of the individual. The organization simply redid the way they operated and eliminated many positions. I took him back to his old job at our company. Still not working, so another position was found and he went to it for a few months. Again, though no particular fault it did not work out and back he came. This back and forth simply did not work. It was now causing problems between the two of us. Frustrating for the disabled man not to be able to do many of his former duties and frustrating to me that the foreman duties of the job could not be handled in my fashion or at least to keep harmony in the troops. Looking back, I know I did not council and tell him I thought he needed to change. This was hard for me to do with an old friend and someone who had been hurt on the job. The accident was preventable if procedures had been followed, but in our haste many of us take a shortcut and this can get us in trouble as it did in this case. Finally I had to be firm that he would have to adjust to the next new job or ours; the back and forth between our job and another was not working. I was about to have dissension in the rest of the employees. I never liked the way this was handled by me, but I do not know how I could have done anything much different. We both got through it and remain friends today, but it was hard for both of us for a long while. This probably weighed on my heart as bad as anything in my career for years to come.

I was fortunate to have a good crew for most of my years. I remember my early years working with the crew. I know it was hard on them to have a green, young boss's son as a ramrod. By and large we got along without any problems. Peggie and Larry were a pair in the early days. On Sunday morning one or the other was always late, probably a victim of too much Saturday night partying. Most mornings on their hay route putting out small square bales of hay in racks to the cattle was just one big party, laughing at one another and telling stories. I always liked to make work fun. The time went faster and it did not seem like work.

One of the Layton family was on the crew almost always. Jay, the senior Layton, worked as the maintenance man in my early years. Like all Laytons, he could fix anything and did not mind trying to do so. I loved to work with him. I was always a dunce at fixing anything, but it was fun to work with Jay and try. He always told me that he would "fire" a guy who did not carry a pair of pliers. I never carried pliers, so I was probably on Jay's list, but he never said so. I have jokingly told employees thirty years later about Jay and the pliers rule. His son, W. Jay helped many a time when we were short or could not figure out how to fix something. Most of the time he was not on the payroll, but would help when he came around just to be nice. You do not find many of this nature these days. I always appreciated this trait. W. Jay was married to my much older cousin. Their sons Gary and Larry both worked full time for the feedlot until they got on their feet with their own established ranching operations. Both were wilder than a March Hare, but would work their tail off. Gary was the youngest and I always liked to tease him. One day he had been hauling manure by Barber Bill's house. He had told Dad he needed off at noon that day to take care of some personal business. Right at the noon hour break, Barber Bill walks in the office and complains that the manure truck was raising too much dust on the gravel road when it went by his house. Soon Gary came in the door and Dad knowing he was to be off in the afternoon, said, "Gary, Bill says you are raising too much dust over at his house. You just park that truck and hit the road, we won't put up with that." Bill did not see Dad wink at Gary. Bill went to throwing his hands in the air and hollering "I don't want him fired, just slow him down." Dad continued on with Gary, saying "That's alright Bill, Gary you get on out of here, right now." No one told Bill that Gary was not fired and we all had a big laugh. We did make an effort to slow down after that when we went by Bill's house.

In a few years when Gary went out on his own, he was over one day getting some supplies for his cattle from our store. He happened to have a cap on from a competing feedlot, someone had given him. I took his cap off and cut the label with the competing firm's name off leaving a hole in the front of the cap and put it back on his head. I am sure he wore it over to aggravate me, but we both had a big laugh. Before he left, I gave him a new "Neill" hat.

Larry worked for many years full time before going out on his own. He always had time to come back and help us when we had a big bunch of cattle to work and needed extra help. When I took over the West Ranch, I made a deal with Larry to take care of it for me and he did for years. I never second guessed him or looked over his shoulder because I knew he would take better care of it than I. It really hurt him when I sold the ranch. I will talk about that in a future chapter, but sometimes you have to make the decision that is not popular.

Larry's son Rowdy also worked through high school on weekends and summers. Like the rest, he was wonderful to have around and could do most anything. Rowdy broke his leg at his home in a horse accident and it has caused him problems for years. He returned to work for us after college, but the bad foot from the accident did not need to be out in the cold and mud doing the type of work we did. I had always hoped that Rowdy would stay with me and learn the business. I thought he might be the one to run a ranching operation for us when I slowed down. If this had worked out, I probably would not have ever sold. Alas, it did not and Rowdy gave banking a try. This was not his cup of tea, however, and one day while on a hot chase of a car needing repoed down a dusty gravel road, Rowdy told his lady bank boss to pull over and let him out. No job was worth getting killed over. I did not blame him, but laughed to myself, if it had been his dad Lightening, as I called Larry, the chase would have been over in a matter of minutes with the car in front pushed to the ditch. Rowdy's next stop was to the local hay equipment dealer as one of their counter men. Most young men have to try a few positions, before they settle on their life's work. I am not sure if Rowdy has yet or not.

Sometimes, we get hurt by someone without any intent at all. We all get our feelings hurt so easily at times. I am no different. As much as I think of all the Laytons, W. Jay hurt me dearly one time, but I never told him. Shortly after Dad's death, W. Jay decided to take his cattle feeding business to the feedlot up the road at Parsons, Kansas. They had a slightly different feeding program than we did and W. Jay wanted to give it a try. The track record of the other lot was never any better than ours according to all the reports I ever got in the industry, but they did a good job. His leaving us for them just came at a time when we were struggling for numbers to feed and I was trying to get my feet firmly on the ground after losing Dad. Both of W. Jay's brothers-in-law also worked for us. I thought surely, for Arch and Warren's sake if not mine, he would stay with us. It hurt badly, but I never told him it did. I tried to explain the advantages of our program over the other lots. Eventually, he came back.

The two brothers in law of the W. Jay, I mentioned were Archie and Warren. They were my cousins, but about twenty years older that I. Arch started helping Granddad on the farm in 1957 and later came to the feedlot and worked until he retired in the mid nineties. Even after retirement Arch would come back and help run the feed mill from time to time when we were short handed. Warren stared in 1960 and drove the feed truck until his retirement in the mid nineties. Warren could drive circles around anyone else in a truck and make it look so easy. He however, did not ever like having to do anything besides drive the truck. The truck job lasted all day, most of the time so this did not cause too many problems. We never had anyone else who liked to stay with the truck job. Most got bored going back and forth from the mill to the pens. Warren never did and just chugged along in the truck. I know Arch and Warren had to feel some resentment for me in the early days. They sure never showed it however. I was twenty years younger and the johnny come lately, nine to twelve years after they had started. Dad always wished that Arch or Warren one would like responsibility, but he could never get them to take a foreman or manager position. I don't know if that was perceived or real to Dad. I just set back and let him handle them until he died and I had to. For years we did not have company health insurance or a retirement plan. I worked the finances around and talked Dad into insurance first and a few years later a retirement plan. The problem was by the time the retirement plan was started, Warren and Arch were down to less than ten years till retirement. Not a long time to build up a nest egg. This has always bothered me that they put in those years and did not have a retirement plan to rely on. This was not my fault of course and in fairness to Dad, in his day not many small businesses of our size offered these benefits. Dad was the type of guy all the employees loved. I know I gave the employees more benefits than Dad ever would have, but I also know I never enjoyed the respect of the employees he did. He just had a special gift and knack with employee relations.

Another relative, an older cousin of mine or nephew to Dad, had a drinking problem he was trying to lick. Dad ask if I would mind putting up with Bob and try to help him get his life straightened out. He knew as the outside manager of the time that I was the one that would be most in contact with Bob. I had never been around him very much and thus knew very little about him. Of course, I told Dad I would do whatever he wanted. I admired Dad for wanting to help this nephew of his. Bob's own father Bill had given Dad fits when it came time to settle Granddad's estate. He had even wanted to throw my folks house into the estate since Dad and Granddad had been in business together. Bob had nothing to do with this, but many men still would have not taken on a reform effort with the son of a brother who had given so much grief to the family. Bob was nice to work with and stayed a year or so. I thought we were making progress, but alas, one morning he did not show up for work and that was the last of Bob I saw. I have a great friend in Welch also named Bob Neil, but only one "l" on the Neil instead of our family's two. Friend Bob and I have a laugh every few months about the call he got very late one night from someone wanting to buy the car he had for sale. Friend Bob did not have a car for sale. The caller who appeared to be intoxicated persisted that he wanted that car. Bob never convinced him that he was not the Bob he wanted.

Vernon Vail worked at the lot when I first came back and helped me get my feet on the ground in so many ways. Vernon worked hard for us and went home and farmed his own rented place in the evenings. He raised a large family and I think each one of his boys worked at the lot at one time or the other as they grew up. All were good workers. Leon the oldest son came early before anyone else and put out the hay and then left to go to college. One morning he fell off one of the rain slickened pipes on the rack the hay was fed in and fell into a sea of wet manure mud. The manure just slimed over his entire body. It no doubt kept him from being hurt. Nothing to do but laugh when he told of not being able to shed the manure smell even after a shower. No one wanted anything to do with him at college that day. Another morning he was driving the hay truck along in the dark without use of the headlights. He said they had shorted out, so he just followed the fence line as a guide that dark morning. He forgot the next alley stuck out about ten feet farther into the alley than the previous line fence. Drove straight into the concrete feed bunk sending concrete flying everywhere. A project for Jay and I to fix. Everyone laughed and kidded Leon about his episodes. Raymond worked his high school weekends at the lot also, until a late night car wreck put him in a coma for over a month. Raymond was merely riding in the fancy new Plymouth with Denny, who owned the new car. Speed caused the wreck. It also wrecked Vernon's life for years to follow. Eventually Raymond recovered with some brain damage, but he has managed a full life with a family and job. Twins, Jack and Jim worked their high school years as well as the youngest Danny. Fifteen years out of school, Danny came back and worked full time till we closed the custom operation down. Third generation Matt and Randy even spent time with us over the years. Vernon left us for about fifteen years after all his family was grown and concentrated on his own farming. When he retired, I ask him if he would like to be the night watchman for us. He gladly did and made my life much easier for several years. He could handle about anything that came up in the evenings he was on duty. He took a vacation and went to Alabama to visit Leon who now lived there. Leon gave his parents a car while they were there and they started home in it as proud as they could be. The trip from Alabama to Welch went well as they enjoyed the new car to them. Arriving at their home on the highway just outside Welch, Vernon signaled the turn he was to make into their driveway. A pickup behind did not heed the signal or the turning car. It started to speed around the car just as Vernon was square into his turn. The pickup crashed into Vernon's side door, killing him instantly. The pickup driver was drunk. Such a waste. Vernon was in his '70s by now, but in great health and enjoying an easier life than he ever had.

Chuck was a man in his fifties when he went to work for us. I thought he would really do well. For some reason, he could not get along with the other men on the crew. I am sure it was not all his fault, but even mild mannered Vernon Vail and he almost came to blows one day. That was it; I decided Chuck would just have to do jobs by himself. I always prided myself on not firing people if there is any way to make a situation work. Chuck was assigned to feed about forty bales of hay per day. I hated to see him have to do it alone, but it seemed to be the only way and forty bales would not kill him. I watched for two weeks, he would load all the upper bales out of the barn and never pick up the harder bottom bales. Soon he had several rows of only bottom bales left. He came in the office in a huff, wanting help with these bottom bales. I was ready as like I said I had been watching. A few bottom bales picked up each day would have been no problem, but now he had a problem. I told him to take his time and just work out of his situation. He said if he got no help, he was finished working for us. I said "I'm sorry to see you go." He left. I had not had to fire him and he had dug his own hole. Sometimes things just have to work out.

The Chamberlain brothers, Terry and Donald "Tonto," both worked in my early years. Terry was my age and we were good friends at work. We handled the doctoring of the sick cattle in those early years. Terry was good and kept excellent records on the cattle doctored. He stayed several years until he got the chance to go to work for the Goodrich tire plant in Miami where his Dad worked. I didn't blame him for leaving for more money and a good set of benefits, but always missed him. Terry stayed at Goodrich until it closed down in 1986 and then went to work at the state hospital at a job more similar in pay to our. I always wished that he had came back to the feedlot. His brother Donald was called Tonto for the long hair he wore and his Indian looks that made him look like Tonto of the Lone Ranger. Tonto worked after school in high school. After graduation he married and moved into a feedlot house. He also worked his head off and was great at all cattle jobs. I always missed him when he left. Tonto got a chance to better himself and took a new job. Being still young like many workers he had his new job and was eager to leave after a proper notice. The only problem was he got into a problem at work of the magnitude that we had to request he go ahead and leave early. I paid him for the notice time and sent him on his way. I think he was just too eager to get to the new job and let his better judgment get the best of him. I hope he learned a valuable lesson from the incident and I trust he did. I have not had much contact with him all these years later, but I think he has become a good family man and worker. I hope we helped shape his work values with us as so many did that worked over the years for us.

There was so much satisfaction in seeing many of the high school and college kids who worked for us in their spare time during the school years and see them go on to success in life. There were many over the years. Craig Eubanks became an insurance agent. Bryant Vail a banker. Some would be a pain to work with, but most had a work ethic that so many of today's youth have not been taught. One high school lad was the son of long time employee Keith McLain. Keith Junior, or just Junior as we called him, worked weekends during high school. One Saturday he had a small job to accomplish before we all quit for the day at eleven. It was not a hard task or one that should take very long. I got busy and did not miss Junior till nearly quitting time. I finally did and went looking. I found him sleeping in one of the pickups and the job not near finished. It seems Junior had too big a night on the town the night before. He had rode to work with Dad that morning. Everyone was ready to leave. I also, needed to be on my way as we had a family outing to Tulsa planned that afternoon. Still, I felt that these kids needed training and took them under my wing as I would have my own. I told Junior he had better stay until his project was finished. I told him I would give him a ride home when finished. I stood over him till the job was finally finished. It wasn't easy in Junior's state that day, but I never raised my voice, just stayed with him till done. I took him home and hurried back to my home and we got a two-hour late start to our trip. It was worth it. I made my point with Junior and I think it stuck. He worked different times off and on for us. He would stay awhile and then either get tired of working with his Dad or see a greener pasture somewhere and off he would go. We always parted friends. He was pleasant to be around and did a great job. Of course, I only had a very small part in his upbringing, but I am still proud of my part none the less.

Arch Corn was the mill manager when I started at the feedlot. He was an old bachelor and set in his ways. However, he never missed a day of work even to the point that he worked seven days a week. On the weekends in those days he would not have to be there over three hours each day, but still had to get up and get there. He always cooked his lunch in the dirty mill control room in an electric skillet, always using onions. Only mill in the country that smelled of cooked onions I am sure. For several years, Arch was also the night man. Our night man slept on the couch in the small office and seldom had many duties in those days except to be there just in case. I am sure this was too much of the feedlot, but that was what he wanted. Problem was he got to drinking two six-packs of beer every night. It started happening at work some also. The straw that broke the camel's back was one day he drove the pickup to the pasture to help gather some cattle. He apparently had some to drink during the noon hour and he wildly drove the pickup through the cattle and caused all kinds of problems that day. It never happened again. He saw for himself what was happening and I never saw a sign of alcohol consumption on him again. Thank goodness. He would get mad at me when I wanted to change the routine for some reason or add a new product in the mix. He would say, "This isn't nothing but an experiment station." I learned the best way to get along with him was to leave him notes on his desk while he was out checking the feed bunks and then just stay out of his way. This worked great and we got along fine until he retired. I respected Arch Corn for the job he did day in and out for our company after he got over the drinking habit. We got along in our own funny way. He retired and only came back to the feedyard once after. I don't know if he just did not want to face not working any more or if he was sick and tired of the place. I see Arch on the street or meet him on the road once in awhile.

Homer Stepp, Dee Ann's uncle, was another night man. He would walk the cattle pens every night in the summer time checking the cattle and water tanks. Of course we usually in his day did not have over 6,000 on feed during the summer. Very little missed Homer's sharp eye. I related early on in this book of the drinking episode of Homer and Woody's. This was the only dim spot in Homer's days with us.

Archie Neill came in the office one day at noon and I immediately saw he was pale as a white sheet and did not look good. I ask him if something was wrong. He said he didn't know, but that he did not feel well. Everyone but Arch and I had gone to town for lunch that day. Not knowing just what was happening at the time, I told him I had better take him to the doctor in Miami. He agreed. On the seventeen mile drive to Miami, I looked at him about half way there and he looked worse and worse. I knew in the back of my mind by now that he was having a heart attack. I did not have a cell phone in those days, so I just drove faster and faster. At one point I came on to the mailman putting mail in a box along side the narrow highway. Another car was meeting me. It was too late to stop for the mailman, so I sped by him just as I passed the car from the opposite direction. Such a narrow highway with no shoulders for this maneuver. I never knew how we avoided a wreck, but God must have been with us. The seemingly forever trip soon found us at the doctor's and it was determined that Arch was indeed having a heart attack. He survived and returned to work sometime later.

My brother Steve had a brother-in-law, Johnny Hurst who worked at the lot in the early days. He left and came back several years later. I did not know but while gone Johnny had got to drinking too much. This caused trouble over the years when he got to stashing beer in his ice chest during the summer at work. I got to checking his ice chest when he was not looking and throwing out the beer I found. I would talk and talk to him about getting help. I told him I would pay his salary while he went for treatment. He finally did and was gone a month or six weeks. He came back a new man. I thought I have really accomplished something now and felt proud of the role I had played in turning his life around. He also was a much-improved employee. The only problem I had was he soon decided to take a cut in pay and go to work at the county barn driving a road grader so that he would have more free time to be with his family. The county guys got off an hour earlier each day and did not have to work weekends. I lost a good man, but was still glad I had played a role in turning his life around. I just wish he would have stayed after we got him changed. Such is life.

We built a new office in 1981. Was I ever glad! I had done more business on the back step sitting on a concrete block in the old non air-conditioned office. It was really going to be nice to have a proper workspace. I learned from the mistakes of our old inadequate office the pitfalls of not having a proper work environment. You just cannot get the job done right without some simple amenities to make a proper work place. With the new office came a showroom for our retail supply. We had a seventy-foot truck scale to weigh both cattle and grain on. It was now time to add some staff to the office. Up to this time all billing and accounting functions had been done by my mother and Dee Ann at a home office in town. This worked well for them, but gave us no inside help at the feedlot. I persuaded another friend, Diane Cox, to join us. First she worked part-time and soon full-time. She early on could not decide whether to pursue a rural mail carriers job. She did it some as a sub. I did not think this would be a very good job for her with you know neither rain, sleet, or snow of a mailman and with the sorry country roads and miles of them she would have to travel. I just knew she would have a lot of problems to deal with in this job. I soon had her talked into helping me full-time. We worked great together! Diane had a wonderful personality and everyone she came in contact with was just "wowed" by her niceness. All of us have strengths and weaknesses to deal with. We all need to find employment in a field we like, has opportunities, and where are strengths are put to best use with minimal impact from our weak traits. Diane was the best at the telephone and dealing with customers. Her weakness was in the book work or computer side of her job. She always got this part accomplished just fine, but it did not come easy as the customer relations did.

Christmas of 1983 was bitterly cold with a blizzard. The temperature was about five above zero with the wind blowing thirty miles per hour with snow. Dad and I worked all day Christmas Eve and Christmas Day. I did get half the crew off at noon on Christmas Eve and the other half at noon on Christmas. Teresa called and caught Dad warming up a minute in the office. She thought it was awful of us to have her husband working on Christmas. We did too, but the cattle had to be taken care of. We had no choice. The animals needed our extra care and we had to serve our customers. Dad and I, as I said, stayed all day both days while the crew got off a half day on either Christmas Eve or Christmas Day. The day after Christmas we lost power for about six hours. We set up a gasoline air compressor to open the gates in the mill to let corn and protein pellets flow down into a mixer truck we used to mix the feed ration usually mixed inside the feed mill. We got the cattle fed each day during what was the worst week of my entire career. I was sure glad, as were all the employees when the weather turned better. Just part of the job dealing with live animals.

In 1986 when I suddenly had to divide my time at the feedlot and the bank, I soon learned that I would have to have help in my job. I turned the buying of the vet supplies for the feedlot and store over to Diane. I would help her as she learned to know the good prices and what we needed, but soon she had a better handle on this part of her job than I. She knew nothing about buying corn or trade skills in those days. I bought all the feed including the corn. It took several hours per week by the time I visited with all the elevators and farmers. You just had to talk the weather, ag prices, and family before you could trade with these people. I loved to do this, but simply did not have the time to do so now. I thought that Diane with her personality would be a natural at this. I set a price to pay and how many loads to buy and set her loose. She would holler at me for help often early on. Sometimes my price would be too low and we would have to adjust. Diane soon learned to trade. Early on she did not understand the fundamentals of the grain market, but she would somehow get a feel for just the magic number it took to purchase our grain at a fair, but as cheap as we could price. Before long, she was buying all feed products, setting her price, and deciding with the mill manager how many loads were needed. We fed from eighteen to twenty-eight loads of corn per week depending on how full the lot was which was somewhat seasonal. I had the time I had to have to trade cattle, talk to feeding customers, and go to the bank every day. A special right hand assistant is a very good asset. We worked well together and complimented each other's skills.

When we started doing trade shows in 1987, Diane would go to many of the bigger shows with me to help run our booth. She could get a prospect started while I talked to another and then hand them off to me to finish. As usual, we made a good one/two team. Diane stayed with me for twenty-one years. When I was trying to decide whether to shut the feedlot down, which I will talk about later, one of my considerations including my health, Dee Ann's overworked job, and Diane seemed to be stressed to the end. We had grown so much over the years and as we get older none of us take the pressure or pace as well as our younger days. The business was good, but competition would not allow adding more staff and overhead. I will explore this more later. Anyway, I thought that Diane would have an easier job just running the retail store and keeping track of my personal cattle. It would cut her job stress and duties close to half while keeping the same pay. I thought that if I ever sold the ranch/feedlot that we could move the store to town and I would simply turn it over to Diane for the cost of inventory or I would keep the investment and let her run it. It would make a perfect retirement job for her that would be low stress and last as long as she wanted. Alas, with the feedlot shut down and only five employees left, she did not like things the way I had planned. She applied for a government job and got it. It would be doing paper work in a government office, just the thing that was her weakness. I did not see this as best for her, but off she went. Diane gave two weeks' notice before leaving. I decided I did not want to train a new person to manage the store or do so myself. I started an immediate close out sale on our inventory. Over the two weeks left with Diane we sold 75 percent of our inventory. Most was sold at a loss to move in such a short time. I thought it best to just take my lumps and end my store business as fast as possible. Diane went to work for a boss with a different style than mine who liked to be little her for her mistakes. It was tough, but she mastered her duties. I missed my long time helper, but also adjusted. Part of the duties learning how to manage employees. It is much harder with friends and family, but also more rewarding with friends and family.

Jo Callison was another friend who worked in the office. We kept many a telephone caller confused when they would mix up Jo for Joe or Dee Ann for Diane. We always laughed at their frustrations and confusions over which they were visiting with. Jo stayed a few years until one day she heard of a government job with the Farm Service Agency. It would have more holidays off and a better government retirement plan than I could offer. She left our company, but remains a good friend today. Her son Roger also worked several summers during college for us. He came in one day with manure up to his knees real heavy and very stinky. It seems the tractor and brush hog he was operating had become stuck and he had walked in to get help to pull out the tractor. On the way in he tried to walk across a drainage ditch that looked dry. He got half way across it and the seemingly dry manure in the ditch gave way and he sunk to his knees. I ask Roger if the tractor was in the same shape as he. We all laughed when he told of the tractor being just barely stuck and how he thought the ditch was dry as he walked in. We laugh about this episode every few years. Shelia Callison, Roger's little sister and Jo's daughter, also worked during her school years off and on in the office. She was always full of fun and a very good worker. The father and husband of this bunch was Ernie Callison, the vice president at the Welch State Bank. Ernie and I worked well together also. We appraised cattle for loans and seldom ever differed on our appraisals even though we would each write down our value on a piece of paper before telling the other our value.

Scott Tynon was another long time worker. Scott looked and was an Indian. His nickname soon became "Chief." Chief could handle cattle with an ease I have never saw. He was simply a natural at working cattle. He soon became our head cattle doctor and was the lead man on the processing crew. He always did a splendid job. Like many of the work family, Chief went through troubles at home. It is a bad part of our society to have such a large divorce rate. Our work family was not immune to these problems. Chief lived in a feedlot house and worked many hours. One of my shortcomings as I look back was to not make every employee take a day off each week. We had a policy of one day off during the week and work half a day Saturday and for two to four hours on Sunday till chores were done. Many of the younger employees liked to work their day off for extra pay. We usually needed the extra help and I would let them do this if they did not pick and choose days worked or off according to the workload we were to have for the day. In other words, I would not let them work on a slow day for us if they did not work on a busy day for us that were their day off. I always worked many hours and most days so I thought nothing about it. The feed lot industry average is fifty-five hours per workweek. We worked on forty-four hours if the employee took their day off. Looking back over thirty-five years, I am sure I lost Chief, Tonto, Mike Fitz, and probably Mike Day because they burned out from working every day with out taking their days off. It made their budget work for them at the time and helped us out until they burned up and quit. Anyway, back to Chief when he went through his divorce he was like most going through this. He was hard to get along with, started smoking, drank too much at night, and in general was a mess at work. One day Chief was spreading manure on pasture with the truck mounted manure spreader. The field he was working in was mostly a long stretch of grass without trees or other obstacles in the way. There was two electric high line poles in the pasture. Chief came in and I noticed a big "V" in the front bumper of the truck. I ask Chief what had happened. He had gone to sleep driving the truck and hit one of the electric poles. I just asked if he got a headache or whiplash out of it. We all laughed and went on about our work. Like most, Chief got over the divorce and found Tammy. A newfound love and courting don't make for the best employee either. I always said an employee isn't worth shooting for six months after a divorce or six months after a new marriage. Most of the time this is true. Chief made it through his rough spot, got married again, and survived the first six months in-love syndrome. He was now a great employee again. This lasted a few years until he decided to try boat building for a job. This job paid well, but was not stable. After several on and off layoffs, the boat company closed. Today, he is back to his beloved cattle work on the Johnston cattle ranch.

I found you have to handle different people different ways. You have to be fair, give equal treatment, and not play favorites. However, there are more than one way to skin a cat and such it is with people. Some just need a different approach. One such was my best truck driver, Dale Charles. Dale started on the grain truck in 1906 after my old friend Jerry decided after only three loads that driving a grain truck was not for him. Dale handled a truck with ease. Our farmer and elevator customers liked him and he made a good impression for our company. No problem here. However Dale was a little high strung in his younger days. He got paid by the mile. If he had to wait to load or just got a bad load he was not happy. We paid him twenty dollars a pay period to make up for some sitting time, but mostly his pay was by the mile and some loads would always be better than others. Hauling grain does not pay very well for the truck, but it did add a lot of flexibility to our corn buying. Hauling corn would never pay the driver as well as some freight hauling jobs. However, our job was pretty flexible on time to start and finish the workday and the driver was home every night. This made it a good job even though the pay was less compared to other truck driving jobs where you were not home every night. I soon learned that Dale and I would pick a fight with each other if I set the loads or if I saw him too much at work. If I just passed him on the road and waved and smiled great big we got along great. On weekends at the church we both attend, we never talked work and got along great. I just learned to keep both of us work happy it was best if Diane set up his loads and handled his schedule. She had to take a little gruff occasionally, but knew how to handle it. This system of while Diane was not his boss, but his dispatcher worked great. We got along great outside work. Dale was a great driver and company ambassador. He liked his hours and being mostly on his on. We found a way to make a great deal for all of us. However, I am sure in the early years if I had talked to him every day one of us would have ended up mad and Dale would have quit or I would have fired him. He stayed till we shut down the trucking operation. I gave him a good severance pay and he never missed a day of work between our job and his new found job. However, Rhonda, Dale's wife, said the night he came home with the news the feedlot was shutting down and the trucking job was over he just sat down and cried. I hated putting everyone through this stress, but was glad the job was worth crying over. I had a great employee and still have a good friend because we found a different way to handle the boss/employee situation.

In late 1988 with the bank problem gone, I planned our conversion to a new computer system. We had been on a program for several years written by the local junior college computer professor. Jim Grover had done a terrific job writing a program as I told him what I wanted. Jim was great to work with, but our program only went about 25 percent of the way I needed to get to. I had about $9,000 in programming cost. I was going to have to give up some of our individuality I liked for a canned program more than 150 other feedyards used. I chose Turnkey Computer Systems for the new program. Dee Ann and I leaned to operate the new system and in fact I set up most up the accounts, as I wanted them with Turnkey's help. Now I needed another full time employee to help run the system so that Dee Ann could concentrate on being our comptroller and I could get back to my job. I found a very unique individual to do this. I am sure I am the only businessman in the world who can say what I am about to tell you. In my second grade in school, a new young principal was hired for our school. When I moved from grade school to junior high, my old grade principal moved along as the new junior high principal taking the place of a beloved principal, J.R. Spence whom had lost a battle with cancer. Three years later when I was to move to the high school building where the school superintendent also had his office, my long time educator moved to the superintendent's job when Mr. Hollis left. Delbert Lovelace followed every step of my school days in Welch from grade two through my senior year. Nineteen years later he took an early retirement option offered by the State of Oklahoma. When I saw him one day, I thought he looked somewhat bored with his new retirement. I ask him if he would like to help get our new computer system running and then find, hire, and teach someone to do the job full time. Delbert jumped at the chance. I was thrilled to have my old teacher back with me. This time I was the boss. Just a joke, because I respected Mr. Lovelace for those years and he was in charge of his new project. I soon sensed he might not want to hire someone, but do the job himself full time. I asked and he said yes, he would like to do so for a few months or maybe years. He said that when the time to retire again came he would find his replacement before he left. He stayed four or five years and we had a big time in our office together.

One day Delbert told me it was time to start looking for his replacement. We did and soon found a local lady I grew up with and attended church with. She was working part-time at the local grocery store and had helped for years in a family business that was being phased out. Glenda Gamble was a single mom who never married. She raised a wonderful son who became a Minister. Glenda or "Blondie" as I liked to call her was full of life and fun to have in the office. Delbert stayed until she was comfortable in her new job and came back from time to time to fill in for a vacation or some other need. Glenda stayed till we closed the operation.

One man was never on our full time staff, but worked six to twenty weeks many years as a contract fence and corral builder. Richard Smith can work circles around most men. He is simply a master at building fences and corrals and even barns. He also can repair about anything broke. Richard was also my neighbor and a good guy. He took me fishing once when he thought I looked over worked. One night when my fatigue syndrome had me weak as a cat, Dee Ann awoke to a sound of rushing water. Our washing machine hose had broke in the middle of the night and water was running everywhere. I was too weak to turn the water off at our outside cut off. The only place I knew to turn at that hour was my friend, Richard. As soon as he got awake enough to realize I was in trouble, he was on his way to help us. I never questioned how he would do a project for me, because I knew he would do it right and would have a better idea than I. You don't find many people that have the work ethic Richard has. Over the years he had many helpers such as Tim Holt. Tim and Richard would work hard all day and still have enough energy to have a friendly scuffle before going home for the day. I always wished I had half their energy.

In 1991 with things settled down at the feedyard and the business growing, I decided the time was right to add an operations manager. I wanted someone who would help me run the day to day operation. This person would be in charge of the entire outside workings of the business, help with the retail sales some, assist in customer development as time permitted and be my backup for all my duties. It would be a fast paced job with many hats to wear. I turned to my friend Dub Berry of The Helming Group to help me find the right person. We ran an ad in the High Plains Journal and The West Texas Livestock Weekly for the described operations manager position at a northeast Oklahoma location without naming our company. All replies were directed to Dub. He received over forty applications. Two brothers working for Cargill's Excel Corporation, one in Texas and one in Kansas, applied without each other knowing the other had applied. There were seasoned men who had more experience than I to men just out of college that applied. Several would work for our position. I felt very good at the response we had. On paper many people can look good and not be. One such applicant sounded good to Dub, but fortunately I had heard of a fraudulent cattle scheme he had been in on at his last position and nixed him immediately. We did an intense background and qualifications check on about fifteen of the applicants and had about six over for a visit and interview. All of the six finalists would make a fine addition to our staff. I have watched the trade journal over the years and most ended up in good positions somewhere.

I finally decided the one for me was Mike Day. Mike had a degree from Oklahoma State University and had been a cattle foreman at the Hitch lot in Garden City. The Hitch family ran a good organization and had always been good to our family. I called Ladd Hitch and asked permission to talk to one of his employees. He probably did not know Mike, but he appreciated my calling and telling him of my intentions. The Hitches had a good training program that Mike had been in about five years. Mike was very clean cut, bright, energetic, and seemed very honest and sincere. I passed up some men with a lot more experience to pick Mike. I just knew he would fit my style and hopefully would be with us for years to come. He enjoyed the Hitch operation, but did not like living in western Kansas. Moving to Welch would put his family in an area with trees and grass like he knew growing up. It would cut the trip to his folks or his in-laws by many hours. Mike, his wife Shelia, and daughter, Leah moved to Welch and soon Mike was in the middle of everything at work. He thought as I did and before long I could have him look at a pen of cattle and describe them to me at selling time. If I didn't have time to go look for myself, I just asked Mike and always came out as well selling the cattle as if I had looked myself. He was gentle, but firm with the employees, as my style was. I just could not have asked for a better fit. The only problem I could ever see that needed training was that if Mike had been in charge of the company checkbook we probably would have a complete new set of trucks and equipment and might have gone broke in the process. He liked new things for himself and wanted them at work. There is a happy medium in having the equipment you need without being extravagant to the point it hurts the bottom line. Mike could have learned this I am sure in time. I thought I had someone who I would eventually give a financial interest in the operation. I did not raise his starting salary much over the time he was with us, but in the fashion I told him I would operate under, I raised his annual year end bonus every year. In the time he was with us his annual take home was raised by over a third. I thought I was doing pretty good.

Mike had one bad habit; he liked to treat himself with cattle drugs when he had a cold or sore throat. This practice and dust in the feedlots was causing some damage to his lungs. I did not think it was serious, but maybe there was more to it than I knew, or maybe he saw how I walked like an old man during my numerous chronic fatigue outbreaks. Something made him decide to get out of the grueling feedlot industry. He came into my office with a thirty-day notice resignation letter. You could have knocked me over with a feather. I had no idea he was looking or thinking of a change. He worked two weeks and then the last two weeks with us spent most of the time using vacation time looking for a house in the area he was moving to. I sure hated to lose the man that I cared for as my own family. I tried to show Mike as we went along how much he meant to me and the operation. We did not socialize much with any of the employees nor did we with Mike other than to provide odd jobs for his wife Shelia at work when she had time so that she would feel a part of the feedlot family too. Shelia was a schoolteacher.

Mike left. It hurt me and the employees who all liked him. I was very hurt when Mike told the employees the reason he was leaving the feedyard for a bank job was that I had not given him a raise in five years. As I said his base salary had not raised as I had told him on his hiring. I told him as long as the company did well and he did his part he would be taken care of in bonus. He never told me he was disappointed in his wages, which I would have kept raising. I don't know if telling the employees this story made me the bad guy in him leaving and thus still ok in their eyes or what. I could read the disappointment in the employees' eyes over Mike leaving and their thinking I hadn't paid him enough was the reason. Most would have had my head on a plate if in truth they had known Mike's total take home was twice most of theirs. I have never let Mike see my hurt or disappointment in the way he left, but it sure left a mark on me. There was certainly nothing against him leaving for a better job without dust to contend with and better hours. However, anytime we leave I think it is in the best interest of everyone to leave very positive. You never know when you might need a good reference. Mike was as close to me as anyone could get. I respected his judgment and opinions and as I said we saw cattle almost one hundred percent of the time the same way. I had grown so close to him that I never trusted myself to ever get that close to an employee again. Had Mike stayed I am sure I would have one day found a way for him to succeed me completely.

I was now back to the drawing board for an operations manager. I decided I should ask Doug, my son-in-law if he wanted the opportunity to work in the family business. After the announcement of their engagement I had persuaded Doug to try one summer vacation working outside at the feedlot. He worked hard and did well. Doug had grown up in the city and knew little about caring for cattle or operating machinery. He learns fast though. At the end of that summer he had told me that it was fun, but nothing he would want to do for life. Now several years later, he was a quality control manager for Lowrance Electronics in Tulsa. He had several people under him and a very good job. He was getting tired of frequent traveling that went with the job. We had formed a company with some money from Mom's estate for the purpose of Doug and Jodee starting their own business if he found one he wanted to try. I was still surprised, but delighted that he wanted to try the feedyard again.

Doug learned fast in his position at the feedyard. We got along well. I never doubted that we would, but many times family members especially sons-in-law cannot get along in a family business. Both sides have to work at it and we both did. Jodee helped in the office and the granddaughters spent a lot of time at the office as well. It was a great family business. I did not realize just how many things I had picked up growing up in the business and took for granted. Doug on the other hand was a city boy and had to learn everything from scratch, but as I said he was a quick learner. I worked harder than I had the past five years making up the slack from Mike who came with experience and Doug who was learning. I did not mind this at all, but it did cause some extra pain from the chronic fatigue syndrome. The one mistake I made, that so many family businessmen do, is I started another expansion of the feedlot capacity soon after Doug started. It gave Doug a project that he had skills in laying out and supervising the construction of the pen addition.

Many family businesses expand and tie up capital and borrow huge sums of money only to learn that the new generation does not share the passion for the industry the old did. Sometimes this leaves hard feelings, the new generation leaves, and the old has a note to pay off and a larger workload in a time they want to slow down. Fortunately, I financed this addition out of current cash flow and did not build anything that would not pay off in two years time. We also needed the capacity to keep up with customer demand for pens. The industry also was requiring more capacity with the same equipment and people to continue to be successful. We had to do more volume to pay for employee raises, higher cost of employee health insurance, and workers' compensation insurance. All new equipment or repairs on the old continued to rise in price, but competition in the feeding industry held fee raises to a minimum. Doug as I said seemed to be fitting in well. The employees liked his wit and helped him. I think they sensed the viability of the company in many ways rested on his shoulders because all knew the toil the chronic fatigue syndrome was taking on my body. The feedyard business is very intense, fast-paced, and requires long hours. None of this is very conducive to someone with chronic fatigue. I handled the pace with pure grit and determination. There were many days it was so hard to get to work and keep going, but I always managed.

One morning Doug walked in my office and sat down. I could tell he had something on his mind. I put my work aside and listened. Doug told me how he enjoyed his new job, but had determined that it just wasn't how he wanted to spend the rest of his life. That was the deal we had made when he came. Come and try, but not to stay if he wasn't passionate about the business. I feel that he was intimidated by not being in control of his position the way he wanted. In the electronics business he knew one hundred times more about the product and business than those under him, but in the cattle business at this point the employees knew one hundred times more than he did. I felt his pain, but knew he could overcome this handicap as fast as he was learning. I did not, however, try to talk him out of his decision. I could tell he had given it plenty of thought. Our deal was that if he did not want to stay it would be easier working in the family business to research and make the deals needed to start his own family business. This is what he did over the next few months while still working with me. Another chapter will deal with his new venture. We all tried, there were no hard feelings, and I'm grateful the attempt was made. Handling work and family can cause turmoil at home for all if not handled properly. We all worked to see that this was not the case. I enjoyed our time together and we learned a lot about each other. This has helped us today.

I started the search for a new operations manager. My National cattle buyer, Gary Marcus suggested I call a young man he knew in Dodge City when Gary was buying cattle in that area. I called Paul Folsom, on Gary's recommendation. Paul had been an outside assistant manager at a feedlot in Scott City, Kansas for several years and had moved to Dodge City a couple of years before to work in the office of a commission seller of finished cattle. This had gave him some phone experience with customers and greater knowledge of selling cattle. He longed to be back in the feedyard business however. His wife's folks only lived about an hour and a half from us in Kansas. Paul did not think he wanted to go back to the feedyard industry in eastern Oklahoma, but came to look while on a visit to the in-laws. I showed him all around our operation and told him how I operated and what I wanted in an operation manager. He went back and talked to Kathy, his wife. Soon he had agreed to our position and was thrilled to be moving to a county close to family, back to trees and green grass, and a chance to work in a progressive feedyard in a management position. Paul learned fast and we got along well. I could once again slow down a pinch I thought. I did in many ways, but a fast-changing industry did not allow much slowing down by any of us. I enjoy change and for the most part the changes would be positive for the industry. However new regulations and another flare-up in the fatigue syndrome made me realize something had to give. More on this another chapter.

I usually had the ability to sense when I needed to be looking for a new person in the group either for staff expansion, or the feeling a key person was getting ready to depart. My right hand man Mike Fitzpatrick was still with us when I could see discontent in his work and home life. He handled the minor breakdowns and we farmed out the more complicated tasks on trucks and pickups. Mike and I had a lot of fun working together. He helped with the farm shows and looked after many of the outside details for me. One funny incident with Mike involved a new grease tank we purchased to hold fat or grease in a heated tank to keep liquid much like your French fry grease. Our new tank was filled and soon started leaking. A small plug the size of a man's finger had been left out at the factory. Grease was shooting out and making a gooey mess. Mike simply put his finger in the hole to stop it up until we could get a bolt to screw in. I know the grease had to feel hot on his finger, but he never let on and just stood there with a funny look and the finger in the hole. We soon had the plug in and the grease mess stopped.

I could see that our growing organization needed a full time mechanic. A former neighbor and long time friend would be just the man if I could talk him into it. Dick Winfrey was at one of the coalmines, but the job stability at all the local mines was kind of shaky right now. I thought it would be a good time to approach Dick. To my delight, he accepted a offer to join our team. I now had an area of the operation that I was the least qualified to handle with a trusted alley to head up. I hoped Mike would develop as my right hand with the cattle and other employees, but at least if my intuition of his leaving happened I would be able to handle his duties with Dick in place as mechanic. To my dismay Mike did leave, but at least I had been ahead of the curve to be ready. My strength was usually in having a good crew to cover the areas I am weak in. I always got good people to in particular handle the feed call for the cattle and the feed mill management. I also always had a trusted man in the maintenance position. Dick was just great in this position. He not only looked after all the equipment like it was his own, he also shopped hard for the best deals on parts, tires, and other maintenance needs. Dick worked several years for our company. Both of his knees were bad and he walked like a duck the last few years. He even used a cane part of the time. He was still the best there was. Alas, cancer also struck Dick. He and his doctors had caught the cancer in time. An operation was successful. The toll of the cancer and his bad knees however forced Dick to retire. I was first of all glad my friend had caught the cancer in time and would be all right with some life style adjustments. Still we would miss him. Dick also did our farm field prep work. I had bought him a new tractor to use for us in 1995. In the nine years and 2,700 hours we owned the tractor, Dick put all but about 100 hours on this tractor. After he retired, he kept doing all the tractor work for us in the spring and fall. When I decided to shut our operation down, Dick was called first to see if he could help put the feed pens back in grass. I knew he would have good ideas of how to do so and he did. Dick is a wonderful friend and a trusted, great employee. What a great combination.

I knew Arch Neill would be ready to retire in a couple of years and I did not have anyone on staff that I thought would grow into his shoes of running the feed mill and making the bunk calls on the cattle. Arch Neill had taken this job over when Arch Corn retired several years before. It had worked well after his heart attack to have a position where he was in climate controlled conditions and did not have any lifting to do. We had a feeding customer who had quit farming and ask me for a job. I liked Rick Rouse , but the timing was just not right a couple of years earlier when Rick and his dad quit farming. Rick went to Colorado and worked for a small feedlot. When I got in the position to hire someone, I gave my old friend a call. He had got settled in Colorado and wasn't sure he wanted to move again. I don't think he would have, but his employer there was on shaky ground financially and Rick's folks back in Missouri not far from us were getting older and had a few health problems. I soon had him talked into the move. Rick started driving the feed truck behind Cousin Warren and was backup in the mill to Cousin Arch. This was tuff being in the middle of the family cousins who after close to forty years were wanting to slow down their pace and were not quite as adapt, rightfully so after all their years, to changes that I was wanting to make in our feed regime. We all made it work. When Archie retired, Rick moved in as Mill Manager. Rick had never married and I somehow in the back of mind when he came always new he would end my marrying our computer girl, Glenda. I never said anything to anyone or tried to fix them up. Nature just took its course and the two of them worked together a lot in the record keeping of the feed Rick mixed for each pen of cattle. Down the road a while they began dating and soon were married. It was a western wedding with the "feedlot family" in attendance. They make a great couple and are good friends to this day.

The last few years of our operation, I employed five women in the office. Sometimes this can be a challenge especially when one is the Boss's wife. We had our challenges, but always worked through them. Sharon Johnston worked in the office and helped with the store. She was just terrific help, honest, very detailed, and fast. The only problem with Sharon was that she did not have to work, as her family had a successful ranch operation. She worked for the fun of it and to make some "mad money." This was ok, except that Lymon her husband bought a travel trailer and liked to leave in January and not come back till March. This was fine for a few years, as January and February are the slow times in our store. It was however tax time, as we had to have our tax return like qualified farmers who do not file an estimate of tax due have to file by February 28. This caused some resentment among the help when Sharon was gone during these times. They also used to take a two or three week vacation in early fall just as we were filling up with feedlot cattle from the summer lull. Sharon was such a nice person and so good help that I just put up with the situation and tried to keep everyone from killing each other when she was gone. We all liked her so we made due. I was glad she had the opportunity for these extended trips.

We decided to add another part-time office lady to be there when Sharon was gone and then have both when things got real busy in the spring. Kathy Vazquez was another rancher's wife. Her husband Bruce was a good store customer and Kathy was the daughter of Morris Barnes the cattle feeder I wrote of earlier in this book. Kathy fit in well and things were smooth inside again. Not to last for long. Kathy did not come till about nine in the morning. One morning we heard the ambulance siren and saw it streaking north. About thirty minutes later we heard there had been a terrible accident at the Vazquez place. At first the reports were that one of the sons was hurt in a car wreck. Dee Ann took off to the Vinita hospital to find out what was going on. We knew it somehow involved Kathy's family as she had not shown for work at her usual time. In a small business everyone becomes like family, or a least it did at ours. We tried to always care for ours in whatever time of need. Dee Ann soon learned the accident involved Kathy and she had lost her life. Kathy was out walking as was her routine every morning before work. She took a different route that morning, walking in the county roadway, listening to the radio with headphones. She did not hear the truck coming from behind her. The early morning sun shown through a dirty feed pickup windshield in a glare. Kathy's son in the feed truck on his way to school did not see his mother in the road and had hit her. The accident was not all his fault as Kathy was walking in the road path while listening to a radio with head phones. She did not hear him coming from behind her. It was a tragic loss for her family, the community, and our staff. It takes a deep faith in God to get through these things. It was just like losing a member of the family and the "feedlot family" attended the funeral. Kathy's family survived, not without some bumps in the road. Our staff missed the lively Kathy, but we also survived. Bruce was never as good a customer after that. I always figured it was too hard to come in and not see Kathy setting at her desk and ready to help him. We all still missed his business and the fellowship we had we he did come in.

Another attempt to find the right staff mix involved my experiment with hiring a young college graduate with a degree in Animal Science. Stacy was hired to fill in gaps outside with the cowboy crew checking cattle, customer relations, and office accounting duties. I did not know if this varied job description would work or not, but wanted to try. We could not afford three people, but needed additional help in all three areas. We had customers coming by every day and many times several during the day and at the same time to look at their cattle. Stacy could show them their cattle and Mike Day or I could talk to them when they came back in. Helping the cowboy crew check cattle by walking the pens each morning would give her added experience with what we were doing and help the cowboy crew get this part of the day done early so that any sick cattle found would be treated as soon as possible. I soon found out that Stacy did not know many of the fundamentals of the cattle business that I assumed would be taught in her college courses. She also would tend to try to "wing" it through areas she did not know and this was giving her a credibility problem with the customers. The older women in office did not get along too well with this very pretty staff addition. The cowboys wanted to flirt with her and this caused more problems as she was married and they were too. I could see trouble brewing and for once did not know what to do. I enjoyed her enthusiasm for the job, wiliness to do anything, and she seemed to want to succeed. I worked with her the best I knew how and encouraged Mike Day to do likewise. He soon gave up on her, I am not sure out of frustration or whether to preserve peace at home. I never saw the latter symptom but it would have been justifiable. I learned that Stacy and her husband were planning a land purchase and were going to build a new fancy home. I did not think it would be fair to let her take on this financial burden with her job on such poor ground. We had talked enough about her shortcomings and she knew she had to shape up for the job she held to continue. I decided that even though I had planned to give it another month, it would be kinder in the long run to Stacy to terminate her now rather than later after they had started the house. She did not take the termination very well and left in a huff. The only time she ever came back was a few months later acting as friendly as "ol' rover" to pick up some things she had left behind. The real reason for the visit was she wanted a good reference for a job she was seeking at the Ratcliff Ranch, one of our customers. She did not get this position through no fault of ours, but she never came back again. She and her husband went ahead with the land and house purchase, but a year later ended their marriage in divorce. Stacy ended up in Tulsa with a job in a bank. I am sure she will do good in this type of work. She probably learned from her first job experience. I felt sorry for her, don't know how I could have handled things any different, and was sad my experiment had failed. I was sure I had failed just as much as Stacy had. I am still glad I cut my losses and hers too when I did.

Scott Dewall joined our crew with split duties. He would work mostly for our trucking corporation as a cattle hauler, but when things were slow on the truck he would work by the hour for the cattle company doing odd jobs. Like all of us, Scott had some quirks and somewhat of a temper at times. I let Diane dispatch the truck drivers and deal with their frustrations over who got what loads. She handled them better than I and the men didn't take get mad at her as they would me. I always enjoyed Scott. He came in the office every morning before we started to visit a minute. Scott had gone through a divorce, but found a new love and was married again after he went to work for us. Everything was going well, except Scott developed some type of kidney ailment. I did not think too much of it, as he looked healthy and passed his over the road driver physical just fine. It had caused some trouble when we changed insurance companies for health insurance. Four or five of us, including me, had some problems that were giving me fits in keeping our company health insurance. Just another headache you had to face in small business. Scott drove and helped in the lot and did fine. One morning in July, he fed a few bales of hay to some cattle, not over eight or ten. The local quick trip said he stopped by while in town getting the hay out of a barn we had by my house. He ordered some fried food for his late breakfast and ate it on the way back to the feedlot. He put the hay out and then cleaned a couple of feedbunks for Rick. He then went to back to the mill and was going to feed a couple of loads of feed with the extra feed truck before going to get a load of cattle at ten o'clock to haul to Joplin for a neighbor. He sat down in the mill and told Rick he was not feeling quite up to par that morning for some reason. Rick had his back to him, mixing the load of feed Scott was to haul. He turned and Scott was out cold. Rick called for help and laid Scott down on the floor. Diane hollered up the steps that something was wrong with Scott at the mill. I flew down the steps and ran to the mill. Dale Charles had came in with his semi load of corn and he was giving Scott mouth to mouth. I called Marilyn Horner, a retired nurse in town and told her our situation and asked her to help. We have no ambulance or medical help in Welch of any kind. Diane had called an ambulance out of Bluejacket and also the Miami hospital advanced team was on the way. We all did all possible, it was a very traumatic experience, but Scott could not be saved. He was pronounced dead at the hospital. I had to get his wife and take her to the hospital and help her deal with her loss. I was not prepared for this part of the job, but you do what you have to do. Again, our "feedlot family" had another member to bury. I felt terrible for the loss of Scott. I questioned his activities, but none seemed to be out of the ordinary or particularly hard to do. We did carry life insurance on each employee and I was glad that the young widow would have that. She filed for workers' compensation. I did not know what to think. Scott's doctor approached me at a hospital meeting we both happened to be at. Without revealing any confidentiality, he came up and said "Don't feel that you caused Scott's loss or let your work comp pay. He had a condition that we did not think would end the way it did, but it does happen sometimes that the condition he had will cause a heart attack. It was not job related, but just his physical defect." Scott was only thirty-eight. His doctor made me feel better. The work comp case was pushed and the widow collected it. I did not think this was really right since the doctor had told me what he had. She had collected the life insurance policy, but the Oklahoma Work Comp Law sometimes do not pay as they should which I had seen in the past, and other times pay claims probably not due. Just the way the system is.

Craig Duvall was a young man fresh out of high school working in the brick laying construction business. One year around the Christmas holidays it was unusually cold for three or four weeks. The construction business was stopped and Craig was out of work. The cold was taking its toll on our crew and another temporary hand would sure help. Craig dived in and worked his head off. He even came in Christmas morning even though I told him I did not expect that of a temporary employee. I had told Craig I did not have any full time openings, but after watching him work so hard in such harsh conditions through the holidays I could not turn him away. I made a place in the crew for him and he stayed several years. I always tried to find a place when a good worker came along. They are so hard to find when you have to have one in short notice. About ten years after working for us, Craig decided he wanted to work for himself in the building trade as he had started years ago. I could not blame him for wanting to do something for himself, but sure hated to loose him. It was now very hard to find good people that wanted to learn our business and did not mind working the split shifts that involved weekend work to feed the cattle. This was another reason I decided to close. It was just hard to get the same people when you needed one more. I always tried to provide the best I could for employees, but I had to stay in line with industry norms and pay as our own pay from our customers was so competitive. We gave each employee one-day off during the week and they got off at eleven on Saturday and Sunday as soon as chores were done. The feeding crew worked all day either Saturday or Sunday and had another day off during the week. They still put in an average of forty-four hours per week on the job in an industry that has an average of over fifty hours per week per employee on the job. Recently over dinner, I told my host the reason he had not been able to hire Keith after we closed. I had been told by Keith that it was because one of the other employees told him the ranch job offered was such that his friend had not had a day off in three months. My host said in the ranch world, we were considered feed-lot if that makes a difference, they could not afford that luxury. Cowboys had to always be there to care for the cattle. They could not afford anymore extra help. Sad for the industry and maybe true, but we managed. This ranch owner also owned banks and other businesses. He is probably the most wealthy man in the county. Too bad he will not share some of his wealth just enough that his employees can have more time off the job. I think it would pay dividends my friend does not see in the long run in productivity.

Over the years it seems we had more than our share of calamities. I guess that is just life. We tried to always stress safety first, but agriculture can be a hazardous business. This part of the life of a small business was hard on me. The straw that broke the camel's back for me happened one morning as we were weighing cattle. I was the only one in the office that early summer morning. The cowboys were bringing the cattle for shipment that day and I was figuring the bills and getting them on the way as I often did. Derrick came in the office and wanted to buy some fly spray from our store. I thought he was spraying cattle at the ranch he worked on, but later found out he was going to spray some bulls on feed in one of our pasture traps. We had a deal with his ranch to feed and care for the bulls as we would our regular feeding customers. If he wanted extra services done for the cattle we would do and charge him or allow him to use our facilities and he come and do the work with his crew. We did this with several of the breeding stock customers because they did more working of their cattle than finishing cattle required. The way we offered the service allowed the ranchers to save money and do some things themselves or else pay us for the added service. It had worked well this way for years. Anyway the brand of spray Derrick wanted we were out of and he did not want to use what we had on the shelf. I remembered some fly spay in the back room that we had on hand along time. We formerly used it to spray over the feedbunks and out over the cattle while eating, but had quit this practice when we went to a parasite wasp program that killed fly larvae. Under the non-stinging wasp program you could not spray or the wasp would also die before doing their job. I told Derrick that I had it in the back where it had been along time, but that it was still good, which it was. I told him I did not remember how to use it and to be sure and read the directions. He took it and left. About thirty minutes later, I had finished weighing the cattle and sat down at my desk. Derrick called on his cell phone and said he was across the road in the bull pasture at our place spraying the bulls and they were all falling over and dying. He was frantic. We called the local fire truck to come wash the bulls off. The vet was called and came immediately. I called the company who made the chemical and told them what had happened. They gave us instructions. The problem was that Derrick had not read the directions. The spray could not be used to fully wet the animals as most sprays are. This chemical could only be used as a fog or mist over their backs. The bulls had been fully wetted and suffered from organic phosphate poisoning. Ten or twelve bulls died, but the rest were saved by the fast efforts of the fire department washing them down and the vet's fast action. When done, Dr. Myers cautioned all of Derrick's crew and ours that had ran to the rescue to go home and shower and change clothes as they also had got wet from the mixture on the bulls while treating them. Later in the day I found out some had changed clothes but not their wet boots. Toward quitting time Jeff started feeling funny. We sent him to the doctor at the ER. He was suffering from the organic phosphate exposure. He had not changed his boots. I went to calling the crew who had all gone home for the day by now. I rounded all up for a precautionary trip to the ER. Two we like to have not found, as not suffering any symptoms they were doing things away from home that nice summer evening. Finally we had fifteen men of the two crews at the ER. About four were having reactions. Our neighbor and long time friend, Dr. Steve Grigsby was working the ER and took excellent care of everyone. All but two were either normal or back to normal in three or four hours. Two had further tests over the next month and were determined to be fine. We had, by God's grace and Dr. Grigsby's care, escaped what could have been a very bad end result.

I had been on the scene, but directing activities and on my cell phone with the product manufacturer and thus did not get wet from the mixture. I was close enough that I absorbed the spray in my system, which was already keen to these types of products from my thirty years of processing cattle. I could taste the mixture in my mouth for a week. I decided then that I was loosing my touch for such a fast paced work environment. I had always prided myself at being able to do three things at once. This time if I had stopped to read the label with Derrick I would have kept him from the dilemma. I had told Derrick to read, but since he thought of it as spray and I did not remember it was only a mist, he only read the part of how to mix the solution and went to work. The ranch owner wanted our store liability insurance to cover his bull loss. I told our insurance adjuster what had happened. Derrick had ask for spray and I gave him a mist. It would have worked with his equipment and been fine for the bulls if he had only read the label. He had not. My insurance adjustor talked with me and said that they did not think that they nor I were liable, but that because it had happened on our property and they were in the habit of being way above board in claim payment they would pay if I wanted them too. The customer, Derrick's boss, was a good customer so I told them maybe it would be best to pay the claim. The owner wiggled and avoided any responsibility for the happening. It at least should have been shared. In a few months, Derrick was gone from the ranch. I am sure the spray incident in the end cost him his job. He is a bright and very energetic young man. I have always and still do have much respect for his ability and knowledge of the cattle industry. He ended up in another good position. As for us, at insurance renewal our liability company that was so nice to step to the plate of what they said was not my fault, canceled our insurance. The ER bill paid by worker's compensation was several thousand dollars and our premium rate with the workers comp insurance skyrocketed. The ranch and bull owner went on about business as usual without a thank you for bailing them out. I am satisfied that we saw that everyone was done right even above our responsibility. I felt awful, the situation cost us thousands in raised insurance and other costs, and I felt as if my customer had me. I never said a word and continue to do business with him to this day. Life is too short to make waves. I should have made sure the label was read by reading it myself and then telling the manager. The manager should have done as I said, when I told him I did not remember how to use, but that I knew we had used in past. We had and it worked good when applied as directed. A big lesson in life. This lesson involved a customer, but I included in the employee section because our crew became so involved with the incident and many had to be treated at the hospital in the aftermath. Agriculture is listed as one of the most dangerous occupations one can have. I can see why when I look back over the years at the many near miss accidents and the bad incidents related in this chapter. One can never let their guard down an instant in such a fast paced industry that allows little margin for mistakes. We always strived to make a safe environmental for the employees and strived to keep the employees focused on their own safety. I was so thankful when everyone got a clean health release. Again, God took care of us.

So many corners of one's business life will affect the life of the business owner both good and bad. We enjoyed many happy times with our employees. When I ended our custom business and thus had to have layoffs, we gave each a liberal severance and kept most till they had other employment or a least had four or five months to get ready. I think all respected us for the way we handled this closing and feel good towards us today. I feel good in my heart that things were handled in the best manner possible in all the years we had people helping us.

Keith McLain was the last of the employees to leave. Keith spent twenty-two years with us. He was always there and made sure he held up his end of the job. We had been through so many things together. The death of each of our fathers. Keith and his wife Paula renewed their wedding vows just like a wedding of which we were at. Paula suffered a long hard hospital stay with a lung operation. We worried with Keith, visited the hospital, and covered for Keith without loss of his needed pay while he was off with her. My philosophy has always been to take care of the work family. The one area I failed Keith in was my ongoing attempts to get him to quit smoking. This has to be an individual choice and some can get through the withdrawal of smoking and others can not. I encouraged him all I could to quit, but to date he had not. I pray he will soon.

There were many more employee stories good and bad. We were fortunate to have a long list of good employees over our many years. I wish there had been space to tell of all without boring the reader.

Employees can make or break a company. To be successful and to do what is right, treat employees as you would like to be treated. Business conditions and profits may dictate employee pay and benefits, but do not take advantage of employees regarding their pay, benefits, and hours worked just because you can. This will not work or reward the business owner in the long run.

The next chapter will deal with the customers.

24

The Customers

In all small business situations there are a various assortment of customer types. Most are great to work with and make your job fun and rewarding. It gives me a great sense of personal satisfaction to do a good job for a customer that appreciates your effort on his or her behalf. Some customers, however, will try your patience and give you one fit of a time. I always told my employees that these later type of customers just made you appreciate the former even more. My daughter, Jodee, got her first start in the business world working at McDonald's while still in high school. She told me many a story of customers coming through the fast food outlet. One such was on a woman coming through the drive through window. She ordered and in a short wait received her order. On inspection of the order, she found mustard on her burger instead of the ketchup she ordered. The lady just started boo-hooing as she told Jodee of the mistake. The burger was wrong, but nothing that could not be fixed in short order and certainly not worth crying over. Jodee trying to console the poor lady, learned she had experienced a very bad day both at work and home. This was just the final straw that brought her to tears. The burger crew had caught her pent up anger and disappointment over her day. Jodee, in her true fashion, tried to console the lady and felt she had made a difference before she pulled on out. We never know when what we do or say will impact another. Even strangers can have a positive or negative impact based upon our actions.

While still in high school, I remember two old bachelors who fed cattle at the family feedyard. Marshall, was a big, burly guy and Howard, his half brother, a short small man. They lived a very simple life in a modest home. They were very good businessmen and did well with their cattle operation. When both had passed on, they left their nephews a nice estate. One day Marshall and Howard came by to see their cattle that were getting close to sale time. They told Dad they were taking a vacation and would be gone. Dad thought this was unusual for the pair, but glad they were finally going to enjoy the fruits of their hard work. He asked where they were going and how long they would be gone. The answer was the trip was to Jay, a distance of about sixty miles and they would be gone for the one day only. Dad smiled and we all had a nice conversation that night about their concept of their vacation.

Most people in the cattle business were hard working people that took care of business and lived a good simple life. There were a few, however, that were of a different cut. They would drive hard, drink hard, and have more than one woman. One such man was Jake. He was a big man. Jake would buy finished cattle to speculate on in the near term markets. After buying the pen, he would either resell to a packer before the weigh day within seven days of his purchase or at times he would weigh up the pen and put back on feed for another two or three weeks. This type of speculation was very risky and I doubt if Jake ever did real well in this venture, but he tried for several years. He lived in Iowa and would travel from there to Oklahoma and Missouri buying both the finished cattle and also light weight feeder cattle to place on feed at various feedlots including his own home facility and some in our feedlot. One day, in a hurry as usual and with a woman who was not his wife, big Jake came roaring in to look at cattle to buy. He made a quick pass by the cattle for sale that day without taking time to get out for a close look or hardly ever slowing down. He said "I don't have time to talk now, I will call you when I get to Springfield." He was afraid he would be late for the weekly sale in Springfield, Missouri, a distance away of about 110 miles. He operated in this fast-paced, fast-living mode until age caught up with him and he finally slowed down to a more sensible life.

L. Jay Hacker was a local businessman who owned two ladies' wear stores. He also liked to ranch and feed cattle. His nickname, of course, was the "Girdle Man." The Girdle Man always seemed more at home in the ranch and feedlot business than at the dress shop.

Tubby was a big man who smoked cigars and drank a little too much. He was a successful rancher and part time cattle buyer. He worked hard and had things going his way until one night on the way to a school banquet with his wife and son he was rushing as they were late. He did not see a load of hay without lights on at dusk. He served to miss the truck, but caught the passenger side of his car on the truck bed. His wife and son perished in the accident. Tubby never found a true happiness again it did not seem. He was a diabetic, but would not watch his diet closely. Overweight and always eating the forbidden sweets, he soon was losing toes and his eye sight to the disease. He liked to trade pork bellies and cattle on the futures market. Like "Kudey Bear," Tubby did not fare well in his trading ventures. He lost most of his estate he had worked hard to put together. I always felt sorry for the likeable guy who had lost his family and seemed never had the same will to survive and do well again. It is so easy to give up on life when we are dealt a poor hand. If only, we would learn to turn to our Maker in times like these for the comfort and guidance we need. He is always there for us, if we only ask for the help. There is no burden too great that cannot be lifted through trust in the Lord. It is a hard lesson, it seems for many to learn, but such an easy answer for those who do take heed. None of us are guaranteed a trouble-free life on this earth. This "golden life" is our promise for Heaven. We all can enjoy and make the best of our days here if we turn our problems over to the Lord. We will have tragedies, losses, health problems, bad deals, and other earthly problems. We can get over the bad times and survive and live a good life if we only trust in the help available from God. Sometimes the answer we get to our prayers is not the answer we thought was best, but God in his infinite wisdom knows best and will care for us.

Sometimes we would have a good laugh over something simple and remember it for years. One such incident was when Maxine Callahan sent the payment for their monthly feed statement for the cattle her husband Joe had on feed with us. In a hurry one month, Maxine signed her check, Mrs. Joe Cattle. We never let her forget it. Twenty years later when I see her, I have to call her Mrs. Cattle.

Her neighbors, the Brysons also fed with us for several years. Ronald and Glen liked to feed a type of cattle I called "near beers." They would be Herefords and Blacks mixed with a few Charolais and Limousin. Most of their cattle were bought at a discount to the best cattle as they would not be as heavily muscled nor have the proper shape of the better cattle. Twenty years ago, we could often make good money on this type of cattle selling them alive. Today, the majority of the cattle are sold on a hanging basis. The payment is based upon the quality grade and the meat yield of the animal. The "near beer" types look pretty good at first look, but do not have the quality and confirmation to the choice grade nor the high dressing percentage yield. The Brysons had fed cattle on their ranch in self-feeders for years and sold to the small local packers I have wrote about. As the small packers went out of business one by one, they decided they should feed with us. As a commercial feedyard we had access to the regional and national outlets they lacked. The whole Bryson family have been friends over the years. We got along with their cattle for several years and they did well. We valued their choosing us for feeding their cattle. As the markets continued to change and concentration among packers increased, it became harder and harder to sell their type of cattle for the value we had been accustomed to. We had always got the top live price for their cattle, but it was becoming increasing hard to do this. To try to get more choice and yield in the cattle, I fed them another two-weeks longer than we had been. This added to the cost of gain to produce the pounds of beef as cattle are not very efficient in their weight gain in the final days of finishing. We were now selling to only a handful of packers and most went to IBP, the industry giant with a packing-house in Emporia, Kansas, which was the closest major packer to us. I had decided it was in our and our customers' best interest to cater to IBP. I had read quite abit about the "Deeming Theory" and decided that we should do our best to serve IBP and felt in the end they would serve our needs well. I will talk more about this in a later chapter. Larry Haley, the IBP buyer, and I got along well. He was harder than nails to trade with, but we got the job done and in the end both of us had done our job. Many of our locals such as the Brysons did not think Larry was treating them right because they had not gotten along selling to him at their home place. I had learned how to trade with Larry and felt he did his best with the orders his boss gave him to trade. I was several years ahead of most in the industry in selling cattle more for their value instead of all classes and kinds of cattle at the same live price. This helped some of our customers get premiums for their choice cattle, but also made cattle like the Brysons fed sell at a slight discount. I encouraged Ronald and Glen to buy better cattle, but they liked their old plan. In the end, they quit feeding with us and went to another lot. Soon most lots were having the same troubles we were having selling the "near beer" cattle and they got into a bad market time and lost quite a bit of money. Ronald and Glen quit feeding cattle altogether and instead sold their feeder cattle off grass for someone else to feed. Ronald's health failed and he died. Glen has ended up renting their pastures out and took a job at the local coop.

I wished they had followed my suggestions and changed the type of cattle they handled. In the final years of feeding with us, I am sure I did not do as good a job of selling as the lots that sold all cattle at the time for the same money. I also made their cost of gain higher than some lots trying to make their cattle better by feeding longer. The path I took with our customers was not wrong. I got premiums for the choice cattle many times when other feedlots did not. My program just did not work well with the type of animal the Brysons wanted to buy. They stayed with me longer than they probably should have if they were not going to change the type of cattle they handled. We never had a cross word, but one-day they started sending their cattle elsewhere. Like many of us, they probably did not want to face us as much since they were not feeding here so they quit buying the cattle working supplies from us that had been so common for many years in our retail store located in the office at the feedlot. This did hurt me. We still had good prices and good service on these products. The Brysons' son-in-law was my truck driver and his job depended upon our success or failure. I never said anything, but just smiled when we met at some function. I wish I could have done a better job on their cattle, but times were changing and I was trying to be a leader in this change to survive ourselves.

In Chapter Two I told of many of the customers in my early years. I will not repeat those stories here. I will add to Stu Parker's story. Stu continued to feed cattle with us until his retirement. He grew his operation and fed over a thousand cattle at one time for many years with us. He also for a few years fed several cattle with the National Farms Feedlot in Parsons, Kansas. Judd Lackey was the manager at National and had a low interest finance plan for both the cattle and feed for a few years. Stu took advantage of this low interest rate which was cheaper than his bank offered to expand his feeding for a few years until health problems slowed him down some. Stu lived only about five miles from our feedyard and came by often to visit and check out the markets on our wire service. We often would go to lunch together. In 1986 after my Dad's death, Stu was one of the few locals who continued to feed with me. Dad died during the time of the bad markets associated with the Dairy Buyout of 1986. Many of the locals quit feeding because of the market volatile and losses they incurred during this time. Others I felt left because they did not have the trust and confidence in me that they had in my father. I had been pretty much running things for the last several years, but I am sure not all customers knew or realized this. I am sure I was also overly sensitive to the locals leaving me. We had been held in awe by our peers for years when we would tell the other feedlot owners that most of our customers were local. They would nearly all say that their locals fed elsewhere and that their customers came from a distance. My rebuilding after 1986 would find me in this position. Most customers from 1986 forward came from all over Eastern Oklahoma and Kansas, but also all of Missouri, Arkansas, Georgia, Tennessee, Kentucky, Illinois, Indiana, Florida, South Carolina, Virginia, Louisiana, and Mississippi. I enjoyed these new customers from afar and they gave a great satisfaction in being "my" customer and I had earned their business. Stu was still the favorite because he was the one who stood by me when many left. He always had the confidence in what I did with his cattle and how I fed and sold them. Even after he retired he would come by to visit and have lunch. I teased him about being my "shrink" when things were going badly. He never offered advice except to bolster my confidence in how good I was at adapting and handling whatever situation threw my way. Many a time Stu would tell me how I needed to be taking notes for a future book on my episodes I was encountering in my business life. I never took the notes, but how I wish I had. I have always remembered Stu's encouragement to write this book. I wish he were still here to read the finished product. Stu is a good example of how to mix friends and business. Sure, there are times and friendships hurt by doing business together. We however have had many a good time with a customer. We have, after all, very much in common enjoying the ups and sharing the disappointments of the downs of the markets.

One customer in the seventies was a local funeral director, Jack Luginbuel. We very promptly took to calling Jack "Luginbaum" instead of Luginbuel for his profession. Jack is a very successful funeral home operator to this day with multiple locations. He still works many of the funerals himself along side his staff and does a good job in his profession. He was not so adept at cattle feeding. It seemed he always wanted to buy in when cattle prices were high and most of the time ready to go down and thus incur a loss. When cattle were cheap he never wanted to buy in and of course these were usually the times to be buying. A good case of being in when he ought to be out and being out when he ought to be in. Many people in our financial stock markets seem to play this game. When the financial stock market is high everyone rushes to get in, but when the market goes south no one wants in. Anyway, Jack decided cattle feeding was not for him and quit. He knew his business but not ours. Probably a good lesson to be learned here. Nothing wrong with venturing out into something else, but usually our best success will be in what we know something about.

I have told of the fast paced markets by the nineties. We often only had fifteen or twenty minutes during the week to sell our finished cattle. We never knew when this short window of time would come and we had to be ready. I always told our customers that they had to give me permission to sell without notifying them or be readily accessible at all times of the day when I could get a bid. One customer was an Amish gentleman from Pryor, about fifty miles away. The Amish did not believe in having telephones in their homes. When Mr. Yoder brought his cattle in to be fed, I ask him how I should contact him when sale day and a good bid came. He promptly said to write him a letter with the bid price. He did not understand we did not have this luxury of time. I knew about when the cattle would be ready and told him to come up or get to a phone and call me on the date I gave him. I said that we would then have an idea of the markets and he would have to give me some input on his feeling for the market and then give me the latitude to sell his cattle without getting in touch with him. This plan worked and we got along fine.

Another customer, Lennie was a nurse anthesologist at a hospital in Kentucky. He liked to be called with every bid and I always caught up with him without any problems. I did not realize for a very long time that many of my calls were took while in the operating room. He would monitor the patient and talk the markets with me at the same time.

Another, Doctor Mings, was a surgeon in an Arkansas hospital. He loved the cattle and ranching business and spent all his free minutes thinking cattle. I also called "Doc" with every bid. Again, I did not realize that many times we were talking while he operated. When I found out that some of these calls came during a patient's operation I always hoped I didn't cause a slip of the knife if I gave a bad market report or bid. These men were professional and never talked long nor I am sure ever took their eye off the patient and what was happening to them. Doctor Mings fed for several years in the late eighties and early nineties. At one time he told me after about four years of feeding in the late eighties that he had not made a great deal of money. He always hedged his cattle and it seemed his hedging losses were over riding the cattle profits during those years. I fed about the same number of cattle as "Doc" did in those years personally and they were the best profit years of my career. Price protection by hedging is taught by many and encouraged by many bankers. In reality in my career I have seen very few successful in their hedging program. Today, with the market volatility we see, we probably need some form of price protection in place. However, this needs to be studied just as hard as the care and buying of the cattle themselves needs to be.

Carroll Meeks was a cattle buyer and ran a local sale in Wister, Oklahoma, for many years for his brother, Wayne who owned the sale barn. Carroll loved to buy plain cattle to feed. He was a master at buying some of the ugliest cattle. Unlike most men who bought these type of cattle, Carroll knew which ones had enough age to help them grade better than calves without being too old to fit the choice grade. They never had the confirmation to yield or dress a high percentage, but when we sold the plain cattle on the rail they often brought back as much as a seemingly choice pen. Sometimes it seemed there was not justice for this, but Carroll had found a niche in feeding and mastered something many tried and failed at. Carroll was good to me and sent me many customers from his area of the state. One time on one of my airplane trips soliciting cattle I stopped over to Wister. Carroll met me at the airport and showed me around the area the entire day all just to be nice to me. We stopped for lunch at an old place far from town known as the Taylor Inn. In Bob Wills of country music fame in the forties, the Taylor Inn had been a dance hall played at by Wills and his band. There were many pictures around the hall of the Wills band. There was a convenience store of such in one side of the front of the old, now run down inn. On the other side was a café. Two men ran the café. We did not get a menu or see a price board on the wall. Carroll told the owner we would have a T-bone steak. I always figured he priced the meals according to how you looked. I was the stranger and the one buying, so I am sure the price was raised. It was good and quite an experience to remember.

Carroll took me up on the top of a mountain to Jimmy Alford's place. Jimmy also fed with us. We hauled his cattle to the feedlot and I now saw why my driver had such a hard time getting to this place. Jimmy raised sheep and cattle on his ranch. He was quite a character in his own right. His pens would have cattle of all ages, sizes, kind, and qualities. It almost looked like a zoo pen. We sorted and sold on Jimmy's pens for quite awhile before all would be gone in contrast to most feeders that had cattle pretty similar and would finish at the same time and be sold together. Jimmy fed some cattle in his name, some his wife's, and some in his wife's mother's name. I never was for sure just what he was doing. He also liked to partner once in awhile with some pretty shady characters.

Larry Reed was my auctioneer friend. He had persuaded Stu to get me started to attending the weekly sale in Nevada, Missouri. He also worked the Thursday sale in our hometown. I attended Larry's home sale every Saturday for years. In was a small hole in the wall type sale barn, but Larry and the Scottens who owned the barn worked the country and built up their trade. I would get a semi load of cattle by buying four or five different kinds or weights of cattle and track them on different buy numbers and turn them out in one of our pastures till I got a pen full of the same thing. I was a good buyer to have for this type of sale. Larry started putting together Jersey cattle to feed at the sales he worked. Jerseys are a dairy breed and not too popular in beef circles. Very few came through the sales, but what did went cheap. Soon we were calling Larry "Coronal Jersey" after his now regular buying of all the Jersey steers that would come through the sale. He would only get three or four at each sale, but when he got forty or fifty together he sent them to me to feed. In those days, we could get by feeding some of these types and Larry made money. Larry for some reason had always seemed to get into financial hot water every few years. I don't know why, he seemed to live a simple life except for a love of owning a race horse. I suspect that he could never afford to play in this high stakes, high roller game and probably it cost him too much of his income and thus was his downfall. This is just speculation on my part. He had a girlfriend Pat during the nineties that also worked in the office at the sale. Pat was good for Larry and I think would have helped him so much on his finances, but it was not to be. Before they could be married, Pat developed a heart ailment and died in her forties. I felt so sorry for my friend. A nice funeral for Pat was held and her kids treated Larry liked family. In a couple of years, Larry was back in financial trouble and gave some hot checks to some other sale barns. I had let Larry buy me cattle on commission and he always did me a good job. No one knows or remembers cattle as well as Larry does. When his problems caused his downfall, Larry never ask me for help or leaned on me for money. I appreciated this friend who treated me right, but did not ask for money to right his wrongs. I don't know if all the checks ever got made good or not, but I suspect not. Larry dropped out of the cattle circles for several years, but always sent me a Christmas card. I missed my friend and wished things would have turned out better for him. I would hear someone tell of him once in awhile. He was working car auctions and estate sales. About five years later, I got a call one-day from Larry. He had a new job back at the old former sale barn as the auctioneer. The new barn operator was the Walrods who formerly had operated a sale at Ft. Scott, Kansas, near by the Nevada barn. Ft. Scott had been a big sale barn before the Walrods went broke. I suspect that they had a bad habit of guaranteeing the people who brought cattle to their sale more than the market would bring. They thus would incur loses on cattle sold for other people instead of the commission profit they should have been getting. They would do this to get more numbers to their barn in a highly competitive business. Larry ask if I would come back to Nevada again to buy cattle. I had quit several years before when my health would not allow such a long schedule of working ten to twelve hours a day Monday through Friday at the feedlot and then spending ten or twelve hours on the road and in the sale on Saturday only to be back to the feedyard early Sunday morning before Church to check my Saturday buy and help take care of our cattle on feed. I told Larry I would be there. He had been good to me and bought me many cattle that worked well in my own feeding program before he got into trouble and had to quit buying. I had not seen Larry in years and looked forward to catching up with my old friend. I went early to the Saturday sale to visit a minute. I hardly knew my old friend. He had always been quite large and now had lost at least 150 pounds. He looked somewhat hard, but I was glad the weight was off. His voice had lost the old sparkle that first sale, but it grew better each week. I was getting some good buys again and enjoying the old hole in the wall sale. The people of the area that came to the sale each week seemed almost the same as the last time

I had been there thirteen or fourteen years before. Of course some looked older, as I'm sure I did. I appreciated many coming by and welcoming me back and asking how I had been. I probably had given too much for their cattle was the reason they remembered me, but I think not. They are a good set of rural Missouri people. Dale Snead the young boy who used to set by me every Saturday while his mother clerked the sale and would go get us a soda when I would buy us both one was now grown and in charge of the back end of the sale barn. It was like old home week all over. I went to the sale again every Saturday and enjoyed it very much. I had more time to do so now. Alas, it only lasted about four months. It seems that the Walrods were back to the price guaranteeing that had got them in trouble before. They lost the barn and Larry lost his job. Together they had been building the sale up and Larry was getting his old steam back every week. I am not sure what friend Larry is doing now, but I am sure we will cross paths again. I take him for what he is and enjoy calling him my friend.

Another customer whose name I cannot remember, but the story is so fresh in my mind. Our customer development program was working and we gained many new customers during these years. This one account called as many did and wanted me to visit their ranch at Wilburton, Oklahoma. I normally did not have the time to visit each customer's ranch, but should have. I made time to fly my airplane to Wilburton where my contact, the ranch foreman, met me. He showed me the entire large ranch with so many fine cattle grazing the lush grass. I could not help but notice a large number of operating natural gas wells. I thought this will be one great customer. Nice cattle and the income from the gas wells will give him staying power if we encountered a bad cattle market. He liked my pitch and soon had the first of what was to be many loads of cattle in our feedlot. Before the next load could be delivered I received a phone call from the local law enforcement. The story that unfolded was just unbelievable, but sadly true. It seems the foreman's sister had gone to the local nursing home where the now senile ranch owner was a patient. He had no close living relatives. A niece and a nephew in Texas had not paid any attention to their uncle until somehow they found out of the woman's scheme she almost pulled off. She checked the ranch owner out of the nursing home and talked him into marrying her. After the quick marriage he was taken back to the nursing home. The lady moved into his ranch home and with her brother as foreman started managing the ranch as if it really was hers. The court directed us to make the cattle check when sold less feed expenses to the court while they determined that the niece and nephew would get control of the estate. My great new customer blew up with only one load fed. Quite a story of how the woman schemed her way to the marriage.

I fed several pens for Lawton Branscum. We always got along good and I thought we did a good job for him. He started doing less and less business with us. One day he told me how he had found this small farmer feeder in Northwest Kansas who would guarantee this cost of gain for the cattle at a price I knew we could never compete with. We also knew that you cannot guarantee cost of gain. There are just too many variables in weather and type and quality of cattle to do so. Those who do always end up broke in the end. You have heard said what sounds too good to be true usually is not. That was the case here. The Kansas people fed several pens for Lawton and he got along fine. He sent more and more loads of cattle to feed with them. I don't know if they were baiting him or went broke on the guaranteed cost of gain. Anyway in the end he had over a million dollars worth of cattle on feed with them and one day he quit getting checks for cattle sold. He went to check things out and found all his cattle gone. Lawton lost over a million dollars. The people had done fraudulent dealing with him, but he never got his money and it broke an old man who had been a success in the lumber business in his younger days. I felt sorry for him falling into this trap. I felt no good, that I had told him the deal was too good to be true. His sons later fed cattle again with me, but Lawton fell into ill health and died.

The Daniel family of Greenfield, Missouri ,were good customers and became good friends. We fed several pens for the family Charles and his wife, sons Chuck, Chris, and their families and Chuck's son Scott. When they bought a couple of cattle trucks and I had sold mine, I used them for several loads of hauling. They also bought equipment when I retired. Just good hard working people and a joy to work for. We always enjoyed and appreciated these type of customers.

My neighbor, friend, and customer Jim Linthicum is known far and wide for his work in breeding, selling, showing, and judging Limousin cattle. If I were in Kentucky or Tennessee, or wherever someone would always ask when they found out I was from Welch if I knew Jimmy Linthicum of the JCL Cattle Co. Jimmy was a wonderful neighbor for twenty-five years or so until we moved. We would feed several of his bulls each year in our bull development program. Jimmy is always happy as can be and has a grin a mile wide. Jimmy has accomplished so much in the cattle industry while dealing with a handicap of not being able to hear or speak. His handicap would keep many people from doing anything, but not Jimmy. He can write a note five miles a minute as neat as can be. We love to sit and visit with each other. Jim is always up on all the current happenings in the cattle industry. Remember Jim the next time you think you have a handicap and how he deals with his. A good lesson for all.

Sometimes people fool you. Bill Henson was one of those kind of guys. He was always great to visit with and work for, but for the longest time I did not think he had a clue about the cattle business and agriculture in general. He bought sorry, plain type of cattle. They did not do or sell real well. Unlike, Carroll Meeks plain cattle, Bill's did not upgrade to a better quality. Bill was divorced when I first met him, but dating a nice lady who had some money to invest on her own. Bill got her involved in some cattle at one of the times the market did not work out and she lost money. I figured that would end that romance, but it did not and they later married. I don't think the Mrs. ever fed but the one set though. I watched Bill over about fifteen years. He bought a couple of ranches a few miles from Welch when land was at rock bottom price after the land price bust in the eighties. He later sold this land at a handsome profit and kept on ranching at his home base a hundred miles away. I noticed that Bill seemed to always have several pens on feed when the market was good at selling time and in turn had few on feed when the prices had gone scour. At first I laid this to lady luck, but after many years of watching Bill figured out just how good his cattle market judgment was. Bill is a real keen buyer and knows just when to be in and when to be out. Few people master this judgment.

Lost Creek Ranch is owned by Jim and Sara Beck and were good customers. When we first met, Jim was Dr. Beck, M.D., and owned a practice in Scottsdale, Arizona. He was trying to run the family ranch he had inherited from his father located just outside of Senaca, Missouri. He would fly back and forth between Arizona and Missouri every few weeks to check on his hired staff at the ranch. He often would be so tired he would fall asleep just sitting in his chair waiting to see me. You could tell he was both overworked and overextended trying to manage the ranch from a distance. He longed to be back at the ranch full time and one day did just that. He gave up a good medical practice and its good income for the uncertainties of a ranch life. He poured his heart and sole into digging postholes and painting fence and breeding good cattle. I always thought he would return to the better paying medical life, but he has not in at least fifteen years, so I now doubt that he ever will. He made a big life changing decision that seems to have been just what he wanted. He seems rested and fresh now when we meet and I think he is very happy with his choice. I am sure he spent many a night wrestling with his big decision. It sure appears he came up with the right answer. Happiness is the best and most important part of career success.

Duane Pemberton was a large cattle buyer and fed in several different feedlots. He treated me all right, but it seemed he was always somewhat gruff with my staff. Duane had financed a pen of cattle at a local bank where we had helped arrange financing. When one of his pens was sold we were to take the check to the local bank and they would pay off his note and send him the rest. One time, our staff messed up and mailed the entire check to Duane up in Missouri where he lived. It was an honest mistake that all of us make from time to time. Both Duane and his wife got on the phone with one of the ladies in my office and proceeded to cuss them up one side and down the other. Diane passed them to Mike, my assistant manager. He could not make them happy either. Finally I got off another conversation and they passed them to me. I looked the situation over and told the

Pembertons we had screwed up. I also noticed that this was the last load of a multi-load pen and that their bank note had been paid off with the previous load. All we had to do was get the bank name off the check so that they could cash it at their hometown bank in Missouri. They thought they would have to mail it back to us and be without the money for a week while the check was going back and forth. I told them I thought I could get the mistake straightened out and have them their money in a few minutes. I called the local bank and told them our problem. They knew they had their note paid, so they just faxed a release to the Pembertons' home bank allowing them to cash the check without the bank's counter signature. Jim Shelton from the local bank called and explained the deal to the Missouri banker in addition to his faxed release. In less than fifteen minutes, our mistake was corrected and the Pembertons had full use of their money.

Moral to this story is we all will make a mistake or two or several over time. It is how we correct them that makes the difference. Also, remember do not throw a fit until someone has a chance to right his wrong. One night we were having a company employee party at our home. The phone rang and I answered. It was Duane Pemberton and he had a load of cattle he wanted me to partner on and feed with us. I had never partnered with Duane, but decided to this time. I told our crew of my call and decision to partner with Duane. They all roared back at me, "Why in the world would you do business with this guy who just cussed us out so bad a few short days ago?" I said he just makes you appreciate our good, nice customers all the more. We got along fine with the Pembertons after this. They had just been short of money, probably had some new cattle to pay for and needed their money and thought they were going to be without it or have a bad check out. We showed them how we corrected our mistakes and while they never told us of any sorrow in their heart over the way they reacted, they did treat us nice on all future deals. We had made a good business point with the Pembertons and they showed their confidence by sending more cattle. Taking care of the customer is of utmost importance in business.

Bill and John Strom were another father son team who fed for many years with us. I always appreciated their loyalty. John fed some cattle he grazed in partnership at other feedlots to get along with his partner, but Bill and John always fed their home raised calves with us. They would listen to suggestions of improvement that we would hear from our buyers and ran a good operation. Sometimes they would send their calves to us unweaned and we would have more trouble with these calves than their weaned ones. They were limited on space and labor, so we would wean the calves as an additional service to the Stroms as well as several other customers. They knew the unweaned calves would not perform as well as the weaned ones, but it fit their program where little outside labor was hired. One day I was on the phone when a load of their calves arrived. The first one off the truck was a big, long horned steer. I thought what is this and nearly dropped the phone. My next call was Bill calling to tell me of his pet, home-raised longhorn he had on the ranch for seven years. He wanted to feed the steer with his calves and when he was finished would butcher the steer for his freezer meat at home and have the head mounted to hang on the wall. Sounded like a good plan to me. The only hitch came when the time came to mount the steer head, Nancy, Bill's wife, said it wasn't going to hang in her living room. We all laughed and Bill ask if I would want the mounted longhorn. I jumped at the chance. I had always wanted one for my office. The only requirement was to be that if Bill ever got a family room he could come and get the steer for his own wall. About five years after this arrangement, I got a call from Bill asking if I remembered the deal. Of course I did, and when I learned his long wanted family room was now a reality he was ready to come get the steer. Fortunately for me, not long after Bill's steer came to our lot, a trader had bought a steer nearly as big and with a good set of horns to be fed. When his selling time came, I sold the steer to a locker plant friend and bought the head from him and had it mounted by the same people who did Bill's. I had this steer in my home, so it was not the end of the world to give back the other. The Stroms invited me to their fiftieth wedding anniversary after I had closed the feedlot. I went to their ranch home for the first time for this party. I had a good time with my old friends and got to see my mounted longhorn in his rightful place in Bill's family room over looking a pretty valley. I was always too busy too visit our customer's ranches, but I realize now I should have made time to do so. With over 150 customers feeding at any one time and probably close to another hundred not feeding all at the same time it was hard to have the time to visit each one over close to one half of the country. I did not get away over three or four days at a time at most and these trips were few and far between. I am sure by visiting the customer, I would have forged even greater relationships with our customers.

Everett Swafford was a customer that came to us through a friend in deep Arkansas years ago. Everett was a hard working man who raised cattle and hogs on a farm way back in the hills of Arkansas. He rarely left the farm. Everett fed with us for at least seventeen years. Most of this time he had two or three pens on feed at any one time. The sad part of this wonderful customer is that we never met in person. We talked on the phone and knew each other well enough that if I had a good bid on his cattle and could not find him, I just went ahead and sold the cattle. One weekend Dee Ann and I went to Branson, Missouri, for a break and get away. True to a cattlemen's holiday I got up on Saturday morning and told Dee Ann that I would like to drive down into Arkansas to Mountain Home where there was a Saturday cattle sale. We set off to Mountain Home and when we pulled into the sale parking lot and got out the first person we saw was Everett's son-in-law. I had met him once at a trade show and he had come by the feedlot once. I did not realize that Mountain Home was only about fifty miles from Everton, Arkansas, which was Everett's address. The son-in-law immediately recognized us and asked what we were doing in this part of the world. He said we must go by and see Everett. He told us it would be of no use to call as Everett would be out in the pasture, but to go by and we might find him. We got directions and after watching the sale a couple of hours set out to find Everett's farm. We found the turn and followed a long winding lane that I could tell would be very muddy and hard to travel on a wet day. After several miles at the dead-end of the road in a canyon was Everett's place. We found it, but did not find Everett. Everett's wife was home, but she suffered from memory loss and poor eyesight. She could not understand who I was, so I left and never found Everett. I called the next week and told Everett I was sorry I missed him and why I had not called ahead. We never met and he continued to feed until we closed. I learned about a year after our closing of Everett's passing while out in the pasture feeding his cows. He had his wife with him and apparently suffered a heart attack. Mrs. Swafford with her memory and sight problems could do nothing but sit in the pickup until several hours later their daughter missed them and went looking. She found Everett dead and her mother beside herself. I wish I had made the effort to have found this friend before it was too late. A good lesson to heed in life.

The Schwerins moved from Iowa to Arkansas several years ago and promptly started feeding cattle with us. At the time their girls were not in school. They became good customers and friends. Every year at Christmas we got a photo of the girls and a note telling about the girls' year in school. They are now finishing high school and we still look forward to the picture and note on their progress. Getting to know one's customer well makes for a better relationship, but also just makes work more fun. Our circle of friends has become so wide because we listen and talk to our customers. Not just their cattle business, but their family happy times if they want to share them with us.

Bill Stoner became a very good friend and a customer too. One of my biggest mistakes as I look back on my career occurred early on when Bill came to me in about 1987. He had been laid off from his excellent position with a manufacturing company in Miami through no fault of his own, but due to two sons of the owner coming into the business. They thought they knew it all and soon Bill's good judgment was making them look bad to their father. They set out to get rid of Bill and succeeded. The company under these boys went broke in a few short years. At one time it had been one of the most successful family owned businesses in the area. They even had some international connections. Poor judgment and a spoiled second generation have ruined many a business. Bill had a small cattle operation on the side and turned to it full time after he lost his nice position. Bill came to me to apply for a job as my assistant manager. I was just getting over the bad bank and knew I needed help, but had not as yet figured our just what I needed. I felt that with the

changes I could see coming to the industry that I should hire someone to compliment my skills, someone with experience with a number one feeding company. Someone younger than I that had some
experience with one of the top companies, but that would have more
energy than I and hopefully someone who would be with me a long
time and allow me someday to slow down and turn much of the
operation over to this person. Bill did not fit this mold. He is slightly older than me, had no feedlot experience, and could not bring the
new ideas I was seeking to the party. He was the kind of person, I
would learn through the years of doing business together that would
work his head off, be consistent, have progressive ideas, and study
every night on what would make a cattle operation better. He had
grown up locally and still lived here. The young men I hired seemed
to want to move on to something better or so perceived. Many such
as Mike did not have roots close by to keep their attention at our
location. Bill would have been my best choice, if I had only known
then what I know today. This is not to say, I did not make good
choices in my right hand men. I just had the best choice right under
my nose and did not realize it. There was nothing about Bill other
than being my age and lacking some depth of experience I thought I
needed at the time. There is no hard and fast rule to the age or experience or college degree of an employee. Sure, the degree and experience give you a heads up, but in the end, the person makes far
more difference in most businesses. Bill went on to feed cattle with
us and never mentioned any disappointment over not getting the job.
In Chapter 26 I will tell of my good bank partnership going scour.
The partners in this bank were cousins of Bill's. He saved my sanity during a very difficult time during my partner's betrayal by coming to my office one day for a long visit. He could tell the deal was
working on me and assured me I had done no wrong in what he
could see and too not let their actions get me down. He did all this
without slamming his cousins, but he sure helped me get my head
back on straight again. More details of this will come out in the
chapter dealing with this time. When I decided I had to shut the
feedyard down to save my health in 2001, Bill came into my office
again with a paper he prepared just for me. It read---

Good things don't last forever
I've heard it said time and again.
This may be true of Neill Feedlot
But not so for Joe Neill, as my friend.
God Bless you as you begin your new endeavor.
Thank you for being a good friend.
    Bill Stoner   May 10, 2001

It says it all. What a difference a friend can make. Here is my customer I am supposed to be serving and the man I turned my back on when he was seeking a job has now saved my sanity not once but twice. He turned a big corner for me on the bank partnership gone scour. Again, every time I get to feeling blue over closing my cattle operation I look on my wall at the above work of my friend, Bill and realize the good things do last. Business, fame, glory, power, and money can come and go, but how we treat our friends and the friendships we have are always there if we just cultivate our friendships. A good lesson for all to learn here.

Bill had a grandson who helped him a lot killed in a tragic accident. On his way to school he met a semi hauling a boat mold right at a railroad underpass. The mold was too tall, struck the railroad above, and fell on the car killing the grandson instantly. This devastated the entire Stoner family. Their faith in God got them through this difficult time. I went to see my friend Bill during this time, but felt like I was very inadequate in comforting him. My friend who had helped me so many times now needed the help, but I could not do the job as well as he did for me. This is an area I, as well as many others, need to work on.

We had many more customers who would be a good story in themselves, but I sure you have got the idea by now just how important relationships are both for family and business. Take the time to develop these relationships in your life.

The next chapter is a good time to stop and tell how important it is to have and cherish friends.

25

Cherish Friends

Today returning from a funeral for the father of my long time friend Pat Guest, I began thinking just how important friends are. Pat and I became good buddies in the first grade and have been friends for nearly fifty years now. We have shared ups and downs of a lifetime including the burial of both my parents and my older brother and today Pat's father, Dick. We, like all friends will neglect each other from time to time. Six months to sometimes a year have passed without contact and then we catch up. The important thing to remember is we always remember each other in time of need and enjoy the happy times such as a daughter's wedding. We all need a friend that is there through thick and thin.

The one thing I have always liked about small towns is the friends you have and cherish. So many of my city friends seem to have a host of business associates and casual friends, but most seem too busy in this fast paced world we live in today to really cultivate the true life long friend. Small town people are great at being there for each other in good and bad times. It has such a special meaning. We all need to find our special friends and then nourish the relationship no matter what. We may not always agree with the direction of life's choices take our friend, but unless they are really off the deep end, it is not our place to second guess these choices, but to support our friend. My friend, Pat, is a great CPA with his own company and very successful. Like all of us, he at times sees greener pastures and has tried side ventures with a quick lube venture that saw his partner rob the till. He spent months in England and most of a year in the Philippines on a project that apparently did not turn out as planned. I didn't ask and he didn't volunteer. He did not have to tell me these things to have my friendship.

When Pat's school days sweetheart and our life long friend, Fonna married we were so happy and enjoyed many a happy time together. Almost blew away in a tornado in Missouri during college days when we visited their mobile home. Alas their happiness did not last and the couple split. We never ask why, but continued to be a friend to both. When Pat found his second love, Janet, she became our friend too. Again, we have fun and enjoy each other's company. My friend is happy again and we are happy for him. We also have another great friend we would not have met, Janet.

When we were kids, Pat's father, Dick would help lead the Boy Scout Troop and was our Explorer Scoutmaster. Dee Ann reminded me of Mary, Pat's mother, telling her how she would devote special times to each child as they had eight. She would take one shopping with her and leave the rest with Dick or someone. If most of the kids were gone on a school outing or something and she just had a couple home for supper, she would fix bacon and tomato sandwiches or French fries, a treat that was hard to fix at one time for the tribe.

Take time to call one of your best friends today and tell them how much you have missed them and how much you appreciate their friendship. Like all good things in life we have to work to maintain our friendships.

Another long time friend, Bob Neil, and I have shared many a family outing. While friend Pat has always lived his adult life in the city several miles away, my friend Bob lived in the same town. Bob never could spell his last name, mine has two "l's" and his one. People have taken us for brothers and once a coworker of Bob's saw us walking down the street and ask Bob at work the next day if that was his boy he was walking with. I have never let him forget that one. When Bob and his wife Patricia's kids were growing up we went on many camping and canoeing trips as a family. We remember nonsense stories of burning the bacon over the campfire. We

borrowed a tent and went to set it up in the dark and could not figure out where all the poles went, so we left a couple off. We thought
we had a good spot away from the crowd in the campground. We
found out why the next morning when it rained and the water flowed
into the tent we had pitched in a swag. We got the tent wet and took
it home to hose it down to get it clean. We forgot to stake it down
properly and the wind came up and broke two poles. We learned a
good lesson in borrowing by the time we found two new tent poles.

Bob has many talents, including art. He painted me a large
landscape scene of a favorite location on our ranch. It hangs proud-
ly in our living room.

Bob worked for the telephone company for years until he could
take early retirement. He worked many a holiday and a lot of over
time. He also received six weeks vacation in his last years and did not
have any of the worries that go with running a small business. He
took early retirement when offered the opportunity and asks me what
I would think of his idea to put in an assisted living home for elderly
people in our little town. I looked at him and said, "You and Trisha
would really be good for the people that chose to have you help care
for them, it would be a great ministry, and the town certainly needs
such a facility." Then I said, "Do you know what you're getting yourself in for?" I never mentioned this again, but Bob laughed and said I
tried to warn him many a time. Like all small start up businesses, Bob
had to worry about his product, his client care, if the help would all
show up, and how to pay the bills when the facility was not full during the early years. Then to be successful and meet his clients needs
and to spread his overhead out enough, like many small businesses
he had to expand. This doubled the loan and many of the problems,
but it also solved some of the overhead problem and let each client
have a private room they wanted. It also brought more help problems,
larger payments and many other headaches.

Like many small business people, Bob and Patricia, jumped
into the business with all their vigor. They cooked, cleaned, and
hauled their clients to the doctor and then played games with the
rest of the residents. It was not an eight-hour job, like most small
businesses. They, unlike most of us though, had to be on call 24/7.

If the night girl didn't make it, you know who did. If a client got sick in the night, you know who was called to help. They did it all in great style. Their clients loved them and they provided a very needed service in the community, a ministry for the elderly, if you will. It took its toll on them both. You could see the sparkle leave their eyes. Like so many small business people they carried on, did well, made money, and the clients loved them. About ten years into the project they were approached about selling to a man that owned another facility. What an answer to their prayers. They were ready to retire again. The sale was made. Today, the sparkle is back in their eyes and they are having so much fun. Was it a wrong turn made when they set out in business for themselves. No, it was not. They did well and most importantly provided a much-needed service in town and for their clients. Were they glad to sell out? You bet they were. The town still has a needed facility and it probably would not have it if not for the hard work of my friends, the Neils. Business does not have to be our entire life, it can be a few chapters of a life with a new direction taken again. Life's choices are what it is all about.

My friend, Chane Duvall has also been a life long friend. We have always went to Church together and enjoyed many things together. Today, Chane is the church board chairman and takes the money to the bank. I pay the church bills. Once a month we get together and balance the books and get ready for the board meeting. Afterwards, we have our time together over dinner. We have a great chance to visit and talk over all the world's problems. Chane has spent thirty-seven years in the auto parts supply business. He started as the deliveryman fresh out of trade school for auto mechanics. Worked his way up to partner and finally owner of the store and later two more. He did well and knew his parts from A to Z frontward and backwards. It was good to him for years and he enjoyed it. Like many of us, though he tired of the pitfalls in business ownership and dealing with customer problems every day. After all, his customers were usually broke down when they came hunting parts. Chane was ready for a change. Was his career a waste, or should he have taken a different direction? No, he just needed a change after so many years in the same business. Some of us get a charge out of the same business for fifty years and some of us are ready for change after ten years or thirty-seven in Chane's case. Like most of us, Chane worried about getting out. What would he do to make a living until retirement age in eight years or so. It's hard to face change good or bad. The best answer I have found in these kind of life decisions is to just lay our problem or choice on the Lord. Ask in our prayers for help and guidance. I have found the Lord will lift my worries if I just turn these problems over to Him. I think Chane has and he has sold out to a long time employee and part owner. Does he have the answers to what is next, I don't think so, but he will be fine, because I know he trusts in the Lord. I have not asked, but I am sure my friend has asked for guidance from the Lord and he will receive the help he needs in making his next vocation choice.

My opposite sex friend, Billye, has been my friend for a lifetime also. We grew up a half block apart. Billye is four years older than me. We were not close as kids when that age difference is a lot, but in adulthood we have been friends forever. For years we lived across the way from each other. We spent many summer Sunday afternoons swimming in our pool with our kids. Billye is the nurse for our lifetime friend, Doctor Steve Grigsby. When I have a bad spell with my chronic fatigue syndrome, Billye gets me right in to Doctor Steve. She notices things about me and tells the doctor. On more than one occasion, I have had all the classic symptoms of a heart attack. Fortunately I have never had heart trouble, but Billye has came to the house at night or took me right in at the clinic to see for sure I am all right. I appreciate someone who will go the extra mile to see to my needs. Of course both, Doctor Steve and Nurse Billye will do the same for anyone and make us all feel special. Billye's place in life is serving others in their health needs with a compassion that is special, true, and sincere.

These are just a handful of the so many friends I am blessed with. As I say, you don't just get these kind of friends on any street corner. You have to work and cherish the friendship. We each have to do our part for the friendship to be so special. The blessings of these friendships are countless.

Make a resolution to do something for a friend of yours today. Your life will be richer as a result.

The following chapter deals with business friends who betrayed me. Take heed and a lesson from this chapter, but do not miss an opportunity because you are afraid of partnerships.

26

The Good Bank Partnership
Goes Sour

Owning a share of a community bank and serving on its board of directors is a natural side venture for many small business owners. Most small business owners, including myself, use a great deal of borrowed capital early on in their business life. A strong relationship with one's banker is necessary to have the mutual trust that each, the banker and the borrower, will serve the other's needs. Of course, the banker wants his principal and interest paid back on the terms agreed upon. The borrower needs someone who understands his business, cash flow needs, and capital requirements. In my case, the cattle business, I often would react to market opportunities and add rather suddenly to my cattle inventory. If I had to wait for a loan committee meeting to get additional funds, I might miss the buying opportunity. My banker always understood this need, we talked about an opportunity would arise unexpectedly in the cattle markets and I would need to be prepared.

Over the years you develop the trust with each other and many times when your banker is putting together a group to buy his bank or perhaps charter a new bank he will turn to his best and strongest borrowers to be partners and directors in the new bank venture. This is exactly how I got my start in banking. In chapter five I told you of acquiring some Welch State Bank stock in a trade for our first house we had recently completed. The stock at the time of our acquiring it had not changed much in price in years, was closely held with only twenty or so shareholders, and paid no dividends. I also knew it was owned by the larger Security Bank in Miami and thought there might be a day soon when the older owners of Security might sell the smaller Welch bank. About five years after our trade talk surfaced of a deal that would result in a local group buying the Welch bank from Security's owners. Welch State Bank's president, Charles Stoner, had been with the bank about twenty years and had guided the bank along a steady growth path. A new facility had been built in 1976 and the bank was in sound condition. Local directors of Welch State included my father, C.E. Neill, Jr. He had inherited stock in the bank from my mother's family. At one time, my Grandfather, H.B. Campbell had even been the president of the bank. This was many years before as Grandfather Campbell had died in his late forties when my own mother was only eight years old. Dad had also bought a few shares of stock from a local family. Bob Richardson served on the board and owned stock. Mr. Richardson had been in the propane gas business and later owned the lumberyard in Welch. He also owned land and other investments. Lloyd Cowgill owned the local grain elevator, which had an office next door east of the bank. Mr. Cowgill was the third local on the board and also a stockholder. President Stoner wanted to buy the bank solely by himself and his cousin, Arthur Cousatte. Art had worked at Security Bank almost as long as Charles had been at the Welch bank. Charles and Art thought their long time mentors and bosses, Mr. Burford, Wallace, and Owens owed them the exclusive right to buy if they could come up with the funds needed. John Burford and his partners John Wallace and Ben Owens felt the bank and community's interest might best be served with a broad-based ownership. I suspect that they knew that Stoner and Cousatte could not come up with the needed cash to buy on their own. Charles and Art tried to persuade their three local board members to buy into the new bank, but that controlling interest would be owned by Art and Charles. Bob, Lloyd, and my dad would not hear of this proposition. They wanted equal ownership by all, with no one person having controlling interest. As they put their plan together, it was decided they would need one more player to get enough stock of outside people involved. The two stockholders most likely to fill the bill of the one more player needed were myself and Jack Rorshaw, a Vinita attorney. Dad, of course was pulling for me, and most if not all the board did not really want to add anyone from Vinita to the Welch bank board. Still a few more shares of stock were needed, more than I owned. Our long time family friends, Arthur and Jewelle McAffrey, were rather elderly now and owned some stock in the bank which had been inherited. The stock was now worth $500 per share and they owned eighty shares. It had never paid any dividends to the McAffreys and now in 1981 if they sold their stock to me they could put the $40,000 in a bank CD and draw interest of about 12 percent. At their age this seemed like a good deal for them and at my age the stock purchase seemed to be a good investment for me. I thought the bank would do well and it has, however we found out later in the Miami National Bank that it certainly is not a cinch that all banks will survive and be a profitable investment. The McAffreys and I made our deal. This gave me the stock the group needed and I was added as the sixth investor and board member. Dad had told me that Charles and Art wanted the controlling interest before I was asked to join and that Bob, Lloyd, and himself had told them they would not allow this. This fact was never mentioned to me by either Charles or Art as I came into the group. I would only know fifteen years later of the intense hatred Charles harbored all these years over not having the controlling interest.

The six of us completed our buy of the bank and received all the proper approvals required by FDIC and Oklahoma State Banking Officials. The small bank held about twelve million dollars in deposits when we took over. Our group rarely differed on the direction the Bank took under Charles Stoner's leadership as both President and Chairman of the Board. Art Cousatte remained at Security Bank in his position as Vice President. This was a strange relationship for two now competing banks fifteen miles apart, but Security acted as our correspondent bank and held our bank stock loan. At our regular monthly board meetings we discussed the bank's loans and talked market strategy. We were a very good group. I stayed fairly quiet in the early days trying to learn my lesson on how to be a good bank director. The others, of course, had been directors for several years. Bob Richardson was a man I respected, but I had never known him as I got to in our board meetings. Bob would be quiet as we talked over a loan, but you could just see the wheels turning in his head about all the ramifications of the discussion and possible extension of credit if we were discussing a line over anyone officer's authority. When Bob had thought of all possible consequences, he would speak with a positive or negative comment along a different line than the rest of us ever thought of. I always appreciated his insight and direction.

Lloyd Cowgill was a nice gentleman and great to get along with. He did not add a lot of substance to the board, but was very amicable in whatever direction we took. Lloyd was in his early seventies when we bought the bank. He was a man who had owned and flown his own airplane until nearly seventy years of age. He worked out regularly and walked or jogged every day well into his seventies. He also loved to play golf and did so at every opportunity. I always have hoped I can be this active and full of life when I reach this stage of my life.

C.E. Neill, my father, was both passionate and firm. He usually went along with the prevailing thought, unless he saw a hole in our line of thinking and he would be as firm as needed to bring us back on track.

Art Cousatte offered insight to how things were done at the Security Bank and some extra expertise to the group. He rarely crossed Charles in his judgment of a loan decision. They were cousins that seemed more like brothers.

Charles Stoner led the group and did a good job in his management of the bank. Once in awhile a funny streak would come out of the blue from Charles and he would want to do some off the wall loan or a silly promotion. Charles could have a mean streak in him if he did not get his way, but this did not happen too often. The bank grew and prospered. The bank examiners always gave us a good report with few corrections to be done. We were proud of our bank and the management Charles provided.

I was the youngest and newest to banking circles, but I think I added a different prospective than the others and spoke my own mind in the discussions. I learned my role fairly quick and feel that I was a positive addition to our group.

Our group never had any big disagreements. We each spoke our thoughts and while we did not always vote the same on all issues, after the vote we went away with a concise direction to take. Charles received a salary comparable to other bank presidents of our size and also had full use of a bank owned automobile. The rest of the board received $300 per month as a director fee. We plowed profits into paying off our stock loan. We each had pledged our previously owned stock and used it as the down payment on the loan for the rest of the stock purchased from the Burford group. The one thing I had not considered in this banking transaction was that to fund our needed money to pay off our stock loan we had to declare dividends on the stock. Our stock dividend went to the loan payment, but for the twenty or so outside shareholders for the first time in their life began also receiving dividends. These outside shareholders received some nice dividends for quite some time. We bought out the small shareholders whenever we could and retired their stock to our holding company stock. Charles had the most stock in our group, but not control. Bob had the next largest amount, and then I. Dad came next, followed by Art and then Lloyd. I enjoyed this time of my life in banking very much.

Things did not stay the same for long. Our group owned the bank for about four years when in February 1986 Dad had his heart attack and died. I was immediately drawn into the Miami National Bank as told in Chapter 14. I ran the feedlot till noon and went to the Miami bank until late each night. On Welch bank board days or in times of special loan committee meetings I altered my schedule and attended the Welch meetings. Everything at Welch was still in good shape. Bob Richardson gave me a good sense of strength and unity to our board. I ask Charles for advice on how to get out of my situation in Miami. At one point when it was decided to try for an assisted buyout by a new group I asked Charles and Art to review our loans and we talked of the possibility of our Welch group trying to purchase the Miami bank through the FDIC assisted buyout program called a 13C. As bad as our bank was, I felt Charles and Art's assessment of the bank was much too harsh. I did not feel that the numbers they purposed would ever fly with the FDIC when the time would come. I had my own evaluation and the hired examination by Clayton Woodrum's Tulsa firm. I also had the opinion of Ron Watkins; our bad bank workout specialist who had been working with us for quite some time. My friend Pat Guest had also added his opinion. I felt that Ron, Clayton, Pat, and I had studied the situation to have a solid number on the losses. I did not want to force, nor would they have allowed me to, a bad deal on my partners at Welch, if they felt the numbers were different than our opinion. Art dreamed of owning a Miami connection and had we acquired this location he could have ran it. Charles and Art did not change their opinion on the numbers in the loss on the bad loans nor did I. The issue was not pushed by me. I certainly wanted our group to get the Miami bank, but not if my partners felt it was not a good deal for the Welch group. On the other hand our family was looking at a huge loss on Miami National and I needed to do what I felt was best for our family. I told Art and Charles and the rest of the Welch board I thought I needed to move on with another group that I felt would have a doable deal with FDIC and the National Bank Comptroller of Currency. I put the second group together and we bid a much higher number on the Miami bank than my Welch group felt comfortable with. I ask my Welch partners to out of respect for me, to stay out of the bidding since my new group was willing to bid higher. The Welch group bowed out and I thought we were all happy with the situation in all aspects of the way each of us handled our feelings and desires.

My new group came in second and thus did not get the Miami bank. I simply went back to running the feedlot and participating in my normal role at the Welch bank. Charles Stoner called me in one day and ask me if I intended to continue to operate the feedlot or sell it. I was now suffering from my chronic fatigue syndrome and he was wondering if I would sell the feedlot and want to work full time at the bank. I never knew what his true feelings on this were. Was he simply worried that one of the town's largest employers and the biggest draw for outside vendors and suppliers to come to town and stop at our cafés and gas stations would close. It doesn't take much to upset the economy of a 600-person town. Maybe he was worried over who might buy his interest in the bank out one day. Charles had most all of his assets tied up in his investment in the bank. He went through a time that I thought he was planning an early retirement and sale of his shares, but this never happened. He may have also just been having one of his soft spots at being nice and worried about me. This was my thought for years until I would one-day find out he always resented his perception of my making him and Art back off the Miami purchase pursuit.

Things leveled out and times got back to normal for a year or two. One partner, Bob Richardson, died. Our group lost a great thinker and ally. We bought Bob's stock for the group. I now owned Dad's stock and thirty-four percent of the bank. Charles decided he would like to sell a few of his shares to have some operating cash. As I had said, Charles owned a home and few acres, but the rest of his wealth was tied up pretty much in the bank stock. With the holding company buying a few shares, it would be a win-win situation for Charles. As the holding company note was paid off, Charles would gain value in his shares still owned as the rest of us would. Kind of like having your cake and eating it too. I did not care because Charles had done a grand job for our group. The bank had grown and prospered.

I had always in the back of my mind wondered if Charles would try to pull a fast one on me someday after Lloyd was gone. I hoped not and really did not think he would, but the inner feeling nagged at me. I would one day find out my feelings were justified. I told Charles that I thought while we were buying some of his shares, it would be a good time to do a buy/sell agreement with each other to have in place if ever needed. My main concern at the time was if something were to happen to me. I had always thought that my bank interest would be my best asset to pass on to daughter, Jodee when I died. I did not think Jodee would like or have the ability to run the feedlot, but I knew she had good judgment and would make an excellent bank director and investor. Charles's son James was the same age as Jodee and while they were not close, they were friends. I thought James and Jodee would be our next generation and good for the town of Welch. Jodee lived in Owasso at this time, but I always figured she would end up with Doug and her family somewhere closer to Welch. This, of course, did happen in a few years. Art had gone through a bitter divorce a few years earlier. His kids had suffered as a result as so often happens in divorce. They were having trouble and seemed to be unstable. This all takes me back to our buy/sell agreement. Charles would not agree to anything in a buy/sell agreement that would allow any of our kids to come into the group. At the time I thought this might be directed at Art's kids, but soon I would believe that this was his plan to get our family out of the bank. You see, Charles is a good banker and I rarely disagreed with his loans or plans. However, he did not ever like to have anyone want a different plan than his. He is a very self-centered man. I had overlooked this aspect of him, because it rarely mattered. I felt with the new revelation of how Charles felt about the second generation, I had little recourse but to have a buy/sell agreement. If something were to happen to me, I was now sure that Charles would force out my family at probably something less than a fair price. Art kept strangely quiet during all these discussions. Lloyd was in his eighties and while alert and in good health no longer added much to any discussion. We all signed the buy/sell formula agreement saying that upon any one of our death our stock must be sold to the holding company. I lost some of my sparkle for this investment this day. I felt I had to sign, but my dream for Jodee was now gone.

We bought the stock Charles wished to sell. I now owned about thirty-seven percent of the bank. Charles had thirty-one percent, Art owned twenty-four percent, and Lloyd about eight percent. I had the most shares, but not control. Art and Charles together could control and they always stood together. We went forward. Ernie Callison a long time vice president of the bank and a good friend of mine was added to the board. I liked having Ernie on the board, as we nearly always saw loans the same way. This would balance the board some. I soon found out how Charles could unleash his wrath on someone. If he disagreed with Ernie he would lash out at him to the point I wanted to hide under the table. This did not happen too often, but when it did it would be quite a scene. Charles liked to be in full control of his employees. I had seen some of his hostility on some of his women employees and did not like it. He was the president though and I did not believe in interference.

Welch was in bad need of some economic development and Charles proposed the bank paying Art as a vice president with the duties of economic development. It was a salary of only about $6,000 per year and Art would still work at Security Bank and do this in his off-hours. We tried over the years to get Art to join Welch full time, but he never would in the days I was involved. I cannot ever think of a time that I ever knew of a project Art worked on for Welch in his new part-time employment. I kept quiet, but it was apparent that the salary to Art was strictly a way to get him some more needed income that he did little to earn. It was not fair, but I did not want to rock the boat over such a small matter. It did start to show me just what kind of partners I was involved with.

In about 1994 or 95 Charles came to us with a plan to build on the bank building with some needed space, start a stock dividend program since we no longer owed on our bank stock and the dividend would go to each of us. He also wanted to pursue a branch bank in South Coffeyville or Miami. We had always been a very conservative group. This three-prong program would be much more aggressive than we had ever pursued. I agreed that I liked all three parts of the plan, but felt doing all three at one time was too fast for me. I told the group I would go along with any two of the three pieces at once, but not all three. I suggested doing two parts and when they were going well, go after the third leg. I, like anyone, would have liked to have received cash dividends, but I was not pushing for it. I had a good income and did not have to have the cash now. The building cost would come out of our available working cash, as would the branch. The money used for a building or branch would be money not available for loans and would impact our earnings to this extent of lost interest income. After my Miami experience, I wanted progress, but at a conservative pace. There just was no need to be this bold in this stage of any of our lives. Things just kind of set still for a long time with nothing happening on any of the three projects. The bank went on and was of course profitable.

I got my first of many surprises in the spring of 1996. Charles proposed that Dee Ann and I go with him and Barbara to New York City on vacation. We had taken several bank trips together and had fun as well as did bank business or learned in a school. However, we had never outside the bank socialized much together. I thought Charles is trying to make amends for the way he has treated me the last couple of years and immediately agreed to go. Soon, Art and his wife Vicki were included. The six of us spent several days in New York City taking in the sights and attending Broadway plays. We had a good time planning the trip and a grand time in New York City. I came home with a new respect for my partners after this June trip in 1996.

Charles's son James was a captain in the Army and ready to get out. He wanted to get a start in banking. Charles told me of his desire and I told him he needed to bring him in to our bank so that he would have some years before Charles's own retirement to teach James his own kind of banking. Charles did not agree with me and proceeded to try to get James a bank job with some of his friends in Tulsa banks. No one wanted to hire James, as they knew as soon as he was trained he would just quit and return to Welch. I had told Charles this and also said that when no one wanted to hire James and he came back to Welch on these terms he would feel like he was not worthy of the position but only getting it because of Dad. Charles shopped James at Tulsa anyway and brought him in only after he could find no one else to take him. What an injustice to the now former Army Captain. It appears to me that this injustice has hurt James's creditability

Our unspoken, but renewed good feeling by all in our partnership did not last long I am sad to say. The following October, I was speaking to my good friend and attorney, Dennis Watson about one of my personal business matters. During our conversation, Dennis made a comment about the Commerce Bank deal we were doing. A long silence on my end of the phone. Dennis realized that I knew nothing of a possible buy of the Commerce Bank. Charles and Art had gone to Dennis to do a contract on the possible buy of the Commerce Bank. Dennis thought it was for our group and that I knew of the deal. I did not. Charles and Art did not have the money to buy a bank without using our Welch Bank for the funds. They were planning to get the deal and shove it down my throat. They assumed I would be against the deal after our talks of the three-prong plan. We had also talked Commerce some over the years and while I did not say I would oppose the deal, I told everyone I thought a South Coffeyville, Oklahoma, or even an Owasso, Oklahoma would make more sense. Commerce joined Miami and like Miami had not grown nor done very well after the Goodrich closing in 1986. It was close enough to Welch that we had some customers from that area and I felt we would do better going to a growing area and have a more diverse loan portfolio.

Dennis made the contract for Art and Charles in their personal names with a clause that it could be transferred to the Welch Bank at Charles's urging. Hard feelings were abound now that my partner's betrayal was known. Dennis was in a hard spot. He did work for Art, Charles, and I individually and also was the bank's primary attorney. Dennis certainly did not want to hurt me and felt a special need to now inform me of what he thought I knew and did not. You cannot start to understand how I felt, finding out what my partners were planning from my friend and attorney by a pure accident. We never had ever disagreed on a point where stock ownership would override our individual votes. Lloyd was put in a spot. He really did not care what we did at this point. He was well into his eighties and just along for the ride. He would side with anything Charles said out of pure loyalty to the man who helped him with his affairs now.

I felt that our partnership was over if they were going to ram a deal of this magnitude down my throat. The bank was making money and I enjoyed being a part of the action. The bank is the center of activity in most small towns and it was in ours. However, I knew if I stayed now I would never have any say in anything again. Partners have to be above board at all times. Everyone needs to agree and plot the course together. We need to feel the right to say our mind, take a vote, and get along after. In this case, a vote was never even talked about. I was hurt and confused by my partner's actions.

I came to my senses and told Charles and Art that I would have no part of the Commerce Bank deal under the way they were doing things behind my back. I offered to sell my stock at the same formula they were buying the Commerce stock at. This was more than our buy/sell agreement, but I also knew our Welch bank would bring more than the Commerce Bank that was in some trouble and in a poor community. None the less, I figured this was my best way out. I did not want a big fight going on in our small town. Everyone including our bank employees would be hurt in a battle over the stock and its price. I told my partners the buy/sell price I would not agree to because it was not my choice to sell. They could drop Commerce and come to their senses or buy me out at the Commerce formula. They chose to buy me out at the Commerce formula.

This would take some time since I was the largest stockholder. The FDIC and State Banking Department would have to approve the sale. Art and Charles would have to line up funding to pay me. I insisted that the contract include that nothing would be done on the Commerce Bank until I was out. I was afraid that they might get the money for it, but not enough to buy me out and I would be stuck with my traitor partners. Dennis advised us to each get a new attorney without the conflicts of interest that existed with him. I told him I would just as soon he do the deal that I trusted him and knew he would point out the pros and cons of the contract. Charles and Art wanted this way also, so Dennis did our buyout contract.

I was crushed. I have never been through a divorce, but from what I have seen of others that have, I must have had the same hurt feelings, insecurities, and betrayed feelings. I did not sleep for weeks. I knew that I would see these guys around town at any major function. The local Lions Club was our civic club and many bank employees belonged. I had also for close to twenty-five years. I was to find I would never have a good time at Lions again as Charles tried to lead it just like he did the bank. At the next Lions Variety Show, James Stoner was the President of the Lions and in charge. He was supposed to be calling the shots, but it soon was shown that Charles, his father, would overrule James and see that it was ran his way. I seldom went back to Lions after that.

As soon as the deal was closed and I was paid, I proceeded to move our banking to Vinita. I would not do my personal banking with these kind of guys. I split my business between the two lead banks in Vinita as each owner did quite abit of business with me at the feedlot and our retail store. Moving the business required an extra trip of twenty-six miles round trip compared to six miles to Welch from our location. This added cost and took a considerable amount of time out of our workday. It still had to be done. I did not bad mouth my partners on the street nor try to get people doing business with them to change. I was hurt, but never showed it when most of my employees and even Jodee did not move their accounts. They probably would have if I had told the full story, but this was not my style.

The final blow came after a long talk with Charles Stoner. We closed on our deal and I had my money. I sat down in Charles's office and told him Welch was too small and life too short to let our differences show. I told him I would always speak to him on the street and try to be nice. We have both done this and several times we have sat at the same table in the local cafe at lunch when we happened in at the same time. However, the surprise of my visit that day with Charles was when I asked what went wrong. He proceed to tell me how he had never wanted the partnership back when I was brought in and had never gotten over it. Fifteen years later and the other original players mostly dead he would remind me how he was wronged. He also resented my not turning the bid process of Miami National over to him no matter what our family loss was or my thoughts in this regard. I had tried to be completely above board in this deal and not try to influence my partners into a deal they might later regret. It was apparent that Charles had no respect for what I had brought to the table in our fifteen-year partnership. He thought I was disagreeable and hard to get along with because I would not support his three-prong plan purposed. I could feel years of resentment toward me come out. I had sure mislead myself. My early suspicions I had felt after Dad's death about how fairly Charles would treat me or my family if something happened to me were right on target. I had decided otherwise many years before, but my first thoughts were the right ones.

I have often wondered what could have been done different. I wanted our partnership to work. I enjoyed my involvement and the bank's success. I tell this story at this stage only to point out there are times and situations we have little control of in our lives. If I had been any different, I would have not been needed. I would have only been a puppet on the Board. Other people's actions sometimes tell their true colors. We cannot change this. There is no use to be bitter or worry about what could have been. I see clearly now, things I would have overlooked before in the way these former partners operate their business for their good only. At least now I am not associated with their actions.

They have continued to be successful and even have their long wanted branch in Miami with Art at its helm. They have upset several people in our community over their high interest charges in a low interest time and a few have moved their accounts. The totals of the bank have grown in spite of this with growth from a large area of Northeast Oklahoma. I wish them well. I am glad I am out, but I still hurt every time I think about how I was treated.

I have always felt community banks best served their communities with a broad-based ownership. Too many owners can result in no one watching the store like our Miami Bank. Five to ten owners will give a bank more perspective and I feel the community will prosper more. One family today owns most all of the community banks in our area. It sure eliminates the problems I had, but I don't think any of the communities have done nearly as well as they would under multi-partner ownership. Just my thoughts.

In 2003 we sold our Welch property. I will tell more of this in a future chapter. However, we felt a need to change communities so as not to have to watch someone else operate our property when I could no longer. I think I could have overcome this as I had lived my entire fifty-four years in Welch. The big blow I could not overcome was my hurt over the bank deal. The bank is the center of all activity in such a small town and I no longer felt a part or comfortable going to a meeting on economic development at the bank where such meetings are usually held. With this feeling it was best for us to move and start over. Kind of like the divorced couple who move to a new town and start anew.

Partnerships can be good and bad. I have watched friends in such deals and it seems more end sadly than go forward with all happy and prosperous. Still, I would not be afraid to enter into another partnership again under the right circumstances. I feel that you cannot avoid things in life that might be grand because you are afraid of being hurt. This makes no sense. I am not sure this chapter makes sense either, but I wanted to explain my story of the pitfalls you can encounter even in long business associations. Just be aware and act accordingly. If you are a partner, remember for a successful partnership all partners have to give and take, speak and be heard, listen to the others. No one can just be a partner as a puppet. Compromise when not in full agreement. Things will be better in the long run. Be alert to all partners needs and concerns. Like marriage, partnerships must have give and take to succeed. Do not let past dealings cause hatred or taint your thinking for the future. Be alert to a partner's feelings as you would a spouse. Also, remember that if all the above is practiced by all the partnership should flourish. Sometimes, however, if one or more partners do not act as just stated the partnership may be doomed in spite of all you do. Then just exit the partnership as quickly as possible with the least damage to all, no matter who is right.

I believe one must forgive others who wrong us. I have truly forgiven these former partners and feel they are the ones who must live by their actions. I feel it is better to move on and live life to its fullest and for us to do what we can to live our four pillars of life. This may or may not mean a physical move of your home. If it helps to ease hurt and pain I think it is best to move rather than to let divisive feelings rob you of a fruitful life.

The next chapter deals with the true meaning of life. My four pillars of life to serve offer you the opportunity for true happiness and satisfaction in this life. Read this chapter closely.

Maranatha Bible Camp

27

Four Pillars of Life to Serve

I have always felt a strong responsibility to serve what I call my four pillars of life.

You see, I feel for all of as individuals to live a happy, satisfying life we need to give back to each of the four pillars. My four pillars of life service are:

1. Service to God
2. Service to Our Family
3. Service to Our Community
4. Service to Our Industry or Vocation

The number one priority in all our lives should be to honor and give glory to our Maker. We should give a portion of what God has blessed us with back to His Kingdom. This not only includes money, as you may have assumed, but also our time and talent. We all do not have the same abilities or talents. Some are ministers, some teachers, some singers with the powerful voice of a songbird, some offer skills in maintenance tasks or building new facilities. Still others may be good at asking neighbors and friends to attend and get involved. One may play a musical instrument or be able to pay the church bills. There is numerous ways we can serve the Lord and as in other walks of life, it is good we all are not good at or like the same tasks. All the above mentioned areas of service are, as well as others, needed and equal in the eyes of the Lord. It is important that we each find our area or areas we can serve in and fill this need. Service to God's Kingdom will be a good example for your family and build on the next pillar.

Our family can not be forgotten as we go about our fast paced life today. Many forget their loved ones and concentrate only on work at their family's expense. I have seen many wonder what happened to a once good marriage or why did a good child grow to be in the drug culture or get in with a group of thugs. We have to cultivate and work our family like a farmer growing his summer crop. We cannot half way do a seed bed, put in half the amount of seed needed, or neglect to take care of the crop when attacked by insects or grass. Our family is the same; we have to spend time to pass our values and wisdom on to our spouse and children. Family can be nurtured in many different ways. A combination of fun and work times is good when working on family relationships. I have written of the business trips that Jodee and I shared as she was growing up. I think each of these outings have as strong of a place in her heart as one of our fun outings camping on the river. We also enjoyed many family outings with our church family. Several times we would help sponsor a canoe trip for the youth and enjoy a family, church outing. So you cannot use the excuse of no time to do the four pillars. You just sometimes have to be creative in working work with family or family with Church, or family with a civic club project. With a little creative thinking, life can be built around the four pillars and still have time for each one on its own.

Service to our community is the third leg. This leg is much more important when you live in a rural town as our family did. The small town environment is great to raise families in, but with so few people to see to all the tasks that are needed to keep the small community and school going it takes all. Even in the cities, a different service may be needed, but to put down roots and feel a part of something, you have to be active and working to preserve a portion of your favorite project in the city. Neighborhood clubs for youth such as scouting programs give kids something to do besides watching television so much or hanging out at the mall all hours. The community big or small is only as good as the people who live in it. We are all needed to fill our space in an area we like and would want to serve in. Hospitals and nursing homes always need volunteers to help patients in small needs. Youth sports leagues need help in coaching and umpiring activities that help youth build their bodies and team spirit. Trash needs to be picked up along about any highway. Schools would love to have help with a special function or party. In a small town a service club like Lions is the life blood of many community projects. Communities also need help in economic and community development. Many towns plant flowers and do other clean up and beautification projects. The list is endless. I guarantee that you will feel the reward from helping your community prosper in the way that fits your interest and skill.

The fourth pillar is service to your vocation or industry. We all make our living in some economic sector. For our sector to prosper and grow for the succeeding generation we have to put some of our time and energy into seeing our industry grow and prosper not just for our own good, but for the sake of those who will follow us when our working days are over. This pillar is most important for self-employed people in different industries, but also applies to those who work for a wage in a particular industry. We cannot in the world we live today expect our vocation to be there tomorrow if we do not progress and change with the times, but also give direction, leadership, and servitude to the industry or association working on our behalf.

I have not been a shining success in my four pillars, but have tried to do my part. As example of what I am trying to get across to you I will outline a few of the different things I have served on in my work on the four pillars of life.

For church, I am not a singer, teacher, or musician. I am also not very good at fixing things. I can oversee projects and did oversee the building of a family life center our church congregation built in the late seventies. I used skills I learned acting as my own building contractor for our homes built and in our business to direct the different skilled craftsmen who worked on the building. I bought all the supplies and materials for the building using my negotiating skills learned first selling cars and later selling cattle. As I have said, I could sponsor and help the youth on a field trip such as canoeing. I am usually in on finding the minister or youth minister when we have needed someone. I saw as a youth what a life impression could be made on youth at a church camp experience. My job and later my illness would not permit me helping with the actual camp, but I have served on the camp board for the sixty some area churches that are associated with our local congregation. In my board role I can help direct policy that will affect the youth. I think I have played a large role in seeing a facility that can be used for all ages from the youth to the elderly. Just as in business, the church must have proper facilities to do its work. When I joined the camp board the finances were in terrible shape. I persuaded the rest of the board that it was better to charge another few dollars to our users to attend than to let the camp go under financially or not be able to build the needed facilities to accommodate a growing camp attendance. My philosophy was for our fees to cover operational costs of the camp such as the director's salary, insurance, maintenance, food cost, and other on going costs. We should raise capital funds from donations to build dorms, chapels, swimming and recreational facilities, and dining halls. We should work with our individual congregations to provide scholarships to those who can not otherwise afford to attend. I have received much satisfaction from seeing the growth of not just facilities, but most of all the Christian growth of all who are impacted by our Camp Maranatha. I have also served as a deacon and later as an elder of our local congregation. Since 1993 I have paid all the bills for the congregation. I see so many that are able to do so much more than I am, but then I remember it takes all of us doing our part to get all jobs done. More Churches need a Mike Harden or Marilyn Horner or Edna Duvall as ours has and I am sure you have in your church also. They seem to be the people that teach several classes, do maintenance work, or secretarial work for the Church. They seem to be involved in all areas. In spite of all these Mike, Marilyn, Edna types do, there is so many areas of service needed to make an impact of every age in the church family. You can be an inspiration and do your part also. Volunteer today, if you are not already doing so. Your life will be the richer for it.

I hope we have not neglected the money side of giving back to God. I will not boast of this or that we have given to the church. However, I will say we have tried to support the Lord and besides our regular church giving have tried to provide extras for Christian needs as we were blessed. Giving of our time, talents, and dollars are all part of what should be our number one pillar of life.

Family is a life time responsibility. A mate's interest and desires must be met to keep the kindle of love glowing for our lifetime. I think that most marriages are not as in TV, where everything is happy ever after. There will always be challenges and trying times. We will all have fights and disagreements or want to go a different direction than the other for our job, vacation, or just an outing. Life and marriage are a give and take. It has taken me several years to learn this. While learning this important task of life, I have suffered the downs and what ifs I am sure most marriages have. At the end of the day, though, we have to remember what drew us to our mate in the first place. My Dee Ann, is pretty much a free spirit, does as she likes without a care. She can be a bit scatterbrained and at times I question her good judgment such as the time she filled my diesel pickup with gasoline. Then I remember how she can have fun doing anything. We have enjoyed hours at different activities such as our early camping days to our mutual interest in flying our airplane for fun on a Sunday afternoon. She always supports my business decisions and is there to console me when I stumble or the Chronic Fatigue flares up. She was the one who took care of my Mother who had all the patience in the world but did not pass that trait on to me. I had so much trouble helping her when she could not walk or do things as fast as she once did. Dee Ann could spend all day or all week helping her and love every minute of it. We have tried to do special things for each other to show we care. At Christmas or for her Valentine Birthday I have always included some special intimate something to keep our flame lit. When it got too embarrassing for an old geezer to buy such products in the retail store I would turn to the Victoria's Secret catalog. They can have a place if used right in life for one's private relationship. We tried to do special things for our daughter, Jodee such as helping her restore her 1966 Mustang as a first car. We taught Jodee respect for others, the value of work, and the need to help others. Her kids and our grandkids now get much of our attention. I was at the hospital for Dakota's birth, calling to cancel a speaking engagement I was scheduled to be at when she was born early. Deonna was born almost on the way to the hospital, so I was not there till later in the day, but as fast as I was found and told we were off to see the new precious little one. Someone had to run the new hardware store that had just opened three days before Dejay was born. That was what I was asked to do and did. You can bet I did not linger long before off again to see the new addition.

For our community I have found different areas of service over the years. I was on the city council of our little town when I was twenty-two. I was president of the Jaycees in my mid twenties and about thirty when I became the president of the Lions Club. Of course other offices proceeded the build up the ladder to the head of Jaycees or Lions in Welch. Both clubs served many different projects for our community in my younger days. When we could not find enough young Jaycees we merged into the Lions and served there. Our Lions Club found the funds and built our local community building and oversees its use and upkeep. Over the years it built and maintained shelters at the local park and cemetery. For years the Lions, ran the summer youth league games. We worked with school officials on projects of mutual interest and the community and school uses the civic auditorium alike. Our local hospital board in Miami, Oklahoma has been a cause I have spent many hours on since about 1990. I have served as chairman of the hospital board. I think I was able to make a difference when a reorganization effort under new ownership and its management was having a difficult time. We can all add something to a community cause if we will only put in a little time and effort. It takes all of us pulling together to make a great community.

For my industry pillar I served as a director for our Oklahoma Cattlemen's Association. Later I served four years as the Northeast District Vice President. I was fortunate to serve this industry as president of the state cattlemen's association for two years. In this position, I served as one of our board members at the National

Cattlemen's Beef Association. At the Oklahoma Cattlemen's office I learned as President just how much time and personal sacrifice our OCA employees gave to our industry. Scott Dewald led a team with Steve McKinley as Operations Manager, A.J. Smith as editor of our association magazine, Michelle Wynn led the charge at our state capital as our lobbyist, and Terri managed the office and Kami the junior program. You can accomplish so much more when you have a team of people such as our OCA team just mentioned. These people give all for a industry they believe in. Our association leaders have done our industry well in putting this crew together and letting them do their jobs without wrongly placed pressures. I enjoyed my time of giving to the cattle industry with my OCA crew. I think I was able to make a difference to this staff and our industry during my term. I set out to serve and not only accomplished this, but was blessed with my new friendships and stronger ties to people like Stanley Barby, the president two terms before me. Stanley is a cowboy's cowboy and runs a first class operation about as far west in Oklahoma as you can go. While I lived as far east as you can go, I never knew Stanley very well until we worked together while he was the immediate past president and I was president elect. I learned to respect this cowboy for a sharp thinker and good businessman. I must admit I was disappointed when I was passed over for president when Stanley was elected. I sure learned a thing or two about life. Stanley was a great man and a great leader. I was honored to be selected later after Stanley had set the stage for some good years in the association. Sometimes it is easy to get caught up in ourselves and not realize how many good people are out there. I always got more out than I put in when I have served organizations such as OCA.

Time has also been spent working on national committees to preserve a court challenged beef checkoff. I have served on our state beef Council that promotes Beef in many different ways. I have served on the board of our state program for future agriculture leaders, called the Oklahoma Agricultural Leadership Program. I have served on the selection committee for the new Dean of Agricultural and Natural Sciences at Oklahoma State University. Numerous times I have worked on the State Extension Service for Agriculture advisory committees. I have had a goal to see an industry better than I have enjoyed for the next generation even though it does not appear any of that next generation of livestock producers will be from my family.

My examples of the four pillars of life are only the way I have seen service in my life. You will have different interest and abilities than I. We all can enrich our personal lives and be such a great example for our family by using our time and talent to further our four pillars of life. Remember to put God on top and to balance the other three in perspective. There will be times in our life where one pillar or the other will slow down somewhat, but do not neglect any one for long. We can get our life goals out of balance in a hurry by forgetting to do our part. I know your life will be enriched if you follow these four pillars. I certainly do not want to hold my blocks in my pillar up as anything special or to give you an impression of bragging on my own accomplishments. They are here merely to give you ideas of service and an impression of breadth in this service. We always will have excuses to not serve, but I have seen bed-ridden people write letters and address envelopes for the church. You can do something. I accomplished much of my pillar work while working and battling my ongoing battle of Chronic Fatigue Syndrome. Some say that health battle would have been served better by not being so involved in these outside work activities. I found that they were also needed to give me new perspective and direction in my personal life. My association with other volunteers has given me so much insight and new zest in my personal work. It will work for you too.

Start your own blocks today in your four pillars of life if you have not already done so. Your life will be filled with joy and satisfaction.

The next chapter deals with the loneliness you can experience in small business life. I have found that the answer to this feeling of being all alone in a giant fish bowl of business life is to engage your own board of directors to share your problems and goals with. The input and direction you receive from your board cannot be beat.

28

Your Board of Directors

Owning and managing a small business can at times seem to be a very lonely existence. Most small business owners wear many hats. They are in charge of policy, safety, government regulations, employee benefits such as health insurance, advertising, product quality and development, and cash flow of the business. Many times, If one is not careful, this seemingly endless list of duties can become overwhelming. There are so many areas of expertise you have to excel in. Some areas can be delegated, but most small business owners have to manage and execute the plans of most important areas. Small business does not have the luxury to have a position for each area for someone to concentrate his or her time and efforts on without interruption.

I feel very strongly that the only way to survive in this jungle is to have your own board of directors just as a large corporation has. Your board may not meet together and discuss all aspects of the business, although that might be a good approach in some instances. I developed my board to work with me in the areas of expertise I needed help in. Each consultant I chose for my board would help in their area during a scheduled time of the month. During this time, all energy would be devoted to that board member's area of expertise.

In our own cattle feedlot business my "board" included the banker, accountant, feed nutritionist, feed supplier, veterinarian, environmental engineer, attorney, cattle and grain price consultant, and a long range business planning consultant . I also use the state university extension service agent and the university consultants available. In the start up days and as long as one is borrowing capital the banker needs to be included on all business boards. I cannot remember during my own bank director times of ever foreclosing on a borrower that kept the bank apprised of the company situation good or bad. The borrow who sought council and talked in plain terms about the company cash flow, profits, and outlook was someone you knew could be trusted and was on top of things. If the company hit a hard spot, the banker knew why and what was happening to cause the downturn and the plan to restore profitability. In most all of these instances, the banker could arrange loan extensions to get his borrower through the tough times he was facing. The borrower who avoided the bank and did not level with his banker about cash flow problems and what actions were being taken to correct was almost always assumed to be out to beat the bank. These borrowers would face foreclosure as fast as possible because the bank had lost confidence in their borrower and felt they were out to beat them out of their borrowed money. Honesty and straightforwardness go a long way in getting through any tough situation.

The accountant is the next pillar on your board. Many years ago before I took over the full time management of our family business we were charging less than our cost for the feed and care of our customer's cattle. It took six months of losses before anything was noticed that something was wrong. We had a large cash flow of customer funds in and out of our account that made it hard to tell just how profitable we really were. When I took over one of the first things I initiated was monthly visits by our accountant to our business. We ran the books up on our computer with the accountant making monthly adjustments for accrual items such as depreciation. We knew exactly how we stood each month after this work up of our profit and loss statement. Before we had only worried about the total picture at year-end tax time or maybe at best once every six to nine months. The cost to do the monthly accounting was not much more than our old method because mistakes were found early on while fresh on our minds. We did not have to pay the accountant to back track information six months old that was found to be in error. Our monthly statement provided by my friend and accountant Gayle Edmondson gave me the up to date information I needed to manage the business. I knew what adjustments to our operations and charges needed to be made in a timely fashion. We would compare the monthly totals to the previous year. Sometimes we would have to watch an item for two or three months to get a firm handle on a trend, but not often. We usually were adjusting our business in a very timely fashion. I cannot over emphasize this basic element that most follow. However, you would be surprised at the number of business people who get so caught up running the business that they neglect the accounting books. If you fall in this latter category, now is the time to shapeup.

I used two accounting firms for the last fifteen years. This is a different approach than you might need or want. The Edmondson accounting firm specialized in income tax business accounting. On complex tax issues or estate tax planning I liked having two opinions to make sure we were doing the right thing to minimize taxes as well as remain legal. My old friend since grade school has an accounting practice in the city that does a considerable amount of audit work, estate planning, and complex tax issue questions. Pat would have done our entire accounting but we had used Gayle before Pat went out on his own. I have always tried to use my own rule to not change advisors, vendors, and contract workers just to be changing. I have to get better service, better price and equal service, or something better than I have currently to change. I do change just because someone else would like our business even if a friend. Pat's firm would not have been quite as effective as Gayle's on the day to day tax work. Gayle has more agriculture background tax experience and was closer to our office for the monthly visits. Pat added expertise where needed and gave a second opinion on complex issues. Neither felt threatened by the other and did not try to take the other's share of our business. We all worked as a team for my benefit. This is the way things should work.

In our own cattle feeding business, the rate of pounds gained per day and how much feed it took to produce a pound of gain on the animals in our care is a very complex issue. The feeding industry is very competitive and a cost per pound of gain even a dollar per hundred pounds gain was often too much. Our feed nutritionist would come monthly for a daylong visit to the feedyard. Cost of gain for pens of cattle closed out during the month were gone over very thoroughly. Feed samples were taken to verify our quality control on the feed ration mixes. The scales in the mill were checked against the scale on the feed truck and then the feed truck weighed on the truck scale to compare it. We could not afford to short change our customer on the feed purchase or give them too much feed for the amount charged. The pen and feed bunk conditions were checked. This would include spot checks of our cattle waterier for cleanliness. No detail was left out that might effect our weight gains. Over the years I worked with several good consultants. I seldom made a change if the consultant was doing his best and we worked well together, I stayed loyal to them. Many had to leave me over time because of changes in their careers or the territory they covered. These included Gary Tibbetts I spoke of earlier in the book. After Gary I used Steve Armbruster until his schedule prohibited him from continuing to work with us. Steve was one of the best in the business, but way overworked and overbooked. I would find that sometimes it is best to have a young, eager, up and comer who has time and is trying to make his mark rather than have the best that does not have the time to devote to you. I next worked with Lee Shell, who is also one of the best in the business. He was pulled out by Purina Mills who he worked for. Purina sent us Ron Scott a young up and comer who taught us many things as he himself learned the feedlot business on the job. Dr. Scott is now in charge of the Purina/Land of Lakes feed companies research department. Greg Catlett convinced us to try a new feeding regime developed by Purina called "Impact." We had no longer went on the "Impact" than my good friend Lee Shell, now on his own called and was available to come back as our consultant. This was a hard call. Lee was the best consultant we had ever had and now we could have him again. Greg was another young and up and coming feed program consultant. He had worked hard to win our account on the new Purina program. It would not have been fair to replace him without doing anything wrong. I explained this to Lee and I stayed with Greg until Purina pulled him out of our yard and replaced him with Tim Murphy. Tim was a lot like Greg and did well for us for a time until he left Purina and the consultant field. I then went back to Lee Shell and we worked together until we closed. I tell of these relationships to show you how much I value loyalty to our company and the good effort and work a consultant can provide your company. I think, in turn, one has to be loyal to those who are loyal to you.

Our principal feed supplement supplier sales representative would also see to quality control of his company product provided. He would make sure delivery of the feed and the condition the product was received in was up to standards. They also would gather data on our costs of gain and compare it against other feedyards they served without showing data from individual yards to another yard. They would also make us aware of trends in the feeding business. At least once a year they would host a meeting of their customers were we could visit about their service and talk one on one with others in the business. David Frieze won our account originally for Purina Mills and served our needs for a good time until promoted by Purina and moved away. John Mareth was another Purina rep that went up and beyond to do his best for us. He left Purina to start a new dream of owning his own ReMax real estate office. To supplement his income during the real estate agency start up phase, John joined the Army Reserves. He is very patriotic and wanted to serve, but it also met a financial need at the time. The only problem is he got called to active duty in the Iraq War. He willing went to serve his country, leaving his able wife Janet in charge of the real estate office and the couple's large family. Janet already worked alongside John in the business, but still has had to adjust to being the boss, only parent, and filling in all of John's other duties. I have a great respect and admiration for our troops and those who serve our Country's needs. Dr. Lee Dickerson was in charge of one of the areas we dealt with Purina. Lee helped Greg Catlett talk us in to going on the "Impact" feeding program. Before changing to "Impact" we fed a conventional Purina feed supplement program with a contract based on feed cost plus seventeen dollars a ton markup to cover their services and profit. The big deal stopper on "Impact" had gone on for quite some time over Purina's desire to have a free rein on what they charged us without us knowing their margin. This is fine in most instances, but I felt that if I were to go to an exclusive program that could not be shopped from time to time, I was opening myself up to price abuse in the future. This would end in a bad relationship for both my company and Purina. One night Drs. Lee and Greg along with John Mareth from Purina and Mike Day, Rick Rouse and myself from our company went out for dinner and to discuss how to get over our pricing impasse. On the way to dinner, things got pretty strained in our discussions. At the restaurant when it came my time to order, I ordered fried chicken. The only time I ever ordered chicken when out with beef people was if I was really mad. My crew knew this trait and shared with the Purina guys. It was a strained evening, but we finally agreed to try the program as presented by Purina complete with no price formulas. I never liked this aspect of the program but went on with our plans because I felt it would be best for our company and customers. To this day, I feel that Purina should have met us at some middle ground with a pricing formula. I lost a great deal of my respect for the company over this one thing.

The veterinarian would monitor our cattle health programs and recommend routine vaccination shots to be given to all arriving cattle for disease prevention. The doctor would also consult with the rancher customer at times if asked to do so and give them advice on how to prepare their cattle for shipment to us. Once in a while disease problems would pop up and the vet would give us a protocol of treatment to follow. He would guide us to proper withdrawal times before cattle harvest on any treatment drugs required. The veterinarian and nutritionist would also work together to coordinate their health and feed programs for best performance. We always used consultants that we knew and trusted. Our veterinarian worked with us for over twenty-five years. Dr. Roger Parker DVM is the son of my old friend and customer Stu Parker. Dr. Parker and I grew up together and he always had our best interest at heart. He also knew the economic side of the equation regarding how far to go on feeder cattle before the cost exceed the possible return on value from the animal. Someone who understands and knows your operation, like my Dr. Parker, will most always be your best choice when selecting a consultant for your board.

The environmental engineer designs our water pollution control system and keeps abreast of the changes in the EPA laws that apply to cattle feedlots. He also obtains needed measurements and other information for our license. He will advise us of any future ramifications that might occur if we change any of the system design or expand it. Ag Engineering owned by John George handled our engineer work for several years. He knows the problems that are unique to our area and can best serve our needs because of this unique area knowledge he has that most feedlot engineers would not have. In the early days of our feedlot business, Alvin Trissell, of the Craig County Soil Conservation Service would serve in this role. Alvin was also great to work with and did so for many years until we became too big for his government agency to help on a day to day basis.

The attorney can keep a business out of many unnecessary corners by doing some simple planning with your business structure. My attorney Dennis Watson has been my friend and attorney for eighteen years. Prior to Dennis, I used one of the founders of his firm, John Wallace, of Wallace and Owens Law Firm. This long continuity of one firm and only two attorneys working for our company has provided seamless information flow for most of our company history. We have worked through our business structure, estate problems when both my parents past on, the bank problems I have spoken of, land buying and selling transactions, and my own estate plan. My friend knows just how I think and act in regard to my business management. Dennis always knows as soon as I walk into his office if I am having a good or bad day with my fatigue syndrome. The total knowledge of how I think and feel gives him a great insight in how to recommend a legal path that is the most in line with our normal operation and what is best for me. Several dollars have been saved by preplanning with the attorney before acting on a project.

For the last fifteen years the cattle market has steadily grown more complex in the issues facing the market. The market has also traded the past several years in a short fifteen to thirty minute window per week. I have always had a market news service teletype and later satellite fed ongoing market news that updates throughout the day. This gives me much of the information of market trends I need, but not enough to have the edge on a market that trades in such a short time window. Cattlefax, a market advisor firm sends updates during the day on what they see in the markets on our satellite service. I have access to them by phone anytime I need to talk one on one with my market person, Kevin Good. Kevin with backup from the entire Cattlefax staff will give me their opinion on the current market as well as market trends out up to one year and projections for the next three years. When major packers start their short trading period, a recorded message is sent to all feedyard clients at once to alert us to the starting trade. Without this knowledge, I would have missed the trade altogether some weeks. They also gave advice on grain prices current and projected to the next crop year.

In 1987 while still dealing with my banking problems I also needed to address our declining customer base. I turned to an old friend I had met when he was the CEO of the National Cattlemen's Association. Dub Berry, was now working part time in Kansas City for an economist, Bill Helming who owned a consultant business known as The Helming Group. I ask Dub to work with me to formulate a new plan to obtain new customers. We put on seminars at Welch that included a feedlot tour and speakers from The Helming Group and our Oklahoma State University. We also used our feed supplier PhD's to speak at some of these meetings. Our seminars usually attracted about three hundred people from a two hundred-mile radius of Welch. They were good for our current customers to gain more knowledge and helped us in expanding our customer base. We also planned how to do trade show exhibits and started working about six shows a year. Dub also encouraged me to start speaking at cattlemen's meetings that needed a speaker. I had no experience in public speaking, but worked up a slide presentation of cattle pictures from our lot that showed it off as I spoke on topics in general to cattle feeding. It was not an advertising message. Soon, I was doing about ten of these talks per year in Oklahoma, Missouri, and Arkansas. I did a few meetings in Tennessee and Kentucky also. The promotional plan Dr. Dub Berry and I developed together worked very well. We soon expanded our customers from about thirty to double this amount. Over fifteen years we grew to an active customer base of about 150 ranchers. We had decided in our plan to seek the smaller customers that most of my competition did not want to service. They were good people and we knew how to work with them for both our benefit. Most large feedlots seldom had over twenty to thirty customers compared to our one hundred fifty. We had to work harder to service this many people, but it was the market niche we chose in our development plan and it worked. The money I spent on the planning consultant team at The Helming Group was money well spent.

Your business will have different needs than ours. You need to pick out the basic same as ours such as the accountant and attorney and go from there. Your board of director consultant team will share much of the management worry load all owners' face. This will make your business flow much easier and save you hours of worry and heartache. Your team can offer expertise that the large corporations have at a price you can afford. You cannot afford in fact to not have your team of experts on retainer for you. You will also enjoy your business planning having an expert to try out your ideas on before putting them into place. They also will add many ideas you might not think of that will take your business to new heights with greater profits.

Don't delay. Start seeking your team today, if you do not have a complete board in place. You will be glad you did. You will lose that sometimes sense of being alone in that big fish bowl of business life. Lastly, do not forget to add God to your board of directors. He more than anyone on this earth can make things so much easier and take all our worry away by trusting in Him.

The next chapter deals with my thoughts on the need to plan, research, and execute your needs and goals.

29

Plan–Research–Execute

As we go through life we need to plan our goals and means to reach these goals. Time frame goals should also be planned and thought about. We all have different life stages in which are goals will be different. Marriage to the right mate might be one of early adult goals. We need to plan and think about the type of mate we want. Don't get me wrong, you do not want to marry for financial or other trait goals. We can however list life goals and traits we want to share. The next phase is to research our goals and figure out how to reach them. If we truly want a Christian mate your research and execution of your plan will lead you to church functions instead of a bar to meet other single people.

I think we need to do planning, research, and execution of many of our life goals just like the one listed above. Career choice, geographic locale we would like to live in, long term financial goals, and when and how we want to retire with proper planning of the financial section are just a few of the goals we need to pay attention to as we go through life. Reading and studying books such as this hopefully will help you to set direction and goals as you plan, research, and execute. I found the book "The Millionaire Next Door" to be very stimulating in my life. It is easy to see our peers buying big houses, big boats, luxury cars, dining out often at the expensive restaurants and a host of other things and wonder why you can't enjoy the same. In too many instances many of these people are simply not saving anything toward retirement or even a rainy day. Many are maxed out on credit cards and payments for their luxuries. There is certainly nothing wrong with having the finer things of life, but do so when you can truly afford and pay for them without robbing your future.

I have tried to plan with different options if my goal went this way or that. One example is my life insurance. Most people will tell you to buy cheap term life insurance. That is a correct answer in many cases. In mine, I did not think this to be the case. I looked at my business and the volatility of the cattle business. In chapter three I told of Morris Barnes making the judgment on the cattle market and losing all he had spent a lifetime building up. I still think of Morris every week, again not in a negative way toward him, but as an example of how I could believe something would be so to the point of putting too much of the farm on the line. We can all be wrong in our judgments at one time or another just as Morris was. He paid the price with his lost assets. I too could fall in his same trap someday. I hope not by thinking of his example every week, but in case I do, I should have another plan. That is where my life insurance comes in. I bought whole life, dividend-paying life insurance. The premium is much higher than term, but I get two added benefits. One is, if I do loose many of my other assets, I have a cash value in the life insurance built up that could be taken as an annual dividend payment to fund my retirement along with my social security. The other benefit is assuming I do not need the cash value to live on, I will have a large death benefit for my heirs to use for inheritance taxes if Congress does not fix this tax or to have to start their dream when I am gone. Thus I had death protection to pay debts when I was starting my business and borrowing large amounts of capital, I have a backup retirement plan, and finally I have cash to leave to my heirs to use. I think this makes the whole life policy a good buy. My cattle business was volatile enough that I did not want to be in investment stocks in my early years. I wanted a more secure backup investment like the whole life insurance.

When I decided I needed a whole life policy, I did not want to just buy from my first friend that sold insurance or the agency on the street corner. I wanted to study for myself what was best for my family and me. When I did this, the Internet was only a dream. I went to the public library and studied the AM Best insurance guides. I looked at each company's track record over the past twenty years. Best had most of the major companies rated in this regard. Past performance does not guarantee future performance, but it is a guide to how a company manages its investments. I picked Northwestern Mutual Life Insurance Company as the best choice for me. They had a good track record, were conservative in their investments, and were told to be one of the best in the projections for the future value of their policies. I did not know any Northwestern Mutual salesmen and there were none listed locally in the yellow pages. I looked to Tulsa, about seventy-five miles away. I got the number for the Northwestern Agency in Tulsa and gave them a call. The salesman who took the call was Kevin Shahan. Kevin was young and green with only a short time in the business. He was eager and ready to serve. The January day I called, the roads were snow packed and somewhat slick. Things were going well at the feedyard, but I was having few phone calls or visits from customers that day because of the weather. I talked to Kevin and told him when the weather cleared up to come up and talk to me. About three hours later, I got a call from Kevin. He was in Vinita and ready to start to Welch, the last fifteen miles of his trip. I scolded him for traveling on such a day, but welcomed him to my office. This eager young man was my kind of guy. He wanted to make a sale. I had done my research, so he did not have to sell me on his company. Kevin quoted the rates for a $400,000 policy. They were as I expected I and signed up right then. He had to have the usual health exam for this large of a policy and get home office approval, but his sale was made. I am sure I was the easiest sale of his career because I knew what I wanted when I called. Kevin did not sell me; I had sold myself by my own research. Kevin selling the policy was my execution of my plan. I have since bought two more policies for myself. We purchased two smaller policies on Dee Ann. As each grandchild was born, I bought a policy on them not for the death benefit but to build them some cash value and so that they would retain some insurability in case of a future health problem when they became adults. Kevin remains my friend who I learned early on in our business relationship was a good Christian man who attended a church of our faith in Tulsa. He is just the kind of guy I like to do business with. You too should research and plan your goal and execute that plan accordingly. Kevin has remained my life insurance consultant since our first meeting back in 1989. Today still with Northwestern Mutual he is evolving his business into more of a wealth coach and financial advisor. Northwestern has bought the Russell Companies, a manager of managers investment company. We are talking of what this relationship could do for us. I am sure it will be a part of our financial plan. The long years of mutual trust in our relationship between Kevin and Dee Ann and I tell so much of how you should cultivate a relationship of this kind with someone you respect and trust will look out after your best interest and not just treat you as another sale.

When I sold my interest in the good Welch Bank, I planned my investment of the sale proceeds. I was still in cattle, so I did not want to invest the time needed in my own research for the paper stock and bond markets. I was ready to have some money in another type of investment. I did not want all my holdings in cattle. I planned to invest some in tax-free municipal bonds and found a bond trader who had treated me well when we met through the bank. Gary Tillman of BOSC investments a subsidiary of Bank of Oklahoma in Oklahoma City knows now after seven years of trading with me what type of bond I like to buy. We have built a bond portfolio together that works for our situation.

The balance of the bank investment I decided to put in good mutual funds. Again, I read and studied all I could about different fund families. I wanted to use a load fund sold by a broker who would help monitor this investment while I was mostly watching the cattle markets. I decided to use one good family of funds since the upfront load fee would be less using one company. I studied fund styles. I did not want a fund up 30 percent one year and down 40 percent the next. I wanted conservative steady growth. American Funds seemed to be the best choice. Again, I sought a broker to work with. My Tulsa accountant and life long friend Pat Guest told me of Glenda Suckey and Elizabeth Carson at BOSC Tulsa, also a unit of the Bank of Oklahoma. I liked using someone from Bank of Oklahoma, a bank with a very strong reputation in our state. Glenda and Elizabeth work together so I had a team to work with. We talked over the various funds offered by American and I made our choice of several of their different focus funds. This proved to be an excellent choice as we went through the long down trend in stock funds from 1999 to 2002. My total fund balance never went below my investment even though I knew of many that were off 50 percent from the original investment. Today the array of funds have come back nicely and performed well. Every choice will not be the correct choice. The point I am trying to make is to plan your goal, do your research, and then execute that plan. Do not be sold a plan by someone who seems like a good old boy. Do your own research and then buy from a good old boy working for a great company. You will not be sorry.

Several years ago I started a company profit sharing retirement plan for my employees. The first couple of years we left the money in short term bonds until each employee had enough to start a good investment strategy. I appointed a committee of employees to research five different companies to place our money with and what family of funds we would invest through our investment councilor chosen. The committee interviewed the choices I gave them and decided to use Glenda Suckey of BOSC. I agreed with this choice as I thought Glenda would serve each employee well. Glenda is a good investment person, but better at selling her firm's plan than she is at having the time to help after the sale. She likes another associate such as Elizabeth to follow through. This would be fine if not for the fact, she would tell the employees to call her. When they did, she did not have time to follow through. Don't get me wrong, I think a lot of Glenda's ability and talent in the investment field and still use her today. We all have weaknesses and hers is overselling what she will do when there is only so many hours in the day to do so. Many sales people have this weakness and it needs to be worked on because it will cause more heartache in the long run than it will increase sales. Anyway the committee picked Glenda and when it came to fund family choices they decided to use Putnam Funds instead of my choice, American. I already had my personal money in American and did not mind using another fund for the company retirement since I would be in it also. I thought it would not be as good overall as American, but would diversify my holdings. I also had given the committee the right to choose what they wanted for all employees. Many of you will know that Putnam Funds fell in some cases over 50 percent during the three bad years. All funds lost quite a lot. They just were not as conservative in their investment programs as American. Putnam also got caught up in the 2003 fund scandals. They did not have a customer-oriented culture that American has. American Funds in 2004 is growing faster than just about any other family of funds. They invest in a prudent, conservative manner and are above board in all dealings with customer funds. They appear to be the model for many companies to learn from and follow.

If your business involves customers pay close attention to what I am about to say. Recently Glenda and Elizabeth left Bank of Oklahoma for the same investment jobs with Smith Barney, also in Tulsa. They felt Smith Barney offered more investment choices to their clients than the BOK products they formerly had. Their employment contract had a no compete clause for a short two weeks if they left BOK. Glenda nor Elizabeth neither could contact us during this two week period. Elizabeth had told me shortly before leaving BOK that very soon she would have more investment products to offer and would be in touch in two or three weeks with the information. Bank of Oklahoma sent us a letter stating that Glenda and Elizabeth had left their company. The letter stated that someone from BOK would be in touch with us very soon in regard to whom would serve our account. We never received this promised call during the time of no compete from Glenda and Elizabeth. We have multiple accounts with BOK in fairly substantial numbers. You would think someone in the BOK organizational management would see that we were called or visited to try to retain our business. I am not sure if I would have moved to the Smith Barney company or not if I had been approached by BOK. Elizabeth called just as soon as her agreement allowed. I am now in the process of moving with her and Glenda to Smith Barney. How we treat and service our customers goes along way in relationships. It is much easier to retain a customer than to find a new one. Many companies and their representatives lose sight of this.

Your working years will pass by rather swiftly. I was told this when I was young and did not really believe it to be true, but it was. It is never too early to plan your life stages and goals for each of these stages. When you get to that last ten years from retirement you will have choices if you have planned. Remember also that illnesses and accidents can change plans such as working till you are seventy. It is much better to be prepared and then when the time comes if we still want to work till seventy it will be on our own terms and not because we have to in order to pay the bills.

Think hard about this when you pass on that next big-ticket item until you get your investment house in order. You, I say once again, will not be sorry.

The following chapter tells of some of the awards we received mainly in the environmental area. It is nice to receive an award, but first priority should always be to do what is right. In our case, the land was our investment and living. We had to take care of this investment.

30

Awards

It is nice to be recognized by one's peers for career accomplishments. I want to tell you about some awards we have been fortunate enough to receive. I relate this to you not for personal bragging rights and glory, but to relate how important it is to be known as a "good citizen" in whatever industry or business sector you work in. Those of us who work with the land realize just how important our actions are in regard to the environment. We know, or at least most know and all should, that we need to leave the land in pristine condition for the next generation. We cannot work all the nutrients out of the land and not replace them. We must work to prevent erosion of the soil. Brush control is not cost prohibitive if maintained on an on going basis. However, to simply avoid brush control will soon see land in an unusable condition except for wildlife only and the cost to restore is often as much as the land value itself. Proper land use practices will allow for abundant wildlife as well as let you have good return on your land investment in the form of excellent crops, grass for livestock, tree production, or other agricultural enterprises.

Our feedlot business also included a need not to pollute our neighbors or the creeks and streams that run into our rivers and lakes. There were times that "Mother Nature" did not allow us to be perfect when we had thirty-three inches of rain in ninety days. Our pollution control lagoons would simply not hold all the water runoff in these circumstances. Rainfall of this magnitude did dilute the tainted water that would run over from our wastewater lagoon. Thus the impact on the streams was very minimal. Our world with tornadoes, hail storms, hurricanes, and other natural calamities will always give man problems to deal with the aftermath of these horrific events. Good management and planning will keep our environment in grand shape. We will leave things better after us than before our management began. We also can use the land to feed our nation in a very cost productive manner.

We have to maintain balance in our business life in regard to maximum production to maintain our country's relative cheap food cost and the impact the production has on the land. This can be done as we have been talking about. I have found that both go hand in hand. Most production practices enhance the land and give a positive return on our production cost.

During our career we were proud to be recognized by the Oklahoma Beef Council as their 1999 Oklahoma Environmental Stewardship Award Winner. We were nominated by the Oklahoma Cattlemen's Association for our work in operating a cattle feedyard in a high rainfall area as well as for our pasture land improvement programs. As the Oklahoma winner we were entered in the National Cattlemen's Beef Association Environmental Stewardship Award program. Our region four includes Texas, Arkansas, and Oklahoma. We were proud to win the region four award, one of seven regional winners in the national award. Our national winner in 1999 was Jim and Brenda Anderson of Colorado. The Andersons farm corn and other crops, maintain a few cows, and have a family farm cattle feedlot in their operation. The other regional winners had varied production enterprises and all were unique in the manner they maintained the environment and cared for their land.

We were also proud to be nominated by our Oklahoma State Regulator, Dan Parrish, of the Oklahoma Department of Agriculture, for a "Keep Oklahoma Beautiful" award in 2000. Mr. Parrish recognized our value in caring for the environmental in our feedyard business. His department was the regulator in charge of inspection of our facility and worked with the federal Environmental Protection

Association in this regard. We received a newly created Oklahoma Business award for "Keeping Oklahoma Beautiful." The award was presented to us by the current chairwoman of Keep Oklahoma Beautiful who also was the chairwoman of the state Sierra Club, a group who is often very critical of animal production practices. This made this award very meaningful to Dee Ann and I not only for ourselves and our employees, but also for our industry.

We shared our awards with our employees by presenting each with a T-shirt inscribed with the award and the words "environmental team member" at a luncheon in their honor for the part each had played in our success. It is important to remember those who help you in your successes. The employees play a vital role in the success or failure of any business. Like the land, employees are a human asset to the company who must be nurtured and cared for in their own right. In the long run, this will add to the success of any business.

Over the years we received other awards from the Oklahoma Conservation Commission for our work in caring for the "land." These included the Governor's Conservation Award and the Goodyear Conservation Award.

I was also proud to receive an Outstanding Leadership Award from the National Young Farmers Education Association for leadership to the cattle industry for my work with the Oklahoma Cattlemen's Association. We do not have to receive an award to have a special feeling for the work we do in our "pillars of life" zones we talked about in Chapter 26. It is however nice to be recognized by one's peers for work accomplished. The award is just the "icing on the cake" that adds to the true fulfillment you can receive when you give back to society. Once again I would implore you to reread Chapter 26 and work on your "Pillars of Life" today.

I would add also the best reward and honor to seek is eternity with our Lord. Riches and awards on this earth mean nothing. Our Eternal Reward is the one that counts. Act accordingly.

The next short chapter is just a few business observations I have observed over the years.

31

Some Business Observations

I have talked at length in this book about how both my father and I managed with usually one of us on site at all time during the course of normal business. In today's world of extended business hours and the hectic pace of the business world this is not always possible. We need to develop and train people to work under and with us. I learned to do this quite well with my various department managers. I did however work more than most owners because I knew my employee was putting in extra effort on our behalf many times and I wanted to share this load. This may or may not have been correct, but it was always my style.

I think that a small business owner has to be heavily involved in the day to day matters because of the ongoing changes that take place in the industry, workers that come and go, and dealing with the competition. When Mike Day left my company on short notice if I had not been heavily involved I would have lost the needed edge with customers, buyers, suppliers, and the working knowledge of my business. It does not take long to lose the edge and feel of managing if you do not stay in contact. My friend Larry Smith has owned a string of Sonic drive-in fast food restaurants. When he owned a few, he turned every tap and aspect of his business. If a store manager quit or perhaps took advantage of Larry by stealing, Larry knew how to step in and run the store. As he grew his chain of Sonics he developed managers to oversee every ten or so stores. He had his reserve if someone quit or had to be dismissed or simply got sick and had to be off for an extended time. This is the advantage a chain has. It has a reserve bench like the baseball team to call on when needed. Larry owned fifty or more Sonics and had a team in place so that he could step back a bit and let his team work. He stayed in touch, but had enough depth to take extended time off without fear. The single outlet business cannot afford this same depth and thus the owner must stay more in touch to insure the continued business success.

In today's cattle business I have saw so many of the new way owners who know very little of the actual business. They buy ranches, hire people to run them, and never help or pay much attention except to collect the checks when their cattle are sold. This makes for a weaker industry and ultimately effects the owner. Some of these owners have little respect for the crews they hire to run their operations. I have seen them speak poorly of their help, cuss them out in front of others, and treat them as inferior people. Why would you want to treat the ones taking care of your operation in this manner. If the employee is not doing his job or looking out for your interest, do both of you a favor and dismiss them. On the other hand if an employee gives you their best and is loyal, he or she should be treated with respect. Employees like all of us have personal problems from time to time. They may need an extra hand during adverse or special times. You will be a better person and your business will do better if you will follow this philosophy.

I feel that in order to teach the next generation the business, if they are interested in carrying on, you should start early. Your offspring should be taught how to work first, know the ins and outs of the business, and then most importantly, how to make deals and run the business. I have spoke of many families I knew who taught the kids to work but never to manage. I have seen other families that never gave the next generation any incentive to learn the family business or any business. They just took care of their needs and gave them the luxuries they desired but had not earned. It is good to provide and do things for your children, but you are doing them a great disservice if you do not give them an incentive to make it on their own. In today's world most anyone wanting to do something on their own will have to have a "money stake" or strong co-signer on a start up note at the bank. To go beyond this, however, and buy your off-spring a business or farm to operate without the debt and growing into the management as the business grows is the wrong way to handle the next generation's start in the business world. We all need to learn where the money comes from. We need to learn to when to buy new equipment because it is more cost effective than fixing the old or how to make do with the old because there is no money for new. We need to learn to meet a payroll or bank payment. We want our children to have things better than we, but if we give everything to them and tell them to go manage it, they will never appreciate the fulfillment we all achieve in building our business or ranch. They also will never learn to scrape to survive if a lean time comes. No one has enough money that the next generation cannot go completely through it if they do not know how to manage properly.

I have also seen family members with drug or alcohol problems in which the older generation just looks aside and tries to pile on more responsibility in running a family operation. If the loved one is already on drugs or an alcoholic they do not need more felt pressure or more or harder duties put on them until they have licked their demon. It certainly is not a time to be changing things in the operation around as far as duties of work are handled or a new purchase or expansion of the business or ranch. The pressure to be as good as Dad in the operation and dealing with employees and suppliers or buyers is hard at best in the eyes of many sons or daughters. Teach the operation and give the responsibility as the next generation is able to take more on. To not teach to manage or to push too fast is not the answer on either end of the spectrum. Expansions, retirements, or major life changing decisions should not be made if anyone involved is still fighting personal problems. As I have said, this will only add to the problems and make the bottle or drug look more attractive.

I also see so many business people who do not keep their spouse informed of their financial dealings. The degree a spouse wants to be involved varies greatly. One's spouse may not even want to know, but they should. We all never know when our time on this earth will end and a spouse needs to know something of the business life. Major expansions of a business or location to a new area should be talked out thoroughly. All these types of decisions will impact a family and they should have some knowledge and input into what is happening.

We all like to make money and be successful. However we need to stop and look at the big picture and not lose the true meaning of life. Teach our children the true values and work ethic. All of us need to practice and teach our off spring the satisfaction in life of living our life for the Lord and following his teachings. We can do so much with our talents besides making millions over millions. At a point money becomes a games and only a means of keeping score. We need so much to prosper and enjoy in this life and that is fine. We also need to provide for the One who has blessed us with our earthly gains. The best legacy one can leave a family is a love and trust for the Lord.

The next chapter will deal with the next generation in business. Read closely some of my observations, it can save a family business.

32

The Next Generation in the Family

Family business is a very rewarding part of life. The older generation most always would like to see the next generation take over the family business. I think while this is very worthwhile and has many benefits; it can also cause an enormous amount of family stress on both the older and younger generation. Businesses change over one generation, let alone two or three generations. The business has to change with the times to remain viable. You can relate to the buggy maker whose trade was not needed except by a few hobbyist after the automobile was invented. We have seen many "mom and pop" stores taken over by the giant corporations and left no room for the family store to compete unless it was reinvented to the new times. Many family businesses do go on to one or two or more generations with a proper changing of the times as needed.

Working with family members can be a truly great experience. I enjoyed working with my father very much. We had different ideas and different ways to get to the same place. However, we respected each other's ideas and methods. As a result, our company grew and changed as needed. My father has also worked with his father in the farming and cattle business. Granddad allowed my father to change the operation and location of the cattle operation as the industry changed in the early years of cattle feeding. I never heard of any major problems with them working together. I must add, I am sure there were problems I was not aware of as Granddad was mostly retired and just a partner in the operation by the time I was old enough to notice such things. One of the biggest considerations in bringing family into the business is how it will affect other family members. The family business may not be big enough to sustain all siblings or some siblings will have other interest in life and may not want to join the business. The non-family business member sibling still is loved and I am sure will want to be remembered in an estate plan and not just leave everything to the sibling in the business.

My father had a great falling out with his own five brothers and sisters after the death of my grandfather. Dad was the only one of the six who became involved in the family farming and cattle business. Neither Dad nor Granddad thought anything about planning for the future of their operation. They both got along together and worked well together. By the time Granddad died in his early eighties, he had been semi-retired for several years. During these years, Dad had grown the operation in size and income. Granddad did have a "will" and left most of his assets to Dad. I am sure this was not only because of the family business they had together, but also for the fact my mother was the one who did most of the care taking for Granddad in his final years when he needed more help. This was probably how he wanted things and the way it should have been. Much of the family success had been accomplished together or Dad had added to during the fifteen or twenty years he had been mostly in charge of the operation.

The problem was the other five siblings were good people, they just went other directions in their lives. Granddad should have explained to all the family that if he was going to leave a larger portion of his estate to my Dad it was because he had helped work and earn much of the estate. He had not done this and before long the family was in an uproar. The brothers and sisters wanted Granddad's will tossed out and to divide the estate the way they saw fit. Dad went along with this pretty well until these siblings wanted to include my folks' home in Welch in the estate. They're reasoning, it had been paid for out of proceeds of cattle ran on the ranch. The house was left out finally, but the land was divided much different than Granddad had planned. The problem with his plan was it did not go far enough.

I know nothing of how Dad and Granddad split the proceeds of their ranching operation. They had formed a family farm business trust, which is basically the same as a corporation in 1960. In 1960 a family farm could not become a corporation, thus a business trust was used to accomplish the same thing a corporation does for a business. This should have set forth the shares each had in the company. They should have paid salaries and dividends to each other. I do not think this happened and most of their assets remained commingled. I could have the wrong conception of this since I was young and not interested in how the business worked in those days.

I do know it was a shame for a fine family to bicker over the family assets. The business trusts should have set out what was whose and so forth. Property outside of the trust should have included their assets before the trust was formed and there personal property and homes. Granddad should have told his kids how and why he wanted his estate divided after he was gone. This is hard to talk about and it is hard to face the fact we all will leave this earth some day. None the less, planning should be done to avoid the family fights that so often happen after the older generation's passing on.

Life insurance is one way of providing for non-business family members. The life insurance proceeds can be used for an inheritance for the non-business family siblings with the business left intact for the sibling who has become involved in the family business. A detailed will with explanations of how and why things are being done in a certain way would also help. Planning by all family members for the passing of one generation to the next while everyone is healthy and in sound mind would also help.

My mother's family was led down the path of Grandmother telling her two daughters and one son exactly how the estate would be divided when she was gone. When the time came, all was divided as set forth. Assets not listed were drawn for or chosen one at a time as they went around the circle of three siblings. A much better plan.

My folks held no resentment to the siblings who made them feel so inadequate in their finances and how Granddad's estate was handled. They had little contact with the rest of the family after the way things were done. They forgave, but just did not have the same feelings for these people again. How sad to see families divided over assets. Proper planning could have avoided all this.

If planning is not going to be seen to, it would probably be better had no siblings become involved in the family business. Take notice of this in your family.

Another aspect of the family business, is to not force it upon the next generation. All of us feel special to the business we have created and want to see it carried on. This is a great ambition. However, few businesses survive to the next generation and fewer still to the third generation. Part of the reason for this I am sure is the family problems talked about above and the changing times that are not adapted to for one reason or the other. The next generation has to have the same passion and business savoy as the previous one. There are times when a son or daughter go to work in the family business just because they feel this is expected of them and not because this is what they want to do. This is a poor way to make choices for your life.

When I started my own short career during college in the automobile business it was because I had a strong passion for this business. I also needed to prove to myself just how good I was. I lacked the confidence I needed. Had I continued in the family business under these terms, I would have always thought of myself as a second class, unworthy worker in the family business. This would have caused problems for both my parents and myself. I know they were disappointed in my choice at the time, but it was better this way than to join their business for the wrong reasons and without passion. We all have different skills. Dad was good at mechanical things and I was terrible. I really had to work at this aspect of the cattle business when I did come home to the family business. I was a better business manager.

When I went off to the automobile business my only living brother was out of college and trying to work in the family business. He was sick with the Cystic Fibrosis and unable to work much of the time. I did not fully understand his illness or realize his days on this earth would be so short. I did not resent him working in the business and felt it was great for our folks to have a business he could help in as his health allowed. I just figured at the time that it would be better for all of us, if I did something different. The automobile business was my first love and the cattle business second.

It turned out I was good in the automobile business and I have no doubts I would have ultimately succeed in this business even though I early on would have went down with my boss who I am sure I would have ended up in partners with, Darrell Kissee as related in Chapter 1. I gained the needed confidence in my own unique skills I brought to the family business when I returned. After my brother died and Dad was suffering from his own health problems I decided to return to the family business. I probably still thought of the automobile business as my first love, but the cattle business ran a close second. I figured with the family start and Dad's need at the time I would be better off with close second than first love. This was the correct decision for my family and me. It would not have been if my love of the cattle business had not been so close to my first choice.

I am sure there are instances where the sibling comes home to help in the family business when it would have in actuality been better for all to have closed out the business. The business owning generation probably would enjoy after a time of adjustment a long and happy retirement instead of continuing to work in the business out of a sense of duty. The younger generation may have just come into the family business out of obligation or duty rather than the passion for the business. To truly succeed in family business you must have passion for the business. Many hours are spent at work, more than you would work in an employment with a corporate job. Thus for a family business to succeed with multi-generations both generations must have passion and an ongoing love of the business.

I never second-guessed my choice of the cattle business over the automobile business. I made the right choice for the time. I also know had I chosen the automobile business, I think this decision would have been fine also. I did enjoy a stronger relationship with my folks by working with them in the family business. I would have never achieved this aspect of our life had I not returned. Don't get me wrong, there were challenges and trying times as with anything in life in my choice of joining the family business. In Dad's later years when I was taking over more and more of the day-to-day responsibilities if I wanted some big change or wanted to do a project a particular way, I would just try to get Dad to take my view for his idea. I don't think he ever saw through my method and most of the time it worked. If it did not, I would not loose sleep over the matter. As I said we enjoyed our almost seventeen years together. We had no family squabble over the estate as related in Chapter 19 as I was the only child still alive.

In Chapter 22 I told of Doug and Jodee our fourth generation working at the feedlot. We all got along well and I enjoyed having them in the business. I have related of Doug's lack of the same passion I had and my father and grandfather before me for our business. He gave it a good try, but had not grown up in a very complex and challenging business. It was not the end of the world when Doug chose to go another route. I wanted him happy in his choice of life's work. It would have been great to have had both Doug and Jodee involved, but it is not my life but theirs.

When Mom died I had bypassed some of her assets to Doug and Jodee. About $240,000, half of which was Doug and Judee's, and was used to form N & W Investments, Inc. Dee Ann and I each owned one fourth of N & W and Doug and Jodee each owned one fourth. We placed the assets of this corporation in treasury bills until it was decided what to invest in. I told Doug and Jodee, this would be their seed money to start their own business either with cattle with me or some other venture. Jodee had done many things for her Grandmother, and I felt she deserved this start from her estate. My total plan for our joint venture was not related to Doug and Jodee. I wanted to be their partner in whatever venture they decided upon. As a partner, I would have the right to help make decisions in the business. If I was not a partner I would have been meddling as a father and father-in-law. I did not want to meddle, but to help smooth the road some as they started out. My plan would be to stay in partners a few years and when their venture was doing well, Dee Ann and I would sign over our share of the company for nothing to the kids.

Doug looked at many things as he sought a business to start after trying the cattle business. I suggested a Hardee's franchise.

Hardee's had been my favorite fast food of the time and I thought one would do well in Miami. Glad he didn't listen to me. Hardee's came to Miami and failed. The national chain of Hardee's has fallen on hard times and poor management and many franchises have failed or not performed as well as they should. I seldom eat at Hardee's today. The food quality is just not there anymore.

A small manufacturing idea was looked at and turned down. Alphagraphics, a franchise printing company, was an idea I liked, but would have required a lot of selling jobs for company printing needs by going direct to companies to solicit their business. This would have been my thing, but Doug does not like cold call selling. For this reason, Alphagraphics would have been a poor choice. Our feed supplier, Purina Mills, had a new urban store concept called "America's Country Store" that sold horse and all kinds of pet and other animal feed along with a selection of country items in a upscale store décor in thriving urban areas. Doug thought a lot about this venture when they still lived in Owasso, which fit the target size and demographic makeup Purina thought would work for these type of stores.

Doug and Jodee ultimately decided they would like to live in Vinita, Oklahoma. This would put them close to both sets of parents, but in a different town than either. Vinita was too small for the Purina new concept store, but they liked something of this nature. They decided that an ACE hardware franchise would work well in conjunction with a Purina feed dealership. They would use many of the best features of the America's Country Store concept but adapt it to a smaller community with ACE. They secured a franchise for ACE and Purina and set forth to begin their store.

Most beginning businesses would be better off renting their facility, but there were not any locations available in Vinita that would begin to work for their store concept. They needed ample parking and a good location, easy to get into and out. My friend Frank Robson offered to build them a building in his Wal-Mart anchored complex. This would have been fine, except that his lease term was ten years and if they could borrow the money needed they had just as well own as lease, as they had the same risk in Frank's lease as ownership would present. They could pay off and own their own building in fifteen years. They found a location across the street from the Wal-Mart strip center. It needed considerable dirt work, but would make a good location. Doug made a good choice.

He looked at several types of buildings to construct. I was somewhat familiar with Morton Buildings and felt their commercial buildings were a good choice for the type of upscale look Doug wanted for his new business. I called a Morton salesman and asked for an informational packet on their buildings. I gave this to Doug and then sat back to see what happened. Doug studied the Morton video and liked what he saw. He met with the Morton salesman and made a deal for a 10,000 square foot building. I stayed out of the choice other than giving him the original packet of Morton information. Our new partnership was starting off well. I gave subtle hints but let Doug make his own choices.

The building looked nice upon completion and soon it was being set up for business. We had sold animal health products and Purina feeds at our country location. I had assumed that when it came time to set the animal health department up in the new store that I would take the lead on purchasing and setting up the inventory in the space Doug wanted to fill with this department. I assumed wrong. Doug, either did not want to bother me with this chore, or wanted to do all of his new venture himself. Either way was his choice. However, I was hurt very much. I had dreamed for years of opening an animal health store in Vinita and now had my chance through our N & W Investments company. The 10 percent or less of the store the animal health would occupy would give me a new interest to supplement my time at the feedlot. I could do this easily because I knew this business very well. It would take little of my time and would give me an excuse to visit the store once in awhile. I no longer had any outside banking interest and yearned for a new challenge that would not take me from the feedlot too much.

I never said a word when Doug decided to do the animal health department his way. He probably just did not want to see me work harder, as I now had a new operations manager at the feedlot to break in as Doug had left this position. I wanted this store to be

Doug and Jodee's dream more than mine. I had my own dreams in my ranch and feedlot operation. So, even though I wanted to do this one department, I stayed quiet. The kids were happy in their choice and they were doing well in starting their business. I did not want to throw a monkey wrench in things. I have worked a few odd times in the store to help out such as when Dejay was born three days after opening. However, my time working at the store has been very limited. I decided it best that I not get too involved and they were doing fine without me. It was hard to walk away from this dream of working with them in this new venture, but I thought it best. The point of all this is that this was not my project. It is Doug and Jodee's. Sure, I was a partner and could have said I wanted to do animal health. Too many times I think we as parents try to replay our lives through our children. Doug's plan was on track and fine, it just did not include my input in one small area. I had my business boat loaded and I am sure Doug did not want to add something to it. Whether it be business or sports we must let the next generation play the game their way.

Soon after the store building was begun in the spring, Doug and Jodee found out they were also building a new addition to there family. Early December, the store was ready to open and was also time for the new baby to be born. Not knowing exactly when the baby would be born, it was decided to open on Tuesday. The following Friday, Dec. 11, Dejay was born. Doug called me at a trade show in Tulsa I was working and said Jodee had gone to the hospital. He wanted me to help work at the store, so I had Diane take my place in Tulsa and I went to the store. I would've liked to have been at the hospital with the rest of the family awaiting the new birth, but I knew I was needed at the store. Late afternoon saw Dejay's arrival. I joined the rest of the family that evening. Dejay and mother went home that weekend. On Monday, I called the store and Jodee answered. Jodee and Dejay were already at work and would be for months to come. Dejay stayed in a backpack with Jodee most of the time, until he grew older. One day Dejay found a button that no one knew about that shut the entire computer system down. Not long after he had to go to a babysitter. I am sure Jodee will never forget having a baby on Friday and going to work on Monday. Just one sacrifice that had to be made in starting a new family business.

Family needs, wants and desires should be remembered first when dealing with multi-generation family businesses. Four years after opening their new store in December, 1998 Dee Ann and I gave Doug and Jodee our stock in N & W Investments at our Christmas. The timing for the family and tax wise was right to do this. I certainly did not want them to build up their new business and then have something happen to Dee Ann or I and them have to pay estate tax on what they had built. The store was accomplished on their own. Our start through the money left me by Mom made their dream possible. In today's business climate it would have been impossible for the kids to have borrowed the money needed in whole for their business. We helped them just enough to get their start. The bank that made their loan for the balance of the store wanted us to cosign the note as co-owners of N & W at the time. This I refused. I thought we had seen that the N & W money was plenty for the needed down payment and I wanted the rest to be on their own. The bank saw the wisdom in this and loaned them the needed money for the project.

Like all new businesses, Ace Town and Country, as their store is called, has not been easy. There is always the challenge of finding qualified help at a price you can afford. Learning who to give credit to and who not is always a challenge. Product displaying and inventory management skills had to be learned. A new chain called Atwood's moved in late 2003. This would be a major competitor selling many of the same products Ace Town & Country handles. To combat this a Radio Shack franchise was added and the store inventory changed around some before the new Atwood's even opened. This would give Doug and Jodee a good mix of product for their small town of about seven thousand.

Dakota is now thirteen, Deonna ten, and Dejay five. The next generation of ACE will be making their own family decisions in a few years. Time seems to pass so very fast the older you get. I wandered if any of the grandkids would have an interest in cattle. I will talk about this in the next chapter.

Remember when doing business dealings with family that family matters first and business second. You will be glad you put other family member priorities ahead of yours.

Next we will look at my big decision. You will have your own big decision in life to make sometime. Read how I handled mine. You might also note it took me awhile to arrive at what might look to you to be an easy answer. Remember also to include God in all your big decisions.

Dakota, Deonna, Jodee, Dejay, and Doug Whitworth

Ace Town and Country

33

The Big Decision

Life presents many challenging opportunities. Sometimes we perceive opportunities as challenges. The way we react to different crossroads as we go through life will determine which road of life we travel for years to come or perhaps the rest of our life. You think of the normal opportunities such as selecting one's mate and getting married. Next comes kids and how many. There are choices of where to live and buying the dream home. One of our biggest decisions is determining our career path in life. Career path can change as we go about our working years. Sometimes career path is changed by our desires. Other times a layoff or company downsizing will signal the next change. Our life's work in many cases will determine where we live, in the city or country, what section of the nation to live, what hours of free time we have, and so many other factors in our daily life.

There are several factors to consider in our vocation choice. Money should not be number one on the list. It is important, but satisfaction in life should be the number one priority in career selection. We spend more waking hours at work than any other activity, so we just as well enjoy what we do. We need a passion for what we do. I have always felt that there is no justification for making this huge decision alone. Family should have an interest since it affects where we live and the hours of freedom we have. You can take a huge load of your shoulders in this choice just by prayer. Our God is there for us in good and bad times if we only let Him into our hearts. Any big life choice needs help and who else should we turn to, but our Maker. He has told us in His Scriptures that He will care for us and help us through any situation. Our answer will come so clearly and easily if we just turn our life over to God and ask for His help.

It is hard to make changes in our life. I am no different than anyone else. I just hate to make even little changes in my life. I lived fifty-four years of my life within three blocks of where I grew up. I have been married nearly thirty-eight years and went about the same work routine most of those years. I was up at five-thirty and off to work between 6:30 and 7:00 each morning. My day at work usually lasted until 6:30 or later in the evening. When things were going well, which was most of the time I enjoyed what I did and thought nothing of the hours spent working. I spent much of my day talking to my customers. I enjoyed a diverse group of people from across the country of different backgrounds as I talked some of in the chapter on customers. It was a joy to serve these people. Like all vocations, we had our problems also. Sometimes we would have harsh weather that was hard on cattle performance. Other times we would have a rash of equipment breakdowns, usually at poor times such as a weekend, holiday, or at night that had to be seen to immediately. I managed normal employee problems, the weather, cattle markets, grain markets, and the equipment problems. It was just part of the landscape I had to deal with. I am sure each of you deal with similar problems in your career. Our pitfalls were narrow and shallow and our good times peaked high and long. It was for the most part, a fun and challenging career. We also enjoyed a good measure of financial success.

The major problem in my life was dealing with the Chronic Fatigue Syndrome. Some of the following was related in the chapter on Chronic Fatigue, but I feel it has impacted my life so much and others have to deal with similar situations with illness that I am going to talk of it again. I have dealt with this illness as told since 1988. It became a part of my life, just like work and play. What I could do and not do was determined largely by what stage of the syndrome I was in. One of the hard to accept parts of Chronic

Fatigue Syndrome is the constant physical swing up and down. Don't get me wrong, I truly enjoyed my upswings when I might go a week or sometimes two or three months at a time when for the most part I enjoyed a good energy level and a pain free life. Then would come a payback time after usually a week of too much activity at play or work. It did not seem to matter whether I was having fun on a weekend outing or working too long hours. When I overdid I paid later in the form of stiff, achy joints and muscle pain. Then I would have a period lasting from days to months that would present a real challenge to my schedule. In the worst form, I would battle a "brain fog" that made it hard to concentrate on my business of the day and my memory would simply leave me. God never gives us more challenges than we can handle and He will be there to help us in life's challenges. He was always there for me. I just dealt with my problems and carried on. I simply tried harder and seldom got the depression that many that suffer from Chronic Fatigue do.

The challenging part of the illness as I started to relate in the above paragraph is how one minute I am bouncing along feeling great and then like a light switch turned off, I cannot walk straight and have all by symptoms hit at once. For those who have not been around someone with Chronic Fatigue Syndrome or one of the related illnesses such as Fibromaligia you cannot imagine the frustrations that go with the illness. So many people think of the illness as a depression, maybe a faked illness, a laziness, or who knows what else. Many do suffer from depression, but I am sure it is secondary and caused by dealing with the type of illness it is. For many years my own Dee Ann questioned what was happening to me and how I could feel so good one minute and have so many troubles the next. She cared and stood beside me, but I know there were times she thought I was just faking or who knows what. This caused me more trouble than dealing with the problem itself. I knew it was real, other people had far worse illnesses, and that I just had to deal with my problem and not let it get the best of me. This is the attitude that I think kept me going in a high stress, long hour days in my work. Other people's doubts including Dee Ann's at times, was always the most hard aspect of the illness. If you know someone with any illness that affects their life style, have a little compassion and respect for what they deal with. You don't know how much you can affect their day just by the attitude you have in regard to them. I hated sympathy and pity. I did not need help. I did require a big dose of understanding to what was happening to me.

Every three or four years out of the blue, I would have a major incident of the affliction that would affect me far more than my usual episodes. Walking would become very difficult. The more effort it took to walk, I would start breathing hard and become short of breath. My chest would hurt; I would get sweaty, and in general have all the major symptoms of a major heart attack. I think I usually knew this was not the case and my long time friend and doctor, Dr. Steve Grigsby, also knew it probably was not heart related, but it looked so real to both of us. I have a family history of heart ailment, a high stress job, and high cholesterol so we had to take serious these attacks. Through the years I have had all the heart ailment tests including stress test, ultra sounds, heart monitoring and other tests. All have shown I have a good heart. It has been determined that the breast bone just above the heart can have the same stiffness and achy feeling as my other joints and the heart muscle itself seems to feel weak just as my other joints do. Still, we have to check these episodes out just in case it is the real thing.

In January 2001 I suffered one of these attacks described above. I wasn't feeling well and went home to lie down for awhile after lunch. I decided maybe I better make a visit to the doctor to check my blood pressure. It has never been my problem, but the doctors were wandering if maybe a spike down in pressure could be part of the problem. I started to Miami by myself thinking I would be fine in doing so as I had other times before. I got to Miami fine, but kept feeling worse as I went. I had to park a good distance from the clinic. As I walked in my legs seemed to just quit. The joints were stiff and the muscles so weak I could hardly stand. This soon had me breathing very hard. I made it in and the receptionist seeing my state of duress immediately called my friend "Nurse Billye" who worked for Dr. Grigsby. She helped me back and the doctor examined me. He told me we both knew my history, but that this looked like the real thing. He wanted to call the ambulance for the trip across the street to the hospital. I balked at this, so instead of making a big point out of the hospital requirement in these situations, Billye simply got her car and helped me to the door and drove me across the street to the hospital ER entrance. I was checked out and sent to the intensive care unit for observation. When I get into these situations, I end up scared and I am sure this leads to hyperventilation. This only makes the symptoms worse, but not any thing real bad in itself. Usually within an hour, the ordeal is over and I feel drained for several hours or days afterward. This was the case this time also.

Dr. Grigsby ask where to find Dee Ann to alert her of my problem and hospitalization. I told him to try daughter, Jodee first. He became alarmed and immediately thought some spat or problem with Dee Ann had maybe intensified my problem. This was certainly not the case. We have a good relationship and everything was fine that day. We had not seen each other too much that day at work as she had several customer checks for cattle in that day that had to be processed and got out to our customers. I knew Jodee had a greater respect for my problem and that she would have a calmer head for whatever she might face. Dee Ann would either doubt or become extremely excited if she thought I was having a heart attack. I wanted to know what was going on before we told her. The problem was, neither could be reached by phone. A major toll telephone cable had been cut between Miami and the switching network in Tulsa. All long distance phone service was out for several hours. Late in the afternoon, Dee Ann missed me at work. Diane told her I had gone home to lie down after lunch, suffering from one of the fatigue spells. Dee Ann went home to check on me when I did not answer the phone. She saw my pickup gone and having a feeling started towards Miami looking for me. Billye was on her way home to Welch by now and met Dee Ann on the road out of town. She stopped her and told her where I was.

I had about four hours I was out of touch with everyone. I felt awful and suddenly so alone. I got over this feeling after I remembered God was with me and would protect me. I knew I was in good hands and said a little prayer. I felt better, but very physically drained.

I knew during this seemingly long time, that I had better make some changes to my life style before something bad did happen. It was not good to put my body through what was happening whether it was heart related or not. How and what to do was the question.

I knew I could not change my method of operation after so many years of being so involved in our operation. Many of today's owners in the cattle business hire managers to run the day to day operation. I guess I could have to, but I knew the many pitfalls first hand and the legal and monetary liabilities that were so great in this business. I thought I needed to be involved. This was our major asset and it just would not work for me to turn the operation over to someone else. I had previously turned over the outside operations to my operations manager. I dealt mainly with the business issues, customer relations, and selling the cattle, which I really enjoyed. I also knew that at our smaller size in the industry that I would always be training good managers and then seeing them leave for a better position. I knew I had to have a steady involvement for our company to survive.

Sometimes there are obstacles placed in our path to get our attention. I had these plainly in sight, but had ignored them. I, like most, had not paid enough attention to the signals God had provided to me for the insight on what I should do. The EPA was going through a process that would result in the first new rules since the 1970s on how feedlots were regulated in the environmental law area. I studied the new laws very carefully. I soon knew that in the high rainfall area I operated that it would be very difficult if not impossible to operate our feedlot as we were. Our award winning work in the environmental area and our infrastructure that far exceeded the current rules would not get us through the new rules without an abundance of new cost. I made a list of my challenges that included—

1. EPA law changes that would affect our operation.
2. Changing marketing of fed cattle
3. Possibility of BSE or "mad cow disease" coming to US after destroying England's cattle industry.
4. Consolidation in the cattle feeding industry
5. No other family member wanting to be in industry after me

6. Where we were in cattle cycle numbers and how this would affect our segment of the industry the next three to five years.
7. Limited value of our feeding facility to sell and need for more investment dollars to meet new standards.
8. My own health and age

I look at my list and it should have been a "no brainier" to my choice, but it does not come easy to pull the plug on a family business spanning soon to be fifty years. The business had just enjoyed two of the best years ever financially and I still enjoyed it. I also was at a place in the industry where I was well respected. I was the president elect of the Oklahoma Cattlemen's Association and could do much to help our industry in the next years.

I realized my need to slow down would not come with all the changes the industry was facing. I would in fact have to speed up my already fast pace. I did not want to give up my volunteer work with the youth camp, hospital, church, and cattle association. They all gave me the true richness of life. My volunteer work gave me not only a fulfilled satisfaction, but also gave me a chance to interact with other volunteers who were successful business people. I always came back from my volunteer meetings with a renewed mental vigor. The time spent with others who worked in many different businesses was stimulating and relaxed my mind from thinking of only the challenges and opportunities in my business world. The extra time spent volunteering tired my body, but the renewed mental vigor made it worth while.

I looked at my list of challenges and thought long and hard. The cost to close the feedlot under the soon to be new EPA regulations I estimated to be $500,000 to $700,000 more than the cost to close under the old regulations still in effect. The changing fed cattle marketing system offered real opportunities and I wanted to be a part of it. I also knew that in the early years of this market change, I would have to spend even more time than I had been helping our customers adjust their cattle to fit the new market. There would be no time for at least three to five years to slow down. I was the only one in our family who could run the operation. Doug had decided the cattle business was not for him. My grandkids were too young to know what life interest they would have. I did not think I could keep our operation going for another fifteen years at the least till they could become involved if they wanted. I also knew that even if they chose the cattle business they would not have the experience and maturity to deal with the industry without a great deal of help from me for another five to ten years beyond the first fifteen. I knew I could not continue at the pace needed for that long. I also feared that if I ever did have a heart attack or accident and pass suddenly, I would be leaving my affairs in quite a mess. The EPA requirements were best to be handled by myself because I knew our system better than anyone did and how to deal with it. Our tax situation in the cattle business and all the equipment it took to operate was complicated. I paid a lot of taxes every year. I also prepaid enough grain and other expenses to give us a cushion in the year that would not be profitable. The cattle business has always had its ups and downs in the markets. For this reason I had always managed this tax carry forward. It was a very legal method of leveling out our tax liability. It was also a fact that when I quit, I would have to face the tax carry forward and pay it. Our entire business structure was just too complicated to dump on my family if something were to happen suddenly to me.

I had known for years that the value of our feedlot property was not for resale to another feeding operation. We just were in a too wet climate to entice anyone to buy the feedlot for its value. I had structured our improvements for a least ten years to add value to a large ranch if the feedlot was ever shut down. When I had added feeding pens or other feedlot improvements, I only did so if they would have a two-year payback or less.

I also looked at the cattle cycle and knew that my segment of the industry would be a hard place to make a good profit in for the next three to five years because of the cattle numbers in the United States were at the low end number wise. Feedlots would bid up the smaller supply of feeder cattle just to keep their pens at capacity. With the higher price of feeder cattle, more ranchers would hold back replacement heifers for cows instead of selling the heifers for feeders. This would start a buildup of cattle numbers in a few years. In short number times, the cow calf man usually makes the most in the industry. When numbers expand, I have found I could make more in my feedlot sector of the business. I would have liked to have kept my feedlot going another five to seven years if not for the just mentioned reasons.

When I looked at my list there was not one compelling reason to continue. The added closure cost would be more than I would probably make during the next five years. The changing market would consume more not less time by me. The threat of BSE or "mad cow" was real and I knew what it had done to England's cattlemen. Most were broke from it. We have suffered BSE since I quit in the U.S. The first few weeks were devastating, but soon prices came back. It has hurt, but not killed our industry. It was and still could be an event that would simply wipe out the earnings of a lifetime, as many of the Canadian cattlemen saw when BSE struck them. The risk was just too great considering my own health and no one else in the family wanting to carry on. It would have been very selfish of me to have continued when I considered the potential impact on the family that was hanging over us.

It should have been plain for no other reason that my own health was not going to get better continuing to work the schedule needed to continue. It was going to be hard to walk away from thirty-two years of the feedlot business that had treated us so well financially. The hard part was not the money though. Shutting down meant laying off my crew that was my second family. It was hard to do, but we managed it the best we could for the employees. With all the mentioned reasons I still would probably not have had the resolve to pull the plug on the family business. It is just too hard to do with such a rich family history in the business. My old friend, board of director-accountant, Gayle Edmondson was at our office one day working on our books. I had one of my weak and quivering spells of the chronic fatigue. Gayle knew I suffered from the syndrome, but had never been around me when it hit hard. From that day on, he started a campaign to get me to close our feedlot. I probably never would have done so, even though all my reasons said I should, without Gayle's urging me to do so. He could see what was best for me and not necessarily for his business. I think he was afraid I would "croak" suddenly and he would be called into action to run the place until closed.

It took months to figure out how to close. We had a feedlot full of cattle that had to be fed to finish. I could not let the employees leave me without any help to finish out what we had started. I had to quit taking new cattle at some date. Finally, I got my plan together and announced in May of 2001 that we would not be taking any more cattle. A letter was sent to all customers explaining that we would finish their cattle in our yard with the same diligence and vigor we always had. We would not take any more cattle. The employees were told and plans were formulated to plant the pens to grass as the cattle went out. I listed the feedlot with a commercial feedlot and large ranch real estate broker, John Wilden. John placed his first ad in the High Plains Journal newspaper and was eager to see if a buyer could be found. I had not elected to try to sell the feedlot as an ongoing operation because I knew it would hard as I have stated to sell as a feedlot in the times the industry was in and where we were located. I thought one of the large feeding companies might buy the property to use as a backgrounding operation for calves to get ready for their feedlots.

John placed his ad, but tragedy struck his family the very next day. John's daughter, a senior in high school was struck by another car in an intersection and killed. John's life was turned completely upside down in just a few short minutes. He took his daughter's loss very hard as one can understand. He knew God had plans for each of us and that she was in a better place. It is still hard to give up a loved one. Three years later, John is starting to get his life back together. It has been a hard adjustment for him, but he is getting the job done. John has been a good friend and I have hated to see him hurt so much. Under the circumstances, we did not have any success in selling our operation. I did not list it with anyone else. I did run some ads myself and had some lookers, but no buyers.

We finished the last cattle in October 2001. It was a long, hot summer. I would be glad when this exercise was over. It is hard to close down a business that has been successful and in your blood for so many years.

I kept the crew busy as we finished the last cattle getting the empty pens sowed to grass. We filled dirt in the holes and places were all the topsoil had washed away over the years. We found an old disc in a ditch on a place I had bought a few years before. It worked just right to scratch the hard pen surface for the grass preparation. It was a small size that would work well in our pens and we would not be tearing up our good equipment. We scratched the pen surface with the disc and then broadcast Bermuda seed. Finally a harrow section was pulled over the newly seeded pens. The new grass would need a lot of water to live under the poor conditions of the hard packed pens. My solution was to take the water values out of our cattle water tanks and replace them with a faucet. I purchased over a thousand dollars worth of garden hoses and plastic water sprinklers like you would use in your home yard. We could water about twenty percent of the pens at one time and then had to move our hoses and sprinklers to the next setting. We pulled hoses all summer. It was hot and hard work, but it did the job. Our new grass started off great. After Bermuda seeding time was over, we switched to fescue for the fall planting of the last pens. Within a year, our pens were back to solid grass.

Our friends at Muller Construction cleaned all of the manure out of our lagoons as soon as we had the water all pumped out of them. Each lagoon was cleaned to fresh dirt and left as a fresh water pond. The cleaned out manure was spread over our fields close by. We had cleaned a good amount of the lagoons in 1999 during a dry summer. The cost of lagoon cleaning in 1999 and the final cleanup in 2001 exceeded $400,000. Under the old and then current regulation we could apply the manure at a heavier application rate than the soon new regulation would allow. This kept the mileage and extra hourly cost down by not having to go as far with the wet, gooey manure mixture. The Muller family business had taken care of my pollution clean out needs for years and always did a superb job. This last cleanup had been scheduled during our usual August dry spell back in May when I announced our closing. I had told

Mark and Larry Muller of my plans. Something happened and they did not get to us at the scheduled time. Two or three weeks went by and they still did not show. This was not like them and I knew something had put them behind. I also knew that I could not get out from under the EPA regulations until we were completely cleaned up and soon the rainy season would start and prevent this cleanup until the next summer when new regulations would be in place and make the clean up cost so much more. I both called with a terse message for Mark and faxed him a letter that was sharp and to the point. This was very hard for me to do to my friends. I knew that they would be at our location if not for some unforeseen hold up. I also knew the rainy season was fast approaching. I had to put the pressure on my friends no matter what had happened on their end. I did not enjoy having to do this. I was relieved that they got moved in right after my actions and got the job done. They held no hard feelings toward me for my harsh actions. I in turn felt relieved that my friends came through. The weather held and the Muller crew got us cleaned up in proper fashion. Sometimes in business you have to put the pressure on, but I never liked doing this especially with good friends. I was glad all ended well.

I decided to keep the feedlot property since a buyer had not been found and use it as a regular cattle ranch. We owned 2,766 acres around the feedyard and another 470 acres about four miles away. I also had the 2,351 acre family bluestem ranch fifteen miles west of Welch. The employee layoff had gone well. I was able to keep all but about three until they had found another job. All received a good severance pay and insurance package. The ones that did not have a job when they left, I think had just not tried because they seemed to want to take someone time off work while unemployment benefits were available to them plus the severance package. I think everyone understood why I had taken the route I had.

We kept our mechanic and two cowboys to work the ranch. I enjoyed my slow office pace and started coming in most days at 7:30 instead of the 6:45 usual. I now had time to go to cattle auction sales myself to buy the calves we now grow on our grass ranch. I love to go to the sale, but had not bought my own cattle for several years with all my duties running the feedlot. I now had time to do so. My only problem I soon realized that I would be the one unloading the cattle when delivered to our place soon after the sale. All my crew lived several miles away and the cattle would not get there until 10:00 or later. I should have insisted on at least one employee living in one of our feedlot homes and doing this job, but I guess I am just too soft. I did not require an employee to be there at night, but did it myself. This made for a long day of sometimes four hours on the road to and from the sale and then six hours or so of the auction. If I bought several, I went in early the next morning to get the processing orders ready for the cattle to be worked and usually helped my small crew process the cattle. This made two long days of work for me. I did not have the old stress of the job and enjoyed every minute of what I was doing. My body just would not stand up to the long hours. I would end up down the next couple of days after the two long days. I thought I would just stay in the office and let the crew handle the work. I simply could not bring myself not to help when we had a lot to do or the weather was real bad. I should have stayed in the office, but I would not. When it snowed, I would run the loader as a snow-plow on the roads to our pastures so the crew could get feed and hay to the cattle. I enjoyed running the heated cab loader with a nice stereo radio. Alas at the end of the day, I could hardly walk. The bouncing around in the loader made my body a wreck.

During November 2002 I relapsed hard with the fatigue syndrome. It was as bad a month as I had spent in several years. For the first time, I felt a depression coming over me. I had always figured that maybe with the stress of running the feedlot gone, I would come back to excellent health and be able to do cattle work. It was not happening. I ached, hurt, and had trouble walking. All the old symptoms were bearing down hard.

I had an offer on the feedlot property by the Tate family of Kansas during this fall, but did not respond to their offer. It was less than I wanted and since I had already went through the hard part of the layoffs and getting out from under the EPA rules I saw no reason to sell the beautiful ranch I was now running. Until November 2002 and the return of the fatigue. I called the Tates and we started dealing. I decided it would be best for me to exit the cattle business. I would never leave my crew to do all the work when we had a lot going on or the weather was bad and my body was not going to hold up to this type of work. It would be better to sell and do something else. A very hard decision to make, but again when God dumps the solution in your lap it is time to take notice.

I figured the Tates were sent to me as a buyer for the 2,767 acres and feedlot to make me slow down and resolve the health issues. It took about four months to resolve all the issues of the sale to both our satisfaction. I could have said no to the Tate deal at anytime and just kept the property. I debated at one time about keeping it and renting it out. I decided renting our highly improved place was probably not a long-term answer. A renter might not take care of the place and destroy some of its value.

We were still debating the issues when out of the blue I get a phone call from Larry Hale, a real estate broker from Missouri who had called numerous times trying to buy our bluestem ranch for the Buford family. Larry Hale had acted as a real estate broker for the Bufords in buying around 9,000 acres on three and one half sides of our 2,350-acre ranch. I had pushed any advances by Hale or the Bufords aside as I did not want to sell this ranch which was very easy to operate compared to our Welch ranch. On the Monday night call from Larry Hale, for some reason I popped off that the only way I would sell the bluestem ranch was if the Bufords would buy our home on 270 acres adjoining Welch. The home in Welch was about 4,500 square feet and way over built for our small town. It would be hard to sell for full value.

I had thought just how hard it was going to be to watch the Tates run my pride and joy ranch that I could see from our home three miles away. I knew it would be tough for me to handle, seeing someone else operating this land. God was working ahead of what I had ever thought of. My off the wall comment on selling the house and the ranch fifteen miles away the night before had hit home. On Tuesday morning around nine, Sam Buford walked into my office and wanted to talk of the deal Larry Hale told him about. We talked and I gave him some prices I would consider on both properties.

Sam left, but his father Dan called and visited about the deal on Wednesday. On Thursday, both father and son walked into my office. This time they wanted to walk through our home. They looked at our home maybe ten minutes, drove by the horse barn, and left.

On Saturday, I told Dee Ann we had better go house hunting because I figured her house was going to be sold soon. We talked to Dan Buford early in the morning by phone. He proposed some valuations on our home and ranch somewhat different than I had. What he proposed would net us more money after taxes than my pricing because the home has a large capital gains exception. Neither figure was over the value, but in Welch as I said who knows the true value of this price home. You have to find the right person to buy a large home in a small town. We talked about his offer and decided to talk later in the day again. Dee Ann and I drove all around the Grand Lake area and into Grove, Oklahoma. We thought we might like this area to move to at least for awhile. We had enjoyed a weekend condo on Grand Lake after we shut the feedlot down. It was quiet, peaceful, and pretty around the lake. We thought it might be a good place to slow down and learn how not to work all the time. It was still close to Jodee and her family in Vinita. It would be hard to leave the town we both grew up at, but harder to watch the Tates run our ranch. I could not talk the Tates into our home. They did not plan to move to Oklahoma, but to have a hired crew only at Welch.

The Buford offer was very attractive. We could sell a house that was very much larger than we needed at a good price. We would not have to watch the Tates on the close by ranch. One other big reason loomed in the background. I told of the partnership falling out on the Welch Bank in Chapter 25. In a small town the bank is the hub of everything as I told you. Seven years after selling the bank interest, I still felt the hurt my partners placed on me. I forgave them and was not bitter. I was still hurt and it was hard to deal with. I just was not comfortable working on town projects with these former partners. I could eat lunch and enjoy their conversation, but I did not want to work with them. I think this all right as long as I am not hateful toward them. I am not and wish them well. The Bufords were offering us the chance to start new in a fresh community close by, but far away as well.

I know God just presented these two offers to us for our well being. I had fought quitting the cattle business. The last details of the Tate offer were worked out to everyone's satisfaction, but no contracts signed during this early April time frame. Dan Buford called my cell phone late Saturday afternoon. Dee Ann and I were looking at a housing addition on the lake near Grove. He made an offer within a very few thousand dollars of what I knew was fair and generous at the time. I held out one more moment. It was hard to sell all our land except two hundred acres. It would be a big life style change moving to a new community. I finally told Dan I would trade if he would throw in three weeks at the Ritz Carlton Hotel he half owned with his brother Bob. I had heard that they owned a Ritz Hotel, but did not know much about it or even where in Florida. I figured a Ritz in Florida would be fine anywhere. Dan said your have yourself a deal. I had added clauses prior to this such as use of the grass till August 1 so that I could graze the pasture one last season. I got six months to move out of the house to give time to find the new home. God planned every move and dumped it in our lap. I was certain that this had to be His will the way it was laid out. We closed with the Bufords and had the money from their transaction within twelve days. They had a tax-free exchange deadline to meet.

We looked at several areas over thirty miles of Grand Lake country. We talked to several active real estate brokers in the area and made an offer on one home. We got within $7,000 of what the owner of this home was willing to take when I got to looking at his waterfront footage. On lakes, the value of the lot lies in how many feet of good shore frontage you own. This home I discovered had about fifteen feet less than we were told. We had already offered too much for the property and then found this out. God came through again. Our offer was turned down and we withdrew the offer and went on looking. I met the man in charge of the housing area the home was located in. Jim told me of another homeowner in the development who was getting up in years and wanted to sell his home. I got the phone number of Bob Vassar and gave him a call. The Vassars had built Chateau #13 in 1980 next to their long time friends the Bernard Wades. The home was well cared for, but in need of a new coat of interior paint and wallpaper. It was 2,900 square feet and priced thousands below the home we had just offered on. It also had 126 feet of the prettiest view shoreline on the lake. The Vassars' only daughter had died suddenly in her early forties a couple of years before. They were getting close to eighty and no longer enjoyed their lake retreat. We loved the home. Bob Vassar and I looked at the home and talked about it for about an hour. Then we just sat down and talked about his life for two or three more hours. He was a retired real estate broker and told me of many projects he had worked on. He still was active, teaching computer classes to retired adults. I made a new friend that I enjoyed very much. I think I also helped fill an empty time in his life with some good conversation.

We remodeled our new home and made the move the last day of September 2003. We had six hours to spare in getting out of our Welch home before the deadline. The Bufords put their ranch manager in our Welch home. They were moving their things in as we moved ours out. They were very anxious to move into our large home with the swimming pool and nice horse barn. The manager had done well also in this trade.

Julie Wolf, a local real estate agent, found a buyer for our small lake condo in short order even though real estate sales had slowed down considerably by now. We closed on it and another problem was solved. The man with the first home we tried to buy and got to within $7,000 of still owns it. It sits empty next to his own lake home he occupies.

The Tates closed on their deal in March 2004 just as they had agreed to. The last months at their new ranch gave me time to sell off all our equipment myself without the need for a farm auction sale. I think I realized a better return this way and the time was spent reflecting on my near life time of being on this property. I slowed my pace down and began to feel better. I have adjusted to not owning cattle. I had originally planned to buy with a tax-free exchange, as both the Bufords and Tates were doing with us another smaller ranch much like the bluestem ranch the Bufords bought. In the year I had to look I did not find a ranch that I thought would be easy to manage and that I liked. I found one in Kansas that would have been nice, but it was two hours from our new home and the kids in Vinita. I did not think this would be good. One ranch near Vinita was very interesting. It laid pretty and would be fun to own. It was not a real productive ranch however and the owner wanted more than it was worth. I finally decided God had other plans for me that did not include ranching.

Interest rates have remained at lows not seen in fifty years. This has caused many to want to invest in land all over our country. I never would have thought rates would be this low for this long. Land prices are higher this year than last. I have not looked back though because I truly believe God planned our sales. We got cash money without a lot of the normal problems associated with deals this large. I also know that there are still ranches I looked at not sold. You always hear of the really high price deals and it is easy to think everything is bringing the high deals. It usually is not so. In case it is and the market keeps going up, that is fine also because I know God looks out for others also. We got a wonderful deal and I am not looking back. I miss our old home and ranches, but our new life is Grand!

We are enjoying our time on Monkey Island on Grand Lake in our new home. It is quiet and peaceful here. I can now walk a mile and one half without playing completely out. I still have days I am not up to par, but for the most part I am feeling better than I have in eighteen years. I now sleep till 7:30 or 8:00 in the morning. The extra rest is what I was needing. I now get nine hours or more sleep every night compared to seven to eight when working. I spend my time on several volunteer projects. I hope I can truly make a difference in this world. I will probably go back to work at something one of these days, but for now I am enjoying my slower pace, time with the grandkids, and my volunteer work.

We all face big decisions at some point or points in our life. Plan ahead for these times. Having options as I talked in Chapter 29 makes life easier. Study your options and list all the pros/cons of a major decision. First, last, and most important turn to God for his wisdom and help. You do not have to shoulder making life decisions alone.

I also have enjoyed writing for you about our life and just how turning our worries over to God works. I told you of my mother's book dealing with her life and my brothers with Cystic Fibrosis. Their illness was a real burden. Mine was never life threatening or any way compared to what they suffered on this earth. I am glad they have peace in their new home with God. Mom taught me well. I hope you get some good out of my thoughts in this book as others did in Mom's.

I will close in the next and final chapter with some recap and final thoughts.

Life is "Grand" today — our view from our back deck on Grand Lake

34

Final Thoughts

My business life has been fun and successful. I was given opportunities by my parents in the form of both wisdom taught and a financial start. The rough times taught me to be a better manager and to trust in not only my ability, but that the Lord would watch over me. The years in the late eighties were long hours of work, stressful work situations, and financial decisions that had they been wrong might have caused us to go broke. These years instilled confidence in my ability. I was successful in turning around a floundering cattle business while managing to get out of the bad bank without losing the family's money. I did develop the Chronic Fatigue Syndrome during this time of long hours, hard decisions, figuring out plans of action, and managing all when money was short. I would have course rather not suffered from the chronic fatigue. I have never been bitter and I know I had to put the hours in to work out of the mess I was in. I have in turn just looked at the positive aspects of my dilemma. I met my million dollar friend, learned to manage money, make deals in short order with informed facts, worked with some top notch people, and grew closer to God. I feel blessed to have had the opportunities I have had and the successes on this earth I have had.

Every business person should learn early on to trust in God and live by His commandments. My own four pillars will round out your life and give meaning to life. Teach your offspring the true values of life, how to work, how to think for themselves, and that success does not always mean huge amounts of money on this earth. Our earthly treasures are great, but more important are our eternal treasure with God.

I have done many things wrong and taken many a wrong turn in life. There was but one perfect on this earth, Jesus Christ. I, like all, learn from my mistakes and try not to repeat them. Some will be repeated though as we are all human. Do not look down a person for his or her past, but look at what their future can be.

Learn to be happy no matter what your situation in life is. Many families who barely make things financially have great family and spiritual relationships. This is the true wealth. Be thankful for the blessings we have and do not worry about what we don't have.

As we talked cherish your family, friends, and most of all your God. Strive to live a good life that you enjoy along the way. Plan for the day you will not be on this earth, for your own eternal life first of all and also plan for an exit from this life that does not leave a pile of troubles for your loved ones to sort out.

Treat others as you would like to be treated. If you are wronged by someone and cannot get them to reconcile, do not dwell on their problem. Forgive and get on with your life.

Life is short. Enjoy, participate, and make your family and friends better for what your have taught and left them in wisdom and knowledge. My own father was such a great teacher and friend. We enjoyed many a good time working together. You can have these same good times and memories. Hopefully your earthly reward will be an offspring like Jodee, who takes after my mother in so many ways. A pretty, bright, energetic, young woman who takes time to instill values in her own three children.

Dakota, Deonna, and Dejay take heed and give service on this earth like your great grandmother and grandfather. This will be the best legacy I can leave you.

Remember, life will be a bumpy road, but God will smooth out the bumps for us if we only let him.

My old friend, Buss Thomas, changed from a farming and hay baling career to the funeral home business at about fifty years of age. Buss's front teeth were missing, but he conducted a very nice, special funeral for all. I remember the farmer side that wore overalls and a beat-up straw hat to the classy dressed with a crisp white shirt and a tie in the new funeral career. He always ended the grave side part of the funeral service by saying "This concludes the services." In the spirit of Buss I now declare that "This concludes the book."

The End